Mathematical Modeling with Differential Equations in Physics, Chemistry, Biology, and Economics

Mathematical Modeling with Differential Equations in Physics, Chemistry, Biology, and Economics

Editor

Arsen Palestini

MDPI • Basel • Beijing • Wuhan • Barcelona • Belgrade • Manchester • Tokyo • Cluj • Tianjin

Editor
Arsen Palestini
Sapienza University of Rome
Italy

Editorial Office
MDPI
St. Alban-Anlage 66
4052 Basel, Switzerland

This is a reprint of articles from the Special Issue published online in the open access journal *Mathematics* (ISSN 2227-7390) (available at: https://www.mdpi.com/si/mathematics/Math_Model_Differ_Equ).

For citation purposes, cite each article independently as indicated on the article page online and as indicated below:

LastName, A.A.; LastName, B.B.; LastName, C.C. Article Title. *Journal Name* **Year**, *Volume Number*, Page Range.

ISBN 978-3-0365-4625-4 (Hbk)
ISBN 978-3-0365-4626-1 (PDF)

© 2022 by the authors. Articles in this book are Open Access and distributed under the Creative Commons Attribution (CC BY) license, which allows users to download, copy and build upon published articles, as long as the author and publisher are properly credited, which ensures maximum dissemination and a wider impact of our publications.

The book as a whole is distributed by MDPI under the terms and conditions of the Creative Commons license CC BY-NC-ND.

Contents

About the Editor vii

Arsen Palestini
Preface to the Special Issue "Mathematical Modeling with Differential Equations in Physics, Chemistry, Biology, and Economics"
Reprinted from: *Mathematics* **2022**, *10*, 1633, doi:10.3390/math10101633 1

Cheon-Seoung Ryoo and Jungyoog Kang
Some Properties Involving q-Hermite Polynomials Arising from Differential Equations and Location of Their Zeros
Reprinted from: *Mathematics* **2021**, *9*, 1168, doi:10.3390/math9111168 3

Daniele Ritelli
A Forgotten Differential Equation Studied by Jacopo Riccati Revisited in Terms of Lie Symmetries
Reprinted from: *Mathematics* **2021**, *9*, 1312, doi:10.3390/math9111312 15

Yu-Cheng Shen, Chia-Liang Lin, Theodore E. Simos and Charalampos Tsitouras
Runge–Kutta Pairs of Orders 6(5) with Coefficients Trained to Perform Best on Classical Orbits
Reprinted from: *Mathematics* **2021**, *9*, 1342, doi:10.3390/math9121342 25

Nazaria Solferino and M. Elisabetta Tessitore
Human Networks and Toxic Relationships
Reprinted from: *Mathematics* **2021**, *9*, 2258, doi:10.3390/ math9182258 35

Vladislav N. Kovalnogov, Ruslan V. Fedorov, Andrey V. Chukalin, Theodore E. Simos and Charalampos Tsitouras
Evolutionary Derivation of Runge–Kutta Pairs of Orders 5(4) Specially Tuned for Problems with Periodic Solutions
Reprinted from: *Mathematics* **2021**, *9*, 2306, doi:10.3390/math9182306 45

Hennie Husniah, Ruhanda Ruhanda, Asep K. Supriatna and Md. H. A. Biswas
SEIR Mathematical Model of Convalescent Plasma Transfusion to Reduce COVID-19 Disease Transmission
Reprinted from: *Mathematics* **2021**, *9*, 2857, doi:10.3390/math9222857 57

Roberto De Marchis, Arsen Palestini and Stefano Patrì
Accidental Degeneracy of an Elliptic Differential Operator: A Clarification in Terms of Ladder Operators
Reprinted from: *Mathematics* **2021**, *9*, 3005, doi:10.3390/math9233005 73

Md Sadikur Rahman, Subhajit Das, Amalesh Kumar Manna, Ali Akbar Shaikh, Asoke Kumar Bhunia, Leopoldo Eduardo Cárdenas-Barrón, Gerardo Treviño-Garza and Armando Céspedes-Mota
A Mathematical Model of the Production Inventory Problem for Mixing Liquid Considering Preservation Facility
Reprinted from: *Mathematics* **2021**, *9*, 3166, doi:10.3390/math9243166 87

Annalisa Fabretti
A Dynamical Model for Financial Market: Among Common Market Strategies Who and How Moves the Price to Fluctuate, Inflate, and Burst?
Reprinted from: *Mathematics* **2022**, *10*, 679, doi:10.3390/math10050679 107

Ilya Boykov, Vladimir Roudnev and Alla Boykova
Stability of Solutions to Systems of Nonlinear Differential Equations with Discontinuous Right-Hand Sides: Applications to Hopfield Artificial Neural Networks
Reprinted from: *Mathematics* **2022**, *10*, 1524, doi:10.3390/math10091524 . . . . **125**

About the Editor

Arsen Palestini

Arsen Palestini was born in 1973. He is currently an associate professor at the Department MEMOTEF in the Faculty of Economics in Sapienza University of Rome, Italy. He completed his PhD in Mathematics at the University of Florence in 2005. He has published more than 30 papers on several international peer-reviewed journals, specializing in game theory, differential games, microeconomic modeling, differential equations, and graph theory.

Editorial

Preface to the Special Issue "Mathematical Modeling with Differential Equations in Physics, Chemistry, Biology, and Economics"

Arsen Palestini

MEMOTEF, Faculty of Economics, Sapienza University of Rome, 00185 Rome, Italy; arsen.palestini@uniroma1.it; Tel.: +39-331-256-0711

Citation: Palestini, A. Preface to the Special Issue "Mathematical Modeling with Differential Equations in Physics, Chemistry, Biology, and Economics". *Mathematics* **2022**, *10*, 1633. https://doi.org/10.3390/math10101633

Received: 9 May 2022
Accepted: 10 May 2022
Published: 11 May 2022

Publisher's Note: MDPI stays neutral with regard to jurisdictional claims in published maps and institutional affiliations.

Copyright: © 2022 by the author. Licensee MDPI, Basel, Switzerland. This article is an open access article distributed under the terms and conditions of the Creative Commons Attribution (CC BY) license (https://creativecommons.org/licenses/by/4.0/).

First of all, I would like to express my warmest thanks to all the scholars who participated by submitting their papers to this Special Issue. As the Guest Editor of this volume, I was delighted to see that the articles that have been proposed over these months are all valuable, interesting and original. My acknowledgements also go to all the reviewers for their commitment, which was extremely helpful to improve the quality of the scientific contributions.

The staff of *Mathematics* (to whom I am very grateful) and I chose to avoid excessive constraints when we conceived this Special Issue in order to keep the number of the possible contributors as high as possible; anyone with brilliant results involving differential equations was welcome. In line with this inclusive approach, we received manuscripts from many disciplines with various lines of research.

I am hopeful that all readers of the papers included in this Special Issue will find them interesting, novel and, above all, inspirational.

The contents of the volume are outlined in this brief introduction, after which I will let you enjoy the papers.

To begin with, we accepted two articles on Runge–Kutta pairs: In Kovalgonov et al. [1], a new Runge–Kutta pair of orders $(5,4)$ is constructed to address problems with periodic solutions and, in particular, the performance of the related method is excellent on a couple of oscillators. On the other hand, Shen et al. [2] consider a family of explicit Runge–Kutta pairs of orders $(6,5)$ to establish a method which performs efficiently on a wide range of orbital problems, such as perturbed Kepler with various disturbances and Arenstorf and Pleiades.

An old but relevant problem is tackled by Ritelli [3], who addressed the issue of a two parameter family of differential equations which was originally treated by Italian mathematician Jacopo Riccati in the 18th century. The closed form integration of a differential equation, more general to the one treated in Riccati's contribution, is obtained, through the use of Lie Symmetries.

A very peculiar application is provided by economists Solferino and Tessitore [4], who derived a theoretical model to shed light on the dynamics leading to toxic relationships, to outline the conditions for the best policy to heal from a toxic relationship.

A dynamic financial model is proposed by Fabretti [5], who investigates the behaviour of a stock price in a given scenario, providing some insights on equilibrium and chaos.

Boykov et al. [6] carry out a study of the stability of solutions to systems of differential equations with discontinuous right-hand sides, providing some applications to Hopfield Artificial Neural Networks.

In our Special Issue, there is also an SEIR epidemiological model by Husniah et al. [7], where the use of convalescent plasma is supposed to reduce the diffusion of a disease such as COVID-19.

Some valuable mathematical results are obtained by Ryoo and Kang [8], whose analysis focuses on q-Hermite polynomials arising from certain differential equations.

Rahman et al. [9] propose an inventory model for mixing liquid considering preservation facility, which is solved numerically.

Finally, De Marchis et al. [10] investigate accidental degeneracy of a linear, second-order elliptic, Schrödinger-type differential operator.

Funding: This research received no external funding.

Conflicts of Interest: The author declares no conflict of interest.

References

1. Kovalnogov, V.N.; Fedorov, R.V.; Chukalin, A.V.; Simos, T.E.; Tsitouras, C. Evolutionary Derivation of Runge–Kutta Pairs of Orders 5(4) Specially Tuned for Problems with Periodic Solutions. *Mathematics* **2021**, *9*, 2306. [CrossRef]
2. Shen, Y.-C.; Lin, C.-L.; Simos, T.E.; Tsitouras, C. Runge–Kutta Pairs of Orders 6(5) with Coefficients Trained to Perform Best on Classical Orbits. *Mathematics* **2021**, *9*, 1342. [CrossRef]
3. Ritelli, D. A Forgotten Differential Equation Studied by Jacopo Riccati Revisited in Terms of Lie Symmetries. *Mathematics* **2021**, *9*, 1312. [CrossRef]
4. Solferino, N.; Tessitore, M.E. Human Networks and Toxic Relationships. *Mathematics* **2021**, *9*, 2258. [CrossRef]
5. Fabretti, A. A Dynamical Model for Financial Market: Among Common Market Strategies Who and How Moves the Price to Fluctuate, Inflate, and Burst? *Mathematics* **2022**, *10*, 679. [CrossRef]
6. Boykov, I.; Roudnev, V.; Boykova, A. Stability of Solutions to Systems of Nonlinear Differential Equations with Discontinuous Right-Hand Sides: Applications to Hopfield Artificial Neural Networks. *Mathematics* **2022**, *10*, 1524. [CrossRef]
7. Husniah, H.; Ruhanda, R.; Supriatna, A.K.; Biswas, M.H.A. SEIR Mathematical Model of Convalescent Plasma Transfusion to Reduce COVID-19 Disease Transmission. *Mathematics* **2021**, *9*, 2857. [CrossRef]
8. Ryoo, C.-S.; Kang, J. Some Properties Involving q-Hermite Polynomials Arising from Differential Equations and Location of Their Zeros. *Mathematics* **2021**, *9*, 1168. [CrossRef]
9. Rahman, M.S.; Das, S.; Manna, A.K.; Shaikh, A.A.; Bhunia, A.K.; Cárdenas-Barrón, L.E.; Treviño-Garza, G.; Céspedes-Mota, A. A Mathematical Model of the Production Inventory Problem for Mixing Liquid Considering Preservation Facility. *Mathematics* **2021**, *9*, 3166. [CrossRef]
10. De Marchis, R.; Palestini, A.; Patrì, S. Accidental Degeneracy of an Elliptic Differential Operator: A Clarification in Terms of Ladder Operators. *Mathematics* **2021**, *9*, 3005. [CrossRef]

Article

Some Properties Involving q-Hermite Polynomials Arising from Differential Equations and Location of Their Zeros

Cheon-Seoung Ryoo [1] and Jungyoog Kang [2,*]

[1] Department of Mathematics, Hannam University, Daejeon 34430, Korea; ryoocs@hnu.kr
[2] Department of Mathematics Education, Silla University, Busan 46958, Korea
* Correspondence: jykang@silla.ac.kr

Abstract: Hermite polynomials are one of the Apell polynomials and various results were found by the researchers. Using Hermit polynomials combined with q-numbers, we derive different types of differential equations and study these equations. From these equations, we investigate some identities and properties of q-Hermite polynomials. We also find the position of the roots of these polynomials under certain conditions and their stacked structures. Furthermore, we locate the roots of various forms of q-Hermite polynomials according to the conditions of q-numbers, and look for values which have approximate roots that are real numbers.

Keywords: q-Hermite polynomials; zeros of q-Hermite polynomials; differential equation

1. Introduction

There is a special case in the Sturm–Liouville boundary value problem the called Hermite differential equation that arises when dealing with harmonic oscillator in quantum mechanics. The ordinary Hermite differential equation is defined as

$$\frac{d^2y}{dx^2} - 2x\frac{dy}{dx} + (\rho - 1)y = 0, \qquad (1)$$

where ρ is a constant. When $\rho = 2n+1, n = 0,1,2,\ldots$, then one of the solutions of Equation (1) becomes a polynomial. These polynomial solutions are known as Hermite polynomials $H_n(x)$, which are defined by means of the generating function

$$e^{(2x-t)t} = \sum_{n=0}^{\infty} H_n(x)\frac{t^n}{n!}, \qquad |t| < \infty. \qquad (2)$$

The numbers $H_n := H_n(0)$ are the Hermite numbers. Hermite polynomials, first defined by Laplace, are one of the classic orthogonal polynomials and many studies have been conducted by mathematicians. These Hermite polynomials also have many mathematical applications, such as quantum mechanics, physics, and probability theory; see [1–6].

We define the q-numbers also referred by Jackson as follows; see [7–9]

$$[x]_q = \frac{1-q^x}{1-q}, \quad 0 < q < 1, \qquad (3)$$

Note that $\lim_{q \to 1}[x]_q = x$. In [8], we recall that the q-Hermite polynomials $\mathbf{H}_{n,q}(x)$ defined by

$$\sum_{n=0}^{\infty} \mathbf{H}_{n,q}(x)\frac{t^n}{n!} = e^{2[x]_q t - t^2} = \mathcal{G}(t, [x]_q), \qquad (4)$$

where $0 < q < 1$. In the definition of q-Hermite polynomials, we can observe that if $q \to 1$, then $\mathbf{H}_{n,q}(x) \to H_n(x)$.

In [10], authors defined the two-variable partially degenerate Hermite polynomials $\mathbf{H}_n(x, y, \lambda)$ as

$$\sum_{n=0}^{\infty} \mathbf{H}_n(x, y, \lambda) \frac{t^n}{n!} = (1 + \lambda t)^{\frac{x}{\lambda}} e^{yt^2}, \quad \lambda \neq 0, \tag{5}$$

and we can see some useful properties of these polynomials. Representatively, we can confirm the following theorems in [10].

(i) $a^m \mathbf{H}_m(bx, b^2 y, \frac{\lambda}{a}) = b^m \mathbf{H}_m(ax, a^2 y, \frac{\lambda}{b})$

(ii) $\mathbf{H}_n(x_1 + x_2, y, \lambda) = \sum_{l=0}^{n} \binom{n}{l} (x_2|\lambda) \mathbf{H}_{n-l}(x_1, y, \lambda).$
(6)

The differential equations derived from the generating functions of special numbers and polynomials have been studied by many mathematicians; see [11–21].

Based on the results to date, in the present work, we can investigate the differential equations generated from the generating function of q-Hermite polynomials $\mathbf{H}_{n,q}(x)$. The rest of the paper is organized as follows. In Section 2, we obtain the basic properties of the q-Hermite polynomials. In Section 3, we construct the differential equations generated from the definition of q-Hermite polynomials:

$$\left(\frac{\partial}{\partial t}\right)^N \mathcal{G}(t, [x]_q) - a_0(N, [x]_q) \mathcal{G}(t, [x]_q) - \cdots - a_N(N, [x]_q) t^N \mathcal{G}(t, [x]_q) = 0. \tag{7}$$

We also consider explicit identities for $\mathbf{H}_{n,q}(x)$ using the coefficients of this differential equation. In Section 4, we find the zeros of the q-Hermite polynomials using numerical methods and observe the scattering phenomenon of the zeros of these polynomials. Finally, in Section 5, conclusions and discussions on this work are provided.

2. Basic Properties for the q-Hermite Polynomials

To derive various properties of $\mathbf{H}_{n,q}(x)$, the generating function (4) is an useful function. The following basic properties of polynomials $\mathbf{H}_{n,q}(x)$ are derived from (4). Hence, we choose to omit the details involved.

Theorem 1. *Let n be any positive integer. Then, we have*

(1) $\mathbf{H}_{n,q}(x) = \sum_{k=0}^{n} \binom{n}{k} 2^{n-k} [x]_q^{n-k} H_k.$

(2) $\mathbf{H}_{n,q}(x) = n! \sum_{k=0}^{[\frac{n}{2}]} \frac{(-1)^k 2^{n-2k} [x]_q^{n-2k}}{k!(n-2k)!}.$
(8)

(3) $\mathbf{H}_{n,q}(x_1 + x_2) = \sum_{k=0}^{n} \binom{n}{k} \mathbf{H}_{k,q}(x_1) 2^{n-k} q^{x_1(n-k)} [x_2]_q^{n-k},$

where $[x]$ is the greatest integer not exceeding x.

Theorem 2. *The q-Hermite polynomials are the solutions of equation*

$$\left(\left(\frac{d}{d[x]_q}\right)^2 - 2[x]_q \left(\frac{d}{d[x]_q}\right) + 2n\right) \mathbf{H}_{n,q}(x) = 0,$$

$$\mathbf{H}_{n,q}(0) = \begin{cases} (-1)^k \frac{(2k)!}{k!}, & \text{if } n = 2k, \\ 0, & \text{otherwise} \end{cases} \tag{9}$$

Proof. From Equation (4), we can note that

$$\mathcal{G}(t, [x]_q) = e^{2[x]_q t - t^2} \tag{10}$$

which is satisfied as

$$\frac{\partial \mathcal{G}(t, [x]_q)}{\partial t} - (2[x]_q - 2t)\mathcal{G}(t, [x]_q) = 0. \tag{11}$$

By substituting the series in (11) for $\mathcal{G}(t, [x]_q)$, we find

$$\mathbf{H}_{n+1,q}(x) - 2[x]_q \mathbf{H}_{n,q}(x) + 2n \mathbf{H}_{n-1,q}(x) = 0, n = 1, 2, \ldots, \tag{12}$$

which is the recurrence relation for q-Hermite polynomials. Another recurrence relation comes from

$$\left(\frac{d}{d[x]_q}\right) \mathcal{G}(t, [x]_q) - 2t \mathcal{G}(t, [x]_q) = 0. \tag{13}$$

The following equation implies

$$\left(\frac{d}{d[x]_q}\right) \mathbf{H}_{n,q}(x) - 2n \mathbf{H}_{n-1,q}(x) = 0, n = 1, 2, \ldots. \tag{14}$$

Remove $\mathbf{H}_{n-1,q}(x)$ from Equations (12) and (13) to obtain

$$\mathbf{H}_{n+1,q}(x) - 2[x]_q \mathbf{H}_{n,q}(x) + \left(\frac{d}{d[x]_q}\right) \mathbf{H}_{n,q}(x) = 0. \tag{15}$$

By differentiating the following equation and using Equations (12) and (13) again, we can obtain

$$\left(\frac{d}{d[x]_q}\right)^2 \mathbf{H}_{n,q}(x) - 2[x]_q \left(\frac{d}{d[x]_q}\right) \mathbf{H}_{n,q}(x) + 2n \mathbf{H}_{n,q}(x) = 0, n = 0, 1, 2, \ldots. \tag{16}$$

From the above equation, we complete the proof of Theorem 2. □

Theorem 3. $\mathbf{H}_{n,q}(x)$ *in the Equation (4) is the solution of equation*

$$\left(\frac{q-1}{q^x \log q} \frac{d^2}{dx^2} + \left(\frac{1-q}{q^x} - \frac{2(1-q^x)}{1-q}\right) \frac{d}{dx} + 2n \frac{\log q}{q-1} q^x\right) \mathbf{H}_{n,q}(x) = 0,$$

$$\mathbf{H}_{n,q}(0) = \begin{cases} (-1)^k \dfrac{(2k)!}{k!}, & \text{if } n = 2k, \\ 0, & \text{otherwise.} \end{cases} \tag{17}$$

Proof. We consider another form of the differential equation for $\mathbf{H}_{n,q}(x)$. We consider

$$\mathcal{G}(t, [x]_q) = e^{2[x]_q t - t^2}, \tag{18}$$

which satisfies

$$\frac{d \mathcal{G}(t, [x]_q)}{dx} - \frac{\log q}{q-1} q^x 2t \mathcal{G}(t, [x]_q) = 0. \tag{19}$$

Substitute the series in Equation (19) for $\mathcal{G}(t, [x]_q)$, in order to find

$$\frac{d \mathbf{H}_{n,q}(x)}{dx} - \frac{2n \log q}{q-1} q^x \mathbf{H}_{n-1,q}(x) = 0, n = 1, 2, \ldots. \tag{20}$$

To use Equation (15), we note

$$\frac{d}{dx}\left(\frac{q-1}{q^x \log q}\frac{d}{dx}\mathbf{H}_{n,q}(x)\right) = \frac{1-q}{q^x}\frac{d}{dx}\mathbf{H}_{n,q}(x) + \frac{q-1}{q^x \log q}\left(\frac{d}{dx}\right)^2 \mathbf{H}_{n,q}(x). \tag{21}$$

By differentiating Equation (15) and using the above Equation (21), we derive

$$\begin{aligned}
&2n\frac{\log q}{q-1}q^x \mathbf{H}_{n,q}(x) + \left(\frac{1-q}{q^x} - \frac{2(1-q^x)}{1-q}\right)\frac{d\mathbf{H}_{n,q}(x)}{dx}\\
&+ \frac{q-1}{q^x \log q}\frac{d^2\mathbf{H}_{n,q}(x)}{dx^2} = 0,
\end{aligned} \tag{22}$$

where the equation is obtained as the required result immediately. □

3. Differential Equations Associated with q-Hermite Polynomials

In this section, we introduce differential equations arising from the generating functions of q-Hermite polynomials. By using these differential equations, we can obtain the explicit identities for these polynomials. Many authors studied differential equations derived in the generating functions of special polynomials in order to derive explicit identities for special polynomials, see [11–20].

Let

$$\mathcal{G} := \mathcal{G}(t, [x]_q) = e^{2[x]_q t - t^2} = \sum_{n=0}^{\infty} H_{n,q}(x)\frac{t^n}{n!}, \quad x, t \in \mathbb{R}. \tag{23}$$

Then, we obtain the following equations using mathematical induction:

$$\begin{aligned}
\mathcal{G}^{(1)} &= \frac{\partial}{\partial t}\mathcal{G}(t, [x]_q) = \frac{\partial}{\partial t}\left(e^{2[x]_q t - t^2}\right) = e^{2[x]_q t - t^2}(2[x]_q - 2t)\\
&= (2[x]_q - 2t)\mathcal{G}(t, [x]_q)\\
&= (2[x]_q)\mathcal{G}(t, [x]_q)\\
&\quad + (-2)t\mathcal{G}(t, [x]_q),
\end{aligned} \tag{24}$$

$$\begin{aligned}
\mathcal{G}^{(2)} &= \frac{\partial}{\partial t}\mathcal{G}^{(1)}(t, [x]_q) = -2\mathcal{G}(t, [x]_q) + (2x - 2t)\mathcal{G}^{(1)}(t, [x]_q)\\
&= (-2 + 4[x]_q^2)\mathcal{G}(t, [x]_q)\\
&\quad + (-8[x]_q)t\mathcal{G}(t, [x]_q)\\
&\quad + (-2)^2 t^2 \mathcal{G}(t, [x]_q),
\end{aligned} \tag{25}$$

and

$$\begin{aligned}
\mathcal{G}^{(3)} &= \frac{\partial}{\partial t}\mathcal{G}^{(2)}(t, [x]_q)\\
&= (-8[x]_q + 8t)\mathcal{G}(t, [x]_q) + (-2 + 4[x]_q^2 - 8[x]_q t + 4t^2)\mathcal{G}^{(1)}(t, [x]_q)\\
&= (-12[x]_q + 8[x]_q^3)\mathcal{G}(t, [x]_q)\\
&\quad + (12 - 24[x]_q^2)t\mathcal{G}(t, [x]_q)\\
&\quad + (24[x]_q)t^2\mathcal{G}(t, [x]_q)\\
&\quad + (-2)^3 t^3 \mathcal{G}(t, [x]_q).
\end{aligned} \tag{26}$$

If we continue this process N-times, we can conjecture as follows.

$$\mathcal{G}^{(N)} = \left(\frac{\partial}{\partial t}\right)^N \mathcal{G}(t, [x]_q) = \sum_{i=0}^{N} a_i(N, [x]_q) t^i \mathcal{G}(t, [x]_q), (N = 0, 1, 2, \ldots). \tag{27}$$

By differentiating $\mathcal{G}^{(N)}$ with respect to t in Equation (27), we find

$$\mathcal{G}^{(N+1)} = \frac{\partial \mathcal{G}^{(N)}}{\partial t}$$

$$= \sum_{i=0}^{N} a_i(N, [x]_q) i t^{i-1} \mathcal{G}(t, [x]_q) + \sum_{i=0}^{N} a_i(N, [x]_q) t^i \mathcal{G}^{(1)}(t, [x]_q)$$

$$= \sum_{i=0}^{N} a_i(N, [x]_q) i t^{i-1} \mathcal{G}(t, [x]_q) + \sum_{i=0}^{N} a_i(N, [x]_q) t^i (2[x]_q - 2t) \mathcal{G}(t, [x]_q)$$

$$= \sum_{i=0}^{N} i a_i(N, [x]_q) t^{i-1} \mathcal{G}(t, [x]_q) + \sum_{i=0}^{N} (2[x]_q) a_i(N, [x]_q) t^i \mathcal{G}(t, [x]_q) \quad (28)$$

$$+ \sum_{i=0}^{N} (-2) a_i(N, [x]_q) t^{i+1} \mathcal{G}(t, [x]_q)$$

$$= \sum_{i=0}^{N-1} (i+1) a_{i+1}(N, [x]_q) t^i \mathcal{G}(t, [x]_q) + \sum_{i=0}^{N} (2[x]_q) a_i(N, [x]_q) t^i \mathcal{G}(t, [x]_q)$$

$$+ \sum_{i=1}^{N+1} (-2) a_{i-1}(N, [x]_q) t^i \mathcal{G}(t, [x]_q).$$

Replace N by $N+1$ in (27), and we obtain

$$\mathcal{G}^{(N+1)} = \sum_{i=0}^{N+1} a_i(N+1, [x]_q) t^i \mathcal{G}(t, [x]_q). \quad (29)$$

Theorem 4. *For $N = 0, 1, 2, \ldots$, the differential equation*

$$\mathcal{G}^{(N)} = \left(\frac{\partial}{\partial t}\right)^N \mathcal{G}(t, [x]_q) = \left(\sum_{i=0}^{N} a_i(N, [x]_q) t^i\right) \mathcal{G}(t, [x]_q) \quad (30)$$

has a solution

$$\mathcal{G} = \mathcal{G}(t, [x]_q) = e^{2[x]_q t - t^2}, \quad (31)$$

where

$$a_0(N, [x]_q) = \sum_{k=0}^{N-1} [x]_q^i a_1(N-1-k, [x]_q) + (2[x]_q)^N,$$

$$a_{N-1}(N, [x]_q) = (-2)^{N-1} N(2[x]_q),$$

$$a_N(N, [x]_q) = (-2)^N, \quad (32)$$

$$a_i(N+1, [x]_q)$$

$$= (i+1) \sum_{k=0}^{N} 2^k [x]_q^k a_{i+1}(N-k, [x]_q) + (-2) \sum_{k=0}^{N} 2^k [x]_q^k a_{i-1}(N-k, [x]_q),$$

$(1 \leq i \leq N-2).$

Proof. Comparing the coefficients on both sides of (28) and (29), we obtain

$$a_0(N+1, [x]_q) = a_1(N, [x]_q) + (2[x]_q) a_0(N, [x]_q),$$
$$a_N(N+1, [x]_q) = (2[x]_q) a_N(N, [x]_q) + (-2) a_{N-1}(N, [x]_q), \quad (33)$$
$$a_{N+1}(N+1, [x]_q) = (-2) a_N(N, [x]_q),$$

and

$$a_i(N+1, [x]_q) = (i+1) a_{i+1}(N, [x]_q)$$
$$+ (2[x]_q) a_i(N, [x]_q) + (-2) a_{i-1}(N, [x]_q), (1 \leq i \leq N-1). \quad (34)$$

In addition, from Equation (27), we get

$$\mathcal{G}(t,[x]_q) = \mathcal{G}^{(0)}(t,[x]_q) = a_0(0,[x]_q)\mathcal{G}(t,[x]_q), \qquad (35)$$

which gives

$$a_0(0,[x]_q) = 1. \qquad (36)$$

It is not difficult to show that

$$\begin{aligned}
&(2[x]_q)\mathcal{G}(t,[x]_q) + (-2)t\mathcal{G}(t,[x]_q) \\
&= \mathcal{G}^{(1)}(t,[x]_q) \\
&= \sum_{i=0}^{1} a_i(1,[x]_q)\mathcal{G}(t,[x]_q) \\
&= a_0(1,[x]_q)\mathcal{G}(t,[x]_q) + a_1(1,[x]_q)t\mathcal{G}(t,[x]_q).
\end{aligned} \qquad (37)$$

By using Equation (29), we can present the following as

$$a_0(1,[x]_q) = 2[x]_q, \quad a_1(1,[x]_q) = -2. \qquad (38)$$

From the Equation (33), we express

$$\begin{aligned}
&a_0(N+1,[x]_q) = a_1(N,[x]_q) + (2[x]_q)a_0(N,[x]_q), \\
&a_0(N,[x]_q) = a_1(N-1,[x]_q) + (2x)a_0(N-1,[x]_q),\ldots \\
&a_0(N+1,[x]_q) = \sum_{i=0}^{N}(2[x]_q)^i a_1(N-i,[x]_q) + (2[x]_q)^{N+1},
\end{aligned} \qquad (39)$$

$$\begin{aligned}
&a_N(N+1,[x]_q) = (2[x]_q)a_N(N,[x]_q) + (-2)a_{N-1}(N,[x]_q), \\
&a_{N-1}(N,[x]_q) = (2[x]_q)a_{N-1}(N-1,[x]_q) + (-2)a_{N-2}(N-1,[x]_q),\ldots \\
&a_N(N+1,[x]_q) = (-2)^N(N+1)(2[x]_q),
\end{aligned} \qquad (40)$$

and

$$\begin{aligned}
&a_{N+1}(N+1,[x]_q) = (-2)a_N(N,[x]_q), \\
&a_N(N,[x]_q) = (-2)a_{N-1}(N-1,[x]_q),\ldots \\
&a_{N+1}(N+1,[x]_q) = (-2)^{N+1}.
\end{aligned} \qquad (41)$$

Choose $i=1$ in (34). Then, we can find

$$a_1(N+1,[x]_q) = 2\sum_{k=0}^{N}(2[x]_q)^k a_2(N-k,[x]_q) + (-2)\sum_{k=0}^{N}(2[x]_q)^k a_0(N-k,[x]_q). \qquad (42)$$

For $1 \le i \le N-1$, by containing this process, we can deduce

$$\begin{aligned}
a_i(N+1,[x]_q) &= (i+1)\sum_{k=0}^{N}(2[x]_q)^k a_{i+1}(N-k,[x]_q) \\
&\quad + (-2)\sum_{k=0}^{N}(2[x]_q)^k a_{i-1}(N-k,[x]_q).
\end{aligned} \qquad (43)$$

Here, notice that the matrix $a_i(j,[x]_q)_{0 \leq i,j \leq N+1}$ is given by

$$\begin{pmatrix} 1 & 2[x]_q & -2+4[x]_q^2 & -12[x]_q+8[x]_q^3 & \cdots & \cdot \\ 0 & (-2) & (-2)2(2[x]_q) & 12-24[x]_q^2 & \cdots & \cdot \\ 0 & 0 & (-2)^2 & (-2)^2 3(2[x]_q) & \cdots & \cdot \\ 0 & 0 & 0 & (-2)^3 & \ddots & \cdot \\ \vdots & \vdots & \vdots & \vdots & \ddots & (-2)^N(N+1)(2[x]_q) \\ 0 & 0 & 0 & 0 & \cdots & (-2)^{N+1} \end{pmatrix} \quad (44)$$

From (33) to (43), we investigate the desired result immediately. □

Theorem 5. *For $N = 0, 1, 2, \ldots$, we have*

$$\mathbf{H}_{m+N,q}(x) = \sum_{i=0}^{m} \frac{\mathbf{H}_{m-i,q}(x) a_i(N,[x]_q) m!}{(m-i)!}, \quad (45)$$

where

$$\begin{aligned} a_0(N,[x]_q) &= \sum_{k=0}^{N-1} 2^k [x]_q^k a_1(N-1-k,[x]_q) + (2[x]_q)^N, \\ a_{N-1}(N,[x]_q) &= (-2)^{N-1} N(2[x]_q), \\ a_N(N,[x]_q) &= (-2)^N, \\ a_i(N+1,[x]_q) & \\ &= (i+1) \sum_{k=0}^{N} 2^k [x]_q^k a_{i+1}(N-k,[x]_q) + (-2) \sum_{k=0}^{N} 2^k [x]_q^k a_{i-1}(N-k,[x]_q), \\ (1 &\leq i \leq N-2). \end{aligned} \quad (46)$$

Proof. By making the N-times derivative for (4) with respect to t, we get

$$\left(\frac{\partial}{\partial t}\right)^N \mathcal{G}(t,[x]_q) = \left(\frac{\partial}{\partial t}\right)^N e^{2[x]_q t - t^2} = \sum_{m=0}^{\infty} \mathbf{H}_{m+N,q}(x) \frac{t^m}{m!}. \quad (47)$$

From (46) and (47), we obtain

$$a_0(N,[x]_q)\mathcal{G}(t,[x]_q) + \cdots + a_1(N,[x]_q) t^N \mathcal{G}(t,[x]_q) = \sum_{m=0}^{\infty} \mathbf{H}_{m+N,q}(x) \frac{t^m}{m!}, \quad (48)$$

which makes the required result. □

Corollary 1. *For $N = 0, 1, 2, \ldots$, if we take $m = 0$ in (45), then, the following holds*

$$\mathbf{H}_{N,q}(x) = a_0(N,[x]_q),$$

where,

$$a_0(N, [x]_q) = \sum_{k=0}^{N-1} 2^k [x]_q^k a_1(N-1-k, [x]_q) + (2[x]_q)^N,$$

$$a_1(N, [x]_q)$$

$$= 2 \sum_{k=0}^{N-1} (2[x]_q)^k a_2(N-k-1, [x]_q) + (-2) \sum_{k=0}^{N-1} (2[x]_q)^k a_0(N-k-1, [x]_q).$$
(49)

For $N = 0, 1, 2, \ldots$, the differential equation

$$\mathcal{G}^{(N)} = \left(\frac{\partial}{\partial t}\right)^N \mathcal{G}(t, [x]_q) = \left(\sum_{i=0}^{N} a_i(N, [x]_q) t^i\right) \mathcal{G}(t, [x]_q) \tag{50}$$

has a solution

$$\mathcal{G} = \mathcal{G}(t, [x]_q) = e^{2[x]_q t - t^2}. \tag{51}$$

The following Figure 1 is the graph representation for this solution by using MATHEMATICA.

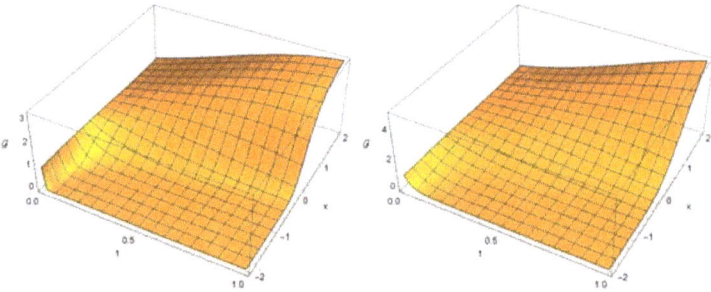

Figure 1. The surface for the solution $\mathcal{G}(t, [x]_q)$.

We can find the left surface of Figure 1 when we choose $-1 \leq x \leq 1, q = 1/10$, and $0 \leq t \leq 1$. Additionally, we can see the right surface of Figure 1 when we choose a condition such as $-1 \leq x \leq 1, q = 1/3$, and $0 \leq t \leq 1$. It particularly shows a higher-resolution density of the plots in the right surface of Figure 1.

4. Distribution and Pattern of Zeros of q-Hermite Polynomials

In this section, we examine the distribution and pattern of zeros of q-Hermite polynomials $\mathbf{H}_{n,q}(x)$ according to the change in degree n. Based on these results, we present a problem that needs to be approached theoretically. Many mathematicians now explore concepts more easily than in the past by using software. These experiments allow them to quickly create and visualize new ideas, review properties of various figures, as well as find and guess patterns. This numerical survey is particularly interesting since it helps them understand the basic concepts and solve numerous problems. Here, we use MATHEMATICA to find Figures 2–4 and approximate roots for q-Hermite polynomials.

The q-Hermite polynomials $\mathbf{H}_{n,q}(x)$ can be explicitly determined; see [21,22]. First, several examples are given, as follows.

$$\mathbf{H}_{0,q}(x) = 1,$$

$$\mathbf{H}_{1,q}(x) = -\frac{2}{-1+q} + \frac{2q^x}{-1+q},$$

$$\mathbf{H}_{2,q}(x) = -2 + \frac{4}{(-1+q)^2} - \frac{8q^x}{(-1+q)^2} + \frac{4q^{2x}}{(-1+q)^2}, \qquad (52)$$

$$\mathbf{H}_{3,q}(x) = \frac{4}{(-1+q)^3} - \frac{24q}{(-1+q)^3} + \frac{12q^2}{(-1+q)^3} + \frac{12q^x}{(-1+q)^3} - \frac{24q^{2x}}{(-1+q)^3}$$
$$+ \frac{8q^{3x}}{(-1+q)^3} + \frac{24q^{1+x}}{(-1+q)^3} - \frac{12q^{2+x}}{(-1+q)^3}.$$

We observe the distribution of zeros of the q-Hermite polynomials $\mathbf{H}_{n,q}(x) = 0$. In Figure 2, plots for the zeros of the q-Hermite polynomials $\mathbf{H}_{n,q}(x)$ for $n = 20$ and $x \in \mathbb{R}$ are as follows.

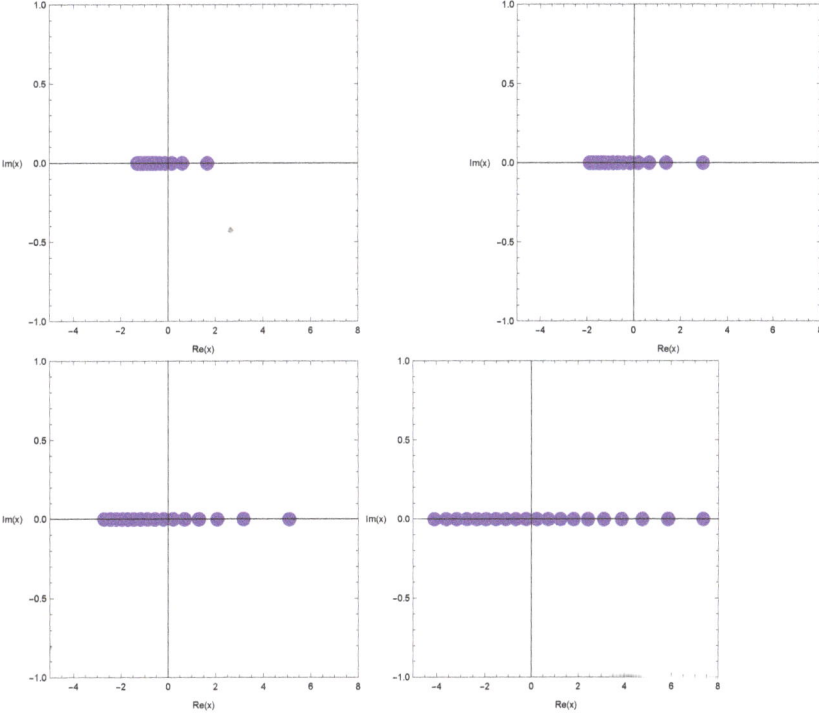

Figure 2. Zeros of $\mathbf{H}_{n,q}(x)$.

In the top-left picture of Figure 2, we choose $n = 20$ and $q = 3/10$. In the top-right picture of Figure 2, we consider conditions which are $n = 20$ and $q = 5/10$. We can find the bottom-left picture of Figure 2, when we consider $n = 20$ and $q = 7/10$. If we consider $n = 20$ and $q = 9/10$, then we can observe the bottom-right picture of Figure 2.

Stacks of zeros of the q-Hermite polynomials, $\mathbf{H}_{n,q}(x)$, for $1 \leq n < 20$ from a 3-D structure are presented as Figure 3.

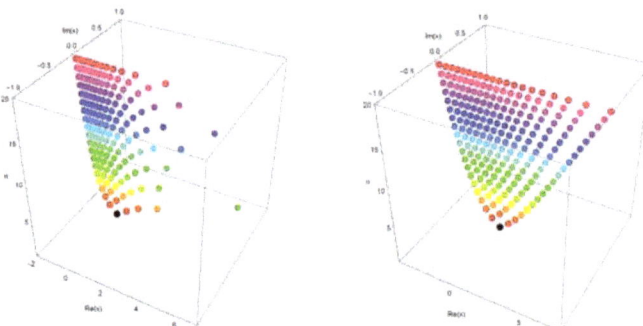

Figure 3. Stacks of zeros of $\mathbf{H}_{n,q}(x), 1 \leq n \leq 20$.

It is the left picture of Figure 3, when we consider $q = 1/2$. Additionally, if we consider $q = 9/10$, we can obtains the right picture of Figure 3.

Our numerical results for the approximate solutions of real zeros of the q-Hermite polynomials, $\mathbf{H}_{n,q}(x)$, with $q = 1/2$ and $x \in \mathbb{R}$ are displayed in Tables 1 and 2.

Table 1. Numbers of real and complex zeros of $\mathbf{H}_{n,\frac{1}{2}}(x)$.

Degree n	Real Zeros
1	1
2	2
3	3
4	4
5	4
6	5
7	6
8	7
9	7
10	8
11	8
12	9
13	10
14	10

The plot structures of real zeros of the q-Hermite polynomials, $\mathbf{H}_{n,q}(x)$, for $1 \leq n \leq 20$ are presented in Figure 4.

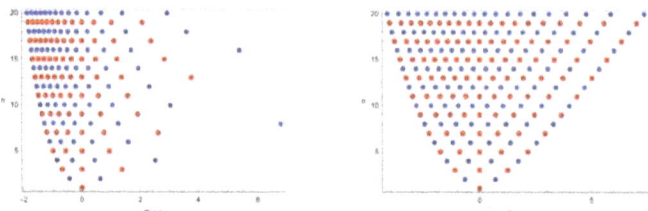

Figure 4. Stacks of zeros of $\mathbf{H}_{n,q}(x), 1 \leq n \leq 20$.

In the left picture of Figure 4, we choose $q = 5/10$. For $q = 9/10$, the right side of Figure 4 is presented. Next, we calculated an approximate solution that satisfies $H_{n,q}(x) = 0, x \in \mathbb{R}$. The results are shown in Table 2.

Table 2. Approximate solutions of $\mathbf{H}_{n,q}(x) = 0, x \in \mathbb{R}$.

Degree n	x
1	0
2	−0.436752, 0.629397
3	−0.689185, 0, 1.36726
4	−0.868165, −0.336082, 0.43894, 2.51738
5	−1.12122, −0.738054, −0.28456, 0.354831, 1.59042
6	−1.12122, −0.738054, −0.28456, 0.354831, 1.59042
7	−1.21784, −0.877176, −0.493795, 0, 0.756682, 2.61507
8	−1.30177, −0.993369, −0.658643, −0.251681, 0.305064, 1.24673, 6.76861

5. Conclusions and Discussion

In this paper, we derive a few solutions of special forms containing q-Hermit polynomials and find several properties of differential equations for these polynomials. Moreover, we find approximate values of real zeros for q-Hermit polynomials and analyze the structure of roots for these polynomials in a special condition from 3D.

We also identified the structure of q-Hermit polynomials under special several conditions. These conditions change the structure of the roots and the form of polynomials, and further research needs to be done on finding various properties. In addition, by simulating the structure of roots for Hermit polynomials through various methods using the results of this paper and multiple software, it is also thought that the characteristics of the roots' structure for higher-order equations will evolve into one area.

Author Contributions: Conceptualization, C.-S.R.; methodology, J.K.; writing—original draft preparation, C.-S.R.; writing—review and editing, J.K.; funding acquisition, J.K. All authors have read and agreed to the published version of the manuscript.

Funding: This research was supported by Basic Science Research Program through the National Research Foundation of Korea(NRF) funded by the Ministry of Science, ICT and Future Planning(No. 2017R1E1A1A03070483).

Institutional Review Board Statement: Not applicable.

Informed Consent Statement: Not applicable.

Data Availability Statement: The data presented in this study are available on request from the corresponding author.

Conflicts of Interest: The authors declare that they have no conflicts of interest to report regarding the present study.

References

1. Andrews, L.C. *Special Functions for Engineers and Mathematicians*; Macmillan. Co.: New York, NY, USA, 1985.
2. Appell, P.; Hermitt, J. *Fonctions Hypergéométriques et Hypersphériques: Polynomes d Hermite*; Gauthier-Villars: Paris, France, 1926.
3. Erdelyi, A.; Magnus, W.; Oberhettinger, F.; Tricomi, F.G. *Higher Transcendental Functions*; Krieger: New York, NY, USA, 1981; Volume 3.
4. Hermite, C. Sur un nouveau développement en série des fonctions. *Comptes Rendus l'Académie Sci.* **1864**, *58*, 93–100.
5. Laplace, P.S. Mémoire sur les intégrales définies, et leur application aux probabilités, et spécialment à la recherche du milieu qu'il faut choisir entre les résultats des observations. In *Mémoires de la Classe des Sciences Mathematiques et Physiques de l'Institut National de France*; Mémoires de l'Académie des sciences: Ière série, France, 1810; Volume 9, pp. 279–347.
6. Temme, N. *Special Functions: An Introduction to the Classical Functions of Mathematical Physics*; Wiley: New York, NY, USA, 1996.
7. Kim, M.S.; Hu, S. On p-adic Hurwitz-type Euler Zeta functions. *J. Number Theory* **2012**, *132*, 2977–3015. [CrossRef]
8. Kim, T.; Choi, J.; Kim, Y.H.; Ryoo, C.S. On q-Bernstein and q-Hermite polynomials. *Proc. Jangjeon Math. Soc.* **2011**, *14*, 215–221.
9. Robert, A.M. *A Course in p-adic Analysis, Graduate Text in Mathematics*; Springer: Berlin/Heidelberg, Germany, 2000; Volume 198.
10. Hwang, K.Y.; Ryoo, C.S. Some Identities Involving Two-Variable Partially Degenerate Hermite Polynomials Induced from Differential Equations and Structure of Their Roots. *Mathematics* **2020**, *8*, 632. [CrossRef]

11. Agarwal, R.P.; Ryoo, C.S. Differential equations associated with generalized Truesdell polynomials and distribution of their zeros. *J. Appl. Pure Math.* **2019**, *1*, 11–24.
12. Hwang, K.W.; Ryoo, C.S. Differential equations associated with two variable degenerate Hermite polynomials. *Mathematics* **2020**, *8*, 228. [CrossRef]
13. Kim, T.; Kim, D.S. Identities involving degenerate Euler numbers and polynomials arising from non-linear differential equations. *J. Nonlinear Sci. Appl.* **2016**, *9*, 2086–2098. [CrossRef]
14. Ryoo, C.S. Differential equations associated with generalized Bell polynomials and their zeros. *Open Math.* **2016**, *14*, 807–815. [CrossRef]
15. Ryoo, C.S. Differential equations associated with the generalized Euler polynomials of the second kind. *J. Comput. Appl. Math.* **2018**, *24*, 711–716.
16. Ryoo, C.S. Differential equations associated with tangent numbers. *J. Appl. Math. Inform.* **2016**, *34*, 487–494. [CrossRef]
17. Ryoo, C.S. Some identities involving Hermitt Kampé de Fériet polynomials arising from differential equations and location of their zeros. *Mathematics* **2019**, *7*, 23. [CrossRef]
18. Ryoo, C.S. Differential equations associated with degenerate tangent polynomials and computation of their zeros. *Dyn. Syst. Appl.* **2019**, *28*, 153–165.
19. Ryoo, C.S.; Agarwal, R.P.; Kang, J.Y. Differential equations associated with Bell-Carlitz polynomials and their zeros. *Neural Parallel Sci. Comput.* **2016**, *24*, 453–462.
20. Ryoo, C.S.; Agarwal, R.P.; Kang, J.Y. Some properties involving 2-variable modified partially degenerate Hermite polynomials derived from differential equations and distribution of their zeros. *Dyn. Syst. Appl.* **2020**, *29*, 248–269. [CrossRef]
21. Agarwal, R.P.; O'Regan, D. *Ordinary and Partial Differential Equations: With Special Unctions, Fourier Series and Boundary Value Problems*; Springer Science & Business Media: New York, NY, USA, 2009.
22. Ruiz, L.M.S.; Blanes, S. *Complementos de Ecuaciones Diferenciales: Resolucion Analitica, EDPs y Mathematica*; Academica Editorial UPV: Editorial Universitat Politècnica de València: València, Spain, 2012.

Article

A Forgotten Differential Equation Studied by Jacopo Riccati Revisited in Terms of Lie Symmetries

Daniele Ritelli

Department of Statistics, University of Bologna, Via Belle Arti 41, 40126 Bologna, Italy; daniele.ritelli@unibo.it

Abstract: In this paper we present a two parameter family of differential equations treated by Jacopo Riccati, which does not appear in any modern repertoires and we extend the original solution method to a four parameter family of equations, translating the Riccati approach in terms of Lie symmetries. To get the complete solution, hypergeometric functions come into play, which, of course, were unknown in Riccati's time. Re-discovering the method introduced by Riccati, called by himself dimidiata separazione (splitted separation), we arrive at the closed form integration of a differential equation, more general to the one treated in Riccati's contribution, and which also does not appear in the known repertoires.

Keywords: splitted separation; Lie symmetries; gauss hypergeometric functions

MSC: 34A05; 33C05

Citation: Ritelli, D. A Forgotten Differential Equation Studied by Jacopo Riccati Revisited in Terms of Lie Symmetries. *Mathematics* **2021**, *9*, 1312. https://doi.org/10.3390/math9111312

Academic Editor: Nickolai Kosmatov

Received: 24 May 2021
Accepted: 5 June 2021
Published: 7 June 2021

Publisher's Note: MDPI stays neutral with regard to jurisdictional claims in published maps and institutional affiliations.

Copyright: © 2021 by the author. Licensee MDPI, Basel, Switzerland. This article is an open access article distributed under the terms and conditions of the Creative Commons Attribution (CC BY) license (https://creativecommons.org/licenses/by/4.0/).

1. Introduction

Given a scalar ordinary differential equation in normal form, say

$$y' = \omega(x, y), \tag{1}$$

where we assume the usual existence and uniqueness conditions, i.e., $\omega : \Omega \subset \mathbb{R}^2 \to \mathbb{R}$ is a Lipschitz-continuous function and Ω is an open set, it is well known that the problem of representing its solutions in terms of elementary, or special, functions is, in general, analytically intractable. In some well known and particular situations, this representation is possible, according to some specific structure of the equation itself. Among the elementary solution methods, the most advanced is that of the search for an integrating factor, which, as we know, is related to the determination of a Lie symmetry, see [1] Section 2.5. When the integrating factor depends on both variables (x, y) some old-school texbooks like, for instance, [2] pages 50–51 or [3] pages 53–55, seek for the integrating factor using an "inspection method", useful when the given equation presents a particular structure. This special technique has a long, and probably forgotten, history. It was, in fact, introduced by the Italian mathematician Jacopo Francesco Riccati (1676–1754) and was published posthumously in 1761, in the first [4] of four tomes of Riccati, Opera Omnia, dedicated to his lectures on differential equations. Riccati called his method "dimidiata separazione" which can be translated as splitted separation. This paper is devoted to one particular family of equations studied by Riccati, revisiting it in terms of Lie symmetry and using the $_2F_1$ Gauss hypegeometric function to express in closed form its integral curves. Moreover, using Lie symmetry we solve a more general equation of the same kind.

2. Materials and Methods

2.1. The Original Equation

The equation proposed by Riccati, written in Pfaffian form, is:

$$y^m(x\,dx + y\,dy) = x^n(y\,dx - x\,dy). \tag{2}$$

Here follows Riccati's argument, given in modern terms; the original source, reference [4] page 486, is shown in Figure 1. The strategy is to seek for the primitive of the two differential forms, which appear in (2). The first step consists in writing (2), dividing both sides for y^2:

$$y^{m-2}(x\,\mathrm{d}x + y\,\mathrm{d}y) = x^n \frac{(y\,\mathrm{d}x - x\,\mathrm{d}y)}{y^2}. \tag{3}$$

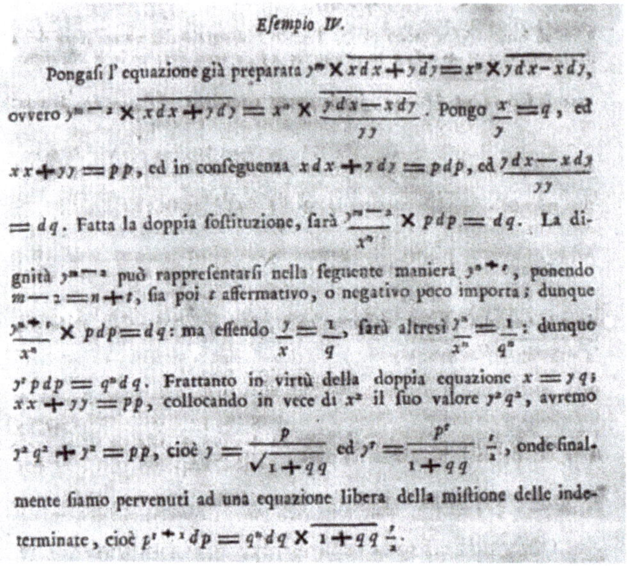
Eſempio IV.

Pongaſi l' equazione già preparata $y^m \times \overline{x\,dx + y\,dy} = x^n \times \overline{y\,dx - x\,dy}$, ovvero $y^{m-2} \times \overline{x\,dx + y\,dy} = x^n \times \dfrac{\overline{y\,dx - x\,dy}}{yy}$. Pongo $\dfrac{x}{y} = q$, ed $xx + yy = pp$, ed in conſeguenza $x\,dx + y\,dy = p\,dp$, ed $\dfrac{y\,dx - x\,dy}{yy} = dq$. Fatta la doppia ſoſtituzione, ſarà $\dfrac{y^{m-2}}{x^n} \times p\,dp = dq$. La dignità y^{m-2} può rappreſentarſi nella ſeguente maniera y^{n+t}, ponendo $m - 2 = n + t$, ſia poi t affermativo, o negativo poco importa; dunque $\dfrac{y^{n+t}}{x^n} \times p\,dp = dq$: ma eſſendo $\dfrac{y}{x} = \dfrac{1}{q}$, ſarà altresì $\dfrac{y^n}{x^n} = \dfrac{1}{q^n}$: dunque $y^t\,p\,dp = q^n\,dq$. Frattanto in virtù della doppia equazione $x = yq$; $xx + yy = pp$, collocando in vece di x^2 il ſuo valore y^2q^2, avremo $y^2q^2 + y^2 = pp$, cioè $y = \dfrac{p}{\sqrt{1+qq}}$ ed $y^t = \dfrac{p^t}{\overline{1+qq}}\,\tfrac{t}{2}$, onde finalmente ſiamo pervenuti ad una equazione libera della miſtione delle indeterminate, cioè $p^{t+1}\,dp = q^n\,dq \times \overline{1+qq}\,\tfrac{t}{2}$.

Figure 1. Riccati original treatment of (2).

In terms of total diffentential $Df = f_x\mathrm{d}x + f_y\mathrm{d}y$, we can consider Equation (3) using the following identities:

$$D\left(\frac{1}{2}(x^2 + y^2)\right) = x\,\mathrm{d}x + y\,\mathrm{d}y, \quad D\left(\frac{x}{y}\right) = \frac{y\,\mathrm{d}x - x\,\mathrm{d}y}{y^2}.$$

It is, then, natural to introduce the change of variables

$$q = q(x,y) = \frac{x}{y}, \quad p = p(x,y) = \sqrt{x^2 + y^2}. \tag{4}$$

To transform Equation (2) via this change of variable, we first write it in normal form:

$$y' = \frac{x^n y - x y^m}{y^{m+1} + x^{n+1}}. \tag{5}$$

For $n = m$ (5) obviously reduces to a homogeneous equation, solvable by elementary methods, whose solution is defined by:

$$\int_{\frac{y_0}{x_0}}^{\frac{y}{x}} \frac{1 + u^{n+1}}{u^n(1 + u^2)}\,\mathrm{d}u = \ln \frac{x_0}{x}. \tag{6}$$

We, thus, may assume $m \neq n$. Therefore, the change of variable (4) leads to the transformed equation

$$\frac{dp}{dq} = \frac{D_x[p(x,y(x)]}{D_x[q(x,y(x)]} = \frac{y(x)^2(x + y(x)y'(x))}{(y(x) - xy'(x))\sqrt{x^2 + y(x)^2}},$$

but, since $y'(x)$ is provided by (5), we obtain:

$$\frac{dp}{dq} = \frac{x^n y^{2-m}}{\sqrt{x^2 + y^2}}.$$

Expressing the original variables (x, y) in terms of (p, q), that is, inverting (4):

$$x = \frac{pq}{\sqrt{1+q^2}}, \quad y = \frac{p}{\sqrt{1+q^2}},$$

we arrive at the transformed equation

$$\frac{dp}{dq} = p^{-m+n+1} q^n \left(1 + q^2\right)^{\frac{m}{2} - \frac{n}{2} - 1}, \tag{7}$$

which is separable, so that the integration of (5) is, as a matter of fact, completed.

2.2. Approach Via Lie Theory

We skip the computation of the integrals generated by (7) since, in view of solving a more general family of equations, we will integrate (5) using the infinitesimal generator of the Lie group of symmetries associated to (5). This means (see [1] page 30 Equation (2.57)) that, given Equation (1), if we are able to find two functions $\xi(x, y)$, $\eta(x, y)$ verifying the linearized symmetry condition:

$$\eta'_x + \left(\eta'_y - \xi'_x\right)\omega - \xi'_x \omega^2 - \xi \omega'_x - \eta \omega'_y = 0, \tag{8}$$

it is possible to obtain the canonical coordinates associated with (5); see for instance [1] (p. 24).

We can formulate the following theorem, which describes the quadrature formula for the solution of the differential Equation (5).

Theorem 1. *If n, m are real numbers such that $n \neq m$ and if (x_0, y_0) lies in the positive quadrant, then the integral curve of (5) which passes for (x_0, y_0) is implicitly defined by:*

$$\frac{1}{m-n}\left(\left(x^2+y^2\right)^{\frac{m-n}{2}} - \left(x_0^2 + y_0^2\right)^{\frac{m-n}{2}}\right) = \int_{\frac{x_0}{y_0}}^{\frac{x}{y}} u^n \left(1 + u^2\right)^{\frac{m-n-2}{2}} du. \tag{9}$$

Proof. To integrate Equation (5), since we know the Riccati variable transformation, we can use the method indicated in [1] page 26 in order to reconstruct the Lie symmetries when canonical coordinates are given. In our situation we found that, defining

$$\xi(x, y) = \frac{x}{(x^2 + y^2)^{\frac{m-n}{2}}}, \quad \eta(x, y) = \frac{y}{(x^2 + y^2)^{\frac{m-n}{2}}}, \tag{10}$$

the linearized symmetry condition (8) is satisfied: This is a matter of algebraic computation. We explain the "reverse enginerinng" procedure employed to obtain (10). Following the argument of [1] page 26, if $(X, Y) = (X(x, y), Y(x, y))$ are canonical coordinates for the differential Equation (5), expressing the original variables (x, y) in terms of (X, Y) as $x = f(X, Y)$ and $y = g(X, Y)$ the invariance condition requires that the transformed coordinates must satisfy the following translation property:

$$\begin{cases} \hat{x} = f(X(x,y), Y(x,y) + \varepsilon), \\ \hat{y} = g(X(x,y), Y(x,y) + \varepsilon). \end{cases} \tag{11}$$

17

Now, also if it is not the case, we assume for a while the change of variable (4) as canonical, and since for it we have

$$f(X,Y) = \frac{XY}{\sqrt{1+X^2}}, \quad g(X,Y) = \frac{Y}{\sqrt{1+X^2}},$$

thus, the expressions in the right hand side in (11) read as:

$$\begin{cases} \hat{x} = x + \dfrac{x\,\varepsilon}{\sqrt{x^2+y^2}}, \\ \hat{y} = y + \dfrac{y\,\varepsilon}{\sqrt{x^2+y^2}}. \end{cases} \quad (12)$$

Differentiating with respect to ε (12) should provide, in case of canonical coordinates, the infinitesimal generator of the Lie symmetries of the differential Equation (5). In our situation from (12) we obtain:

$$\check{\xi}(x,y) = \frac{x}{\sqrt{x^2+y^2}}, \quad \check{\eta}(x,y) = \frac{y}{\sqrt{x^2+y^2}}.$$

The couple $(\check{\xi}, \check{\eta})$ misses the linearized symmetry condition (8); in fact, the left hand side of (8) evaluated when $\xi = \check{\eta}$ and $\eta = \check{\eta}$ is indeed:

$$\frac{(m-n-1)y^m x^n \sqrt{x^2+y^2}}{(y^{m+1}+x^{n+1})^2}.$$

This means that $(\check{\xi}, \check{\eta})$ is the infinitesimal generator for (5) only in the particular occurrence $m = n+1$ and, more importantly, gives us the suggestion to look for an infinitesimal generator of the form:

$$\xi_a(x,y) = \frac{x}{(x^2+y^2)^a}, \quad \eta_a(x,y) = \frac{y}{(x^2+y^2)^a},$$

where a is a real parameter which we choose in order to meet condition (8). Thus, evaluating the left hand side of (8) for (ξ_a, η_a), we get:

$$\frac{y^m x^n(-2a+m-n)(x^2+y^2)^{1-a}}{(y^{m+1}+x^{n+1})^2}. \quad (13)$$

It is clear that (13) is zero if $m-n-2a = 0$ and this explains why (10) is the infinitesimal generator of the Lie group of (5). Hence, using (10) we arrive at the canonical coordinates:

$$X(x,y) = \frac{x}{y}, \quad Y(x,y) = \frac{1}{m-n}(x^2+y^2)^{\frac{m-n}{2}}.$$

Thus, differential Equation (5) is fully separated in:

$$Y' = X^n \left(X^2+1\right)^{\frac{1}{2}(m-n-2)}. \quad (14)$$

Hence, integrating (14), we obtain:

$$Y(X) = \int_{X_0}^{X} u^n (1+u^2)^{\frac{1}{2}(m-n-2)} du + Y_0, \quad (15)$$

where $X_0 = x_0/y_0$. Formula (9) follows, turning back to the original variables (x,y). □

Remark 1. *Keeping in mind the elementary limit, for $p, q > 0$*

$$\lim_{\varepsilon \to 0} \frac{p^{\frac{\varepsilon}{2}} - q^{\frac{\varepsilon}{2}}}{\varepsilon} = \frac{1}{2} \ln \frac{p}{q},$$

we can take the limit for $m - n \to 0$ in (9), obtaining

$$\frac{1}{2} \ln \frac{x^2 + y^2}{x_0^2 + y_0^2} = \int_{\frac{x_0}{y_0}}^{\frac{x}{y}} u^n \left(1 + u^2\right)^{-1} du,$$

which, after some elementary computations, agrees with (6).

3. Results

3.1. Hypergeometric Integrations

In some particular situations it is indeed possible to evaluate the integral at the right hand side of (15) in closed form. To this aim, since some notions and terminology are needed. For the sake of completeness, we recall the integral representation of the Gauss hypergeometric function, which is, as is well known, defined in terms of power series, which converges for $|x| < 1$

$$_2F_1\left(\begin{array}{c}a,b\\c\end{array}\bigg|x\right) := \sum_{n=0}^{\infty} \frac{(a)_n (b)_n}{(c)_n} \frac{x^n}{n!}.$$

When $\operatorname{Re}(a) > 0$, $\operatorname{Re}(c - a) > 0$ then $_2F_1$ can be represented by the integral, see [5] Section 2 Equation (30):

$$_2F_1\left(\begin{array}{c}a,b\\c\end{array}\bigg|x\right) = \frac{\Gamma(c)}{\Gamma(a)\Gamma(c-a)} \int_0^1 \frac{s^{a-1}(1-s)^{c-a-1}}{(1-sx)^b} ds. \quad (16)$$

Equation (16) provides the analytical continuation of $_2F_1$ to the complex plane excluding the half line $(1, \infty)$; in the following we will use this fact. Thus integral (15) can be evaluated in closed form, if the hypotheses of the integral representation (16) are fulfilled.

Theorem 2. *If n, m are real numbers $n \neq m$ and if $n > -1$ for any (x_0, y_0) in the positive quadrant, then the integral curve of (5) which passes for (x_0, y_0) has equation $\Phi(x,y) = \Phi(x_0, y_0)$ where:*

$$\Phi(x,y) = \frac{n+1}{m-n}\left(x^2 + y^2\right)^{\frac{m-n}{2}} - \left(\frac{x}{y}\right)^{n+1} {}_2F_1\left(\begin{array}{c}\frac{n+1}{2}, \frac{n-m+2}{2}\\ \frac{n+3}{2}\end{array}\bigg| -\frac{x^2}{y^2}\right). \quad (17)$$

Proof. If $n > -1$ it is possible to invoke (16); in fact, we express the integral in the right hand side of (15) as

$$\frac{1}{2}\left(\int_0^{X^2} u^{\frac{n-1}{2}} (1+u)^{\frac{m-n-2}{2}} du - \int_0^{X_0^2} u^{\frac{n-1}{2}} (1+u)^{\frac{m-n-2}{2}} du\right) + Y_0. \quad (18)$$

Notice that we must assume the convergence of the integrand in the origin, which is guaranteed by the assumption $n > -1$. Then, normalizing the integration intervals with the change of variable $s = X^2 \sigma$ and $s = X_0^2 \sigma$ in the first and the second integral, respectively, in (18) we use (16), to rewrite (14) as:

$$Y(X) = \frac{1}{2}\left(\frac{2X^{n+1}}{n+1} {}_2F_1\left(\begin{array}{c}\frac{n+1}{2}, \frac{n+2-m}{2}\\ \frac{n+3}{2}\end{array}\bigg| -X^2\right) - \frac{2X_0^{n+1}}{n+1} {}_2F_1\left(\begin{array}{c}\frac{n+1}{2}, \frac{n+2-m}{2}\\ \frac{n+3}{2}\end{array}\bigg| -X_0^2\right)\right) + Y_0.$$

Going back to the original variables, we get Equation (17). □

Remark 2. Since the argument of $_2F_1$ in (17) is strictly negative, and so we operate in the analytic continuation of $_2F_1$ itself, function $\Phi(x,y)$ is well posed in the interior of the first quadrant.

Remark 3. The hypergeometric structure of (17) allows algebraic implicit solutions of (5) provided that the quantity $(n+2-m)/2$ turns out to be a negative integer, so that the $_2F_1$ collapses to a polynomial, that, of course, is strictly connected to the fact that in this case integral (9) is computed in terms of elementary functions. Other solutions of (17) expressible in terms of the elementary transcendental occur for half integer values of $n+1/2$ and $(n+2-m)/2$. We provide a couple of illustrative examples.

Example 1. For instance, for $n=2$, $m=6$ (17) allows algebraic solutions: in fact, the differential equation for $x_0, y_0 > 0$

$$\begin{cases} y' = \dfrac{x^2 y - xy^6}{x^3 + y^7}, \\ y(x_0) = y_0, \end{cases}$$

has an implicit solution given by:

$$\frac{3}{4}\left(x^2+y^2\right)^2 - \frac{3x^5+5x^3y^2}{5y^5} = \frac{3}{4}\left(x_0^2+y_0^2\right)^2 - \frac{3x_0^5+5x_0^3y_0^2}{5y_0^5}.$$

Of course, in this situation it is possible to represent the integral curves in polynomial form, which in this case for simplicity we took $x_0 = y_0 = 1$:

$$30x^2y^7 + 15y^9 - 12x^5 + 15x^4y^5 - 20x^3y^2 - 28y^5 = 0.$$

Example 2. If we take $n=2$ and $m=3$ in (17) relation

$$_2F_1\left(\begin{array}{c}\frac{3}{2},\frac{1}{2} \\ \frac{5}{2}\end{array}\bigg| -z\right) = \frac{3}{2z^{3/2}}\left(\sqrt{z(1+z)} - \operatorname{arcsinh}\sqrt{z}\right)$$

comes into play, see [6], http://functions.wolfram.com/07.23.03.2889.01 (accessed on 5 June 2021), so that the solution to

$$\begin{cases} y' = \dfrac{x^2 y - xy^3}{x^3 + y^4}, \\ y(x_0) = y_0, \end{cases}$$

for positive initial data is:

$$\frac{(2y^2-x)\sqrt{x^2+y^2}}{y^2} + \operatorname{arcsinh}\frac{x}{y} = \frac{(2y_0^2-x_0)\sqrt{x_0^2+y_0^2}}{y_0^2} + \operatorname{arcsinh}\frac{x_0}{y_0}.$$

If $n > -1$ hypotheses for the integral hypergeometric representation (16) are not fulfilled, but it is still possible, and the second parameter m is chosen suitably to obtain a hypergeometric representation of the solution of (5) as shown in the following Theorem 3.

Theorem 3. If n, m are real numbers $n \neq m$ such that $n \leq -1$ and $m < 1$ then for any (x_0, y_0) in the positive quadrant, the integral curve of (5) which passes for (x_0, y_0) has equation $\Xi(x,y) = \Xi(x_0, y_0)$, where:

$$\Xi(x,y) = \frac{1-m}{m-n}\left(x^2+y^2\right)^{\frac{m-n}{2}} + \left(\frac{y}{x}\right)^{1-m} {}_2F_1\left(\begin{array}{c}\frac{1-m}{2}, \frac{n-m+2}{2} \\ \frac{3-m}{2}\end{array}\bigg| -\frac{y^2}{x^2}\right). \tag{19}$$

Proof. Since we cannot use the integral representation to evaluate integral (15) we change variable $u = 1/v$ so that

$$Y = \int_{\frac{1}{X}}^{\frac{1}{x_0}} v^{-m}\left(1+v^2\right)^{\frac{1}{2}(m-n-2)} dv + Y_0. \quad (20)$$

At this point, integral (20) can be handled with the same technique used in Theorem 2 to arrive at thesis (19); we omit the computational details here. □

Example 3. *Taking $n = -2$, $m = -3$ differential Equation (17) becomes*

$$\begin{cases} y' = \dfrac{y^4 - x^3}{x^2 y + xy^3}, \\ y(x_0) = y_0, \end{cases}$$

and its solution via (19) is given by:

$$\frac{2x^2 - x + y^2}{x\sqrt{x^2 + y^2}} = \frac{2x_0^2 - x_0 + y_0^2}{x_0\sqrt{x_0^2 + y_0^2}}.$$

3.2. A More General Equation

The use of the Lie symmetries, until now has not improved what Riccati found, if we leave aside the hypergeometric integration of (14) that was of course unknown in Riccati's age. However, having a more general perspective enables the discovery of a richer family of differential equations which can be treated with this method. Let r, s be two positive reals and let m and n be two real numbers such that $n \neq m$. Consider the differential equation in Pfaffian form:

$$y^m D\left(\frac{1}{r}(x^r + y^r)\right) = x^n y^{s+1} D\left(\frac{x^s}{sy^s}\right). \quad (21)$$

Equation (21) can be written in normal form as

$$y' = \frac{x^{n+s-1}y - x^r y^m}{y^{m+r} + x^{n+s}}. \quad (22)$$

We are in position to provide the generalization of Theorem 1.

Theorem 4. *If n, m, r, are real numbers $n + r \neq m + s$ and if (x_0, y_0) lies in the positive quadrant, then the integral curve of (22) which passes for (x_0, y_0) is implicitly defined by:*

$$\frac{1}{m-n+r-s}\left(\left(x^{1+r} + y^{1+r}\right)^{\frac{m-n+r-s}{1+r}} - \left(x_0^{1+r} + y_0^{1+r}\right)^{\frac{m-n+r-s}{2}}\right) = \int_{\frac{x_0}{y_0}}^{\frac{x}{y}} u^{n+s-1}\left(1 + u^{1+r}\right)^{\frac{m-n-s-1}{2}} du. \quad (23)$$

Proof. The thesis follows observing that in this situation the infinitesimal generator of the Lie group of transformation associated at the Equation (22) is

$$\xi(x,y) = \frac{x}{(x^{r+1} + y^{r+1})^{\frac{m-n+r-s}{r+1}}}, \quad \eta(x,y) = \frac{y}{(x^{r+1} + y^{r+1})^{\frac{m-n+r-s}{r+1}}}. \quad (24)$$

Therefore the canonical coordinates are readily obtained:

$$Y(x,y) = \frac{(x^{r+1} + y^{r+1})^{\frac{m-n+r-s}{r+1}}}{m-n+r-s}, \quad X(x,y) = \frac{x}{y},$$

and using these coordinates Equation (22) is transformed into:

$$Y' = X^{n+s-1}(1 + X^{r+1})^{\frac{m-n-s-1}{r+1}}. \tag{25}$$

Equation (23) follows in a similar fashion as Theorem 2. □

Remark 4. *For $r = s = 1$ Theorem 4 reduces to Theorem 1.*

At this point it is also easy to generalize Theorem 2 using again the integral representation (16).

Theorem 5. *n, m are real numbers $n + r \neq m + s$ and assume:*

$$n + s > 0. \tag{26}$$

If (x_0, y_0) lies in the positive quadrant, then the integral curve of (22) for (x_0, y_0) has equation:

$$\Psi(x,y) = \Psi(x_0, y_0), \tag{27}$$

where:

$$\Psi(x,y) = \frac{n+s}{m-n+r-s}\left(x^{r+1} + y^{r+1}\right)^{\frac{m-n+r-s}{1+r}} - \left(\frac{x}{y}\right)^{n+s} {}_2F_1\left(\begin{array}{c}\frac{n+s}{1+r}, \frac{1-m+n+s}{1+r} \\ \frac{n+r+s+1}{r+1}\end{array} \middle| -\frac{x^{r+1}}{y^{r+1}}\right). \tag{28}$$

Proof. To solve (22) we have to integrate the canonical (fully separated) differential Equation (25) and, as in Theorem 2, in order to express the integral in terms of ${}_2F_1$ we need to extend the integration interval including the origin and so we have to impose conditions (see the right hand side of (23)) $1 - n - s < 1$ which is ensured by (26). Thus we can adapt the argument of Theorem 2 to rewrite the right hand side of (23) as:

$$\frac{1}{1+r}\left(\int_0^{X^{1+r}} \frac{u^{\frac{n-r+s-1}{1+r}}}{(1+u)^{\frac{n-m+s+1}{r+1}}} du - \int_0^{X_0^{1+r}} \frac{u^{\frac{n-r+s-1}{1+r}}}{(1+u)^{\frac{n-m+s+1}{r+1}}} du\right) + Y_0. \tag{29}$$

Normalizing the intervals of integration on the right hand side of (29), we can use the same argument of Theorem 2 to arrive at (28). □

Example 4. *We take, for instance, $r = 2$, $s = 3$, $m = 2$, $n = 3$ and the initial data $x_0 = 1$, $y_0 = 2$ (22) takes the form:*

$$\begin{cases} y' = \dfrac{x^5 y - x^2 y^2}{x^6 + y^4}, \\ y(x_0) = y_0. \end{cases}$$

Using (27) and (28) we can provide the solution in implicit form, which to the best of our knowledge, is not yet reported in any repertoire and not obtainable via computer algebra:

$$\frac{2x^3 + 3y^3 + y}{y(x^3 + y^3)^{2/3}} = \frac{2x_0^3 + 3y_0^3 + y_0}{y_0(x_0^3 + y_0^3)^{2/3}},$$

or in algebraic form, for a suitable constant of integration c:

$$\left(2x^3 + 3y^3 + y\right)^3 = c^3 y^3 \left(x^3 + y^3\right)^2.$$

In the case that integral representation condition (26) is not fulfilled, theorem (5) cannot be invoked, but it is possible, using exactly the same techniques, obtain the analogous of Theorem 3.

Theorem 6. *If n, m are real numbers $n + s \neq m + r$ such that $n \leq -s$ and if condition*

$$\frac{m+r}{1+r} < 1, \tag{30}$$

then for any (x_0, y_0) in the positive quadrant, the integral curve of (22) which passes for (x_0, y_0) has equation $\Lambda(x, y) = \Lambda(x_0, y_0)$, where

$$\Lambda(x,y) = \frac{1-m}{m-n+r-s}\left(x^{r+1} + y^{r+1}\right)^{\frac{m-n+r-s}{1+r}} \\ + \left(\frac{y}{x}\right)^{1-m} {}_2F_1\left(\begin{array}{c} \frac{1-m}{1+r}, \frac{n-m+s+1}{1+r} \\ \frac{r-m+2}{1+r} \end{array} \middle| -\frac{y^{1+r}}{x^{1+r}}\right). \tag{31}$$

Proof. Since in this situation the integrand at the right hand side of (23) is not integrable at the origin we use, as we did in theorem 3, the variable transformation $u = 1/v$, obtaining:

$$Y - Y_0 = \frac{1}{1+r} \int_{\frac{1}{x^{1+r}}}^{\frac{1}{x_0^{1+r}}} \frac{v^{-\frac{m+r}{1+r}}}{(1+v)^{\frac{n-m+1+s}{1+r}}} \, dv. \tag{32}$$

Condition (30) ensures the integrability at the origin of (32) and from this point the same hypergeometric integration procedure can be repeated concluding the proof of the theorem. □

Example 5. *Taking $n = -4$, $m = -2$, $r = 1$, $s = 2$ Equation (22) assumes the form*

$$y' = \frac{\frac{y}{x^3} - \frac{x}{y^2}}{\frac{1}{x^2} + \frac{1}{y}} = -\frac{x^4 - y^3}{x^3 y + xy^2}.$$

From (31) we infer that integral curves through (x_0, y_0) in the first quadrant are:

$$\frac{(2x^2 + y)\sqrt{x^2 + y^2}}{x^2} - \operatorname{arcsinh}\left(\frac{y}{x}\right) = \frac{(2x_0^2 + y_0)\sqrt{x_0^2 + y_0^2}}{x_0^2} - \operatorname{arcsinh}\left(\frac{y_0}{x_0}\right),$$

Notice that we used the identity.

$$_2F_1\left(\begin{array}{c} \frac{3}{2}, \frac{1}{1} \\ \frac{5}{2} \end{array} \middle| -z\right) = \frac{1}{2}\left(\frac{3\sqrt{1+z}}{z} - \frac{3\operatorname{arcsinh}\sqrt{z}}{z^{\frac{3}{2}}}\right),$$

see [6], http://functions.wolfram.com/HypergeometricFunctions/Hypergeometric2F1/03/07/07/03/0012/ (accessed on 5 June 2021).

4. Discussion

Starting from a two parameter family of differential equations, (5), studied by Jacopo Riccati in the second part of his treatise [4], we interpreted Riccati's procedure in terms of Lie symmetries, extending it to the more general four parameter family of Equation (22). Once the canonical form of both families of equations has been obtained, see (14) and (25) providing quadrature relations, Theorems 1 and 4, we derive, where possible, through integral representation of Gauss hypergeometric function $_2F_1$, the explicit representation of integral curves, Theorems 2, 3, 5 and 6. Finally, some particular cases have been highlighted in which these representations are given in terms of algebraic curves or containing elementary transcendents. Note that none of the particular cases reported in the Examples 1–5 appear in specialistic repertories and are not obtainable via computer algebra. The latter, however, greatly facilitated the search for infinitesimal generators (10) and (24) used in the proofs of Theorems 1 and 4.

5. Conclusions

Hopefully the contribution made in this article is a prelude to further research developments in the field of ordinary differential equations, continuing the historical interpretation approach adopted here, i.e., not limiting it to a chronological description of the results obtained by the founding masters, but rather to mastering their techniques, in the light of both the most recent knowledge, such as Lie symmetries, used in this article, and computer algebra, which allows to tackle computational difficulties that could not be faced previously and to consider generalisations of equations dealt with in the past.

Funding: Work supported by RFO 2018 (Panel 13) Italian grant funding.

Acknowledgments: Jacopo Riccati's lectures on differential equations have been highlighted to me by G. Mingari Scarpello: I take the opportunity to thank him warmly. To access Riccati's book I took full advantage of the on-line resources provided by Biblioteca Europea di Informazione e Cultura https://www.beic.it/it/articoli/biblioteca-digitale (accessed on 5 June 2021).

Conflicts of Interest: The author declares that he has no known competing financial interests or personal relationships that could have appeared to influence the work reported in this paper.

References

1. Hydon, P.E. *Symmetry Methods for Differential Equations*; Cambridge University Press: Cambridge, UK, 2000.
2. Spiegel, M.R. *Applied Differential Equation*, 2nd ed.; Prentice-Hall Inc.: Englewood Cliffs, NJ, USA, 1967.
3. Ritger, P.D.; Rose, N.J. *Differential Equation with Applications*; Mac Graw-Hill: New York, NY, USA, 1968.
4. Riccati, J. *Opere del Conte Jacopo Riccati, Nobile Trevigiano, Tomo I*; Appresso J. Giusti: Lucca, Italy, 1761.
5. Legendre, A.M. *Exercices de Calcul Intégral sur Divers Ordres de Transcendantes et Sur Les Quadratures*; Courcier: Paris, France, 1811.
6. Wolfram. The Mathematical Functions Website. Available online: http://functions.wolfram.com (accessed on 5 June 2021).

Article

Runge–Kutta Pairs of Orders 6(5) with Coefficients Trained to Perform Best on Classical Orbits

Yu-Cheng Shen [1], Chia-Liang Lin [2], Theodore E. Simos [3,4,5,6,7,*] and Charalampos Tsitouras [8]

1. Department of Preschool Education, School of Educational Sciences, Huaiyin Campus, Huaiyin Normal University, Huaian City 223300, China; roscoeshen@gmail.com
2. Department of Visual Communications, School of Arts, Huzhou University, Huzhou 313000, China; tronic1983@gmail.com
3. College of Applied Mathematics, Chengdu University of Information Technology, Chengdu 610225, China
4. Scientific and Educational Center "Digital Industry", South Ural State University, 76 Lenin Ave., 454 080 Chelyabinsk, Russia
5. Department of Medical Research, China Medical University Hospital, China Medical University, Taichung City 40402, Taiwan
6. Data Recovery Key Laboratory of Sichuan Province, Neijiang Normal University, Neijiang 641100, China
7. Section of Mathematics, Department of Civil Engineering, Democritus University of Thrace, 67100 Xanthi, Greece
8. General Department, GR34-400 Euripus Campus, National & Kapodistrian University of Athens, 15772 Athens, Greece; tsitourasc@uoa.gr
* Correspondence: tsimos.conf@gmail.com

Abstract: We consider a family of explicit Runge–Kutta pairs of orders six and five without any additional property (reduced truncation errors, Hamiltonian preservation, symplecticness, etc.). This family offers five parameters that someone chooses freely. Then, we train them in order for the presented method to furnish the best results on a couple of Kepler orbits, a certain interval and tolerance. Consequently, we observe an efficient performance on a wide range of orbital problems (i.e., Kepler for a variety of eccentricities, perturbed Kepler with various disturbances, Arenstorf and Pleiades). About 1.8 digits of accuracy is gained on average over conventional pairs, which is truly remarkable for methods coming from the same family and order.

Keywords: initial value problem; Kepler-type orbits; Runge–Kutta; differential evolution

MSC: 65L05; 65L06; 90C26; 90C30

1. Introduction

The initial value problem (IVP) is

$$y' = f(x,y), y(x_0) = y_0 \qquad (1)$$

with $x_0 \in \mathbb{R}$, $y, y' \in \mathbb{R}^m$ and $f : \mathbb{R} \times \mathbb{R}^m \to \mathbb{R}^m$.

Runge–Kutta (RK) pairs are amongst the most popular numerical methods for addressing (1). They are characterized by the following Butcher tableau [1,2]:

$$\begin{array}{c|c} c & A \\ \hline & b \\ & \hat{b} \end{array}$$

with $b^T, \hat{b}^T, c \in R^s$ and $A \in R^{s \times s}$. Then, the method shares s stages, and when $c_1 = 0$ and A is strictly lower triangular, it is evaluated explicitly. The approximated solution steps from (x_n, y_n) to $x_{n+1} = x_n + h_n$ by producing two estimations for $y(x_{n+1})$. Namely, y_{n+1} and $\hat{y}_{n+1}$, given by

$$y_{n+1} = y_n + h_n \sum_{i=1}^{s} b_i f_i$$

and

$$\hat{y}_{n+1} = y_n + h_n \sum_{i=1}^{s} \hat{b}_i f_i$$

with

$$f_i = f(x_n + c_i h_n, y_n + h_n \sum_{j=1}^{i-1} a_{ij} f_j),$$

for $i = 1, 2, \cdots, s$. These two approximations y_{n+1} and $\hat{y}_{n+1}$ are of algebraic orders p and $q < p$ respectively. Thus, a local error estimation

$$\epsilon_n = h_n^{p-q-1} \cdot \|y_{n+1} - \hat{y}_{n+1}\|$$

is formed in every step and is combined in an algorithm for changing the step size:

$$h_{n+1} = 0.9 \cdot h_n \cdot \left(\frac{t}{\epsilon_n}\right)^{1/p},$$

where t is a tolerance given by the user. When $\epsilon_n < t$, the above formula is used for the new step forward. In reverse, we also use it, but the solution is not advanced and h_{n+1} is a new version of h_n. Details can be found in [3]. As an abbreviation, these methods are named RKp(q) pairs.

Runge–Kutta methods were introduced back in the late 19th century [4,5]. After 1960, RK pairs appeared. Fehlberg gave the first celebrated such pairs of orders 5(4), 6(5) and 8(7) [6,7]. Dormand and Prince followed in the early 1980s [8,9]. Our group has also presented a series of successful RK pairs [10–13].

Runge—Kutta pairs are suited for efficiently solving almost every non-stiff problem of the form (1). The variety of pairs is explained by the accuracy required. Thus, when less accuracy is required, the lowest RK pairs are more efficient. In contract, for stringent accuracies at quadruple precision, a high-order pair should be chosen [14].

Here we focus on RK6(5) pairs, which are preferred for moderate to higher accuracies. We are especially interested in problems (1) that resemble Kepler-like orbits. Thus, we will propose a particular RK6(5) pair for addressing this type of problem.

2. Producing Runge–Kutta Pairs of Orders 6(5) and Training Their Coefficients

Runge–Kutta pairs of orders six and five are amongst the most frequently used. The coefficients have to satisfy 54 order conditions. Thus, families of solutions have been discovered over the years. Here we chose the Verner-DLMP [15,16] family, which has the advantage of being solved linearly. Then, we freely chose the coefficients c_2, c_4, c_5, c_6, c_7 and $\hat{b}_9$. Pairs from this family have been proven to perform most efficiently in various classes of problems [17].

We proceed by explicitly evaluating the remaining coefficients. The algorithm is discussed in [10] and is given as a Mathematica [18] package in the Appendix A.

Although $s = 9$, the family spends only eight stages per step since the ninth stage is used as the first stage of the next step. This property is called FSAL (first stage as last).

The next question to be answered is regarding how to select the free parameters. Traditionally we try to minimize the norm of the principal term of the local truncation error. That is, the coefficients of h^7 in the residual of Taylor error expansions corresponding to the sixth-order method of the underlying RK pair.

We intend to derive a particular RK6(5) pair belonging to the family of interest here. The resulting pair has to perform best on Kepler orbits and other problems of this nature. Thus, we concentrate on the particular orbit

$$\begin{aligned}
{}^1y' &= {}^3y, \\
{}^2y' &= {}^4y, \\
{}^3y' &= -\frac{{}^1y}{\left(\sqrt{{}^1y^2 + {}^2y^2}\right)^3}, \\
{}^4y' &= -\frac{{}^2y}{\left(\sqrt{{}^1y^2 + {}^2y^2}\right)^3},
\end{aligned}$$

with $x \in [0, 10\pi]$, $y(0) = \left[1 - ecc, 0, 0, \sqrt{\frac{1+ecc}{1-ecc}}\right]^T$ and the theoretical solution

$${}^1y(x) = \cos(v) - ecc, \quad {}^2y(x) = \sin(v)\sqrt{1 - ecc^2}.$$

In the above, $v = ecc \cdot \sin(u) + x$, ecc is the eccentricity, and the components of y are denoted by the left superscript. They should not be confused with $y_1 = \left[{}^1y_1, {}^2y_1, {}^3y_1, {}^4y_1\right]^T$, $y_2 = \left[{}^1y_2, {}^2y_2, {}^3y_2, {}^4y_2\right]^T$, $y_3, \cdots$, which represent the vectors approximating the solution at $x_1, x_2, x_3, \cdots$.

This problem can be solved with an RK6(5) pair from the family we are interested in here. After a certain run, we recorded the number fev of function evaluations (stages) needed and the global error ge observed over the mesh (grid) in the interval of integration. Then, we formed the efficiency measure

$$u = fev \cdot ge^{1/6}. \tag{2}$$

Running DLMP6(5) twice for Kepler we obtained the efficiency measures $\hat{u}_1$ and $\hat{u}_2$ as reported in Table 1. For example, we needed 1121 stages in order to achieve a global error of $2.14 \cdot 10^{-6}$ when running Kepler for $ecc = 0$, $x_{end} = 10\pi$ and $tol = 10^{-7}$. Thus, we obtained $\hat{u}_1 = 1123 \cdot 2.14 \cdot 10^{-6} \approx 127.22$, as reported in Table 1. Analogously, for a second run with $ecc = 0.6$, $x_{end} = 20\pi$ and $tol = 10^{-11}$ we observed $\hat{u}_2 = 833.27$.

Let us suppose that any new pair NEW6(5) furnishes corresponding efficiency measures $\tilde{u}_1$ and $\tilde{u}_2$ for the same runs. Then, as a fitness function we form the sum

$$u = \frac{\hat{u}_1}{\tilde{u}_1} + \frac{\hat{u}_2}{\tilde{u}_2},$$

and try to maximize it. That is, the fitness function is actually two whole runs of initial value problems. The value u changes according to the selection of the free parameters c_2, c_4, c_5, c_6, c_7 and $\hat{b}_9$.

The original idea is based on [19]. For the minimization of u we used the differential evolution technique [20]. We have already tried this approach and obtained some interesting results in producing Numerov-type methods for integrating orbits [21]. In this latter work we trained the coefficients of a Numerov-type method on a Kepler orbit. We observed very pleasant results over a set of Kepler orbits as well as other known orbital problems.

Table 1. Efficiency measures for both runs and pairs.

	ecc	x_{end}	tol	DLMP6(5)	NEW6(5)	Ratio $\hat{u}/\tilde{u}$
First run	0	10π	10^{-7}	$\hat{u}_1 = 127.22$	$\tilde{u}_1 = 50.64$	2.51
Second run	0.6	20π	10^{-11}	$\hat{u}_2 = 833.27$	$\tilde{u}_2 = 386.64$	2.16

The optimization furnished six values for the free parameters. They are included with the rest of the coefficients in the resulting pair NEW6(5) presented in Table 2.

Table 2. Coefficients of the proposed NEW6(5) pair, accurate for double precision computations.

$c_2 = 0.173146279530013,$	$c_3 = 0.163620769891761,$	$c_4 = 0.245431154837642,$
$c_5 = 0.452502877641229,$	$c_6 = 0.902924768667267,$	$c_7 = 0.8101151362080617,$
$c_1 = 0, c_8 = c_9 = 1,$	$b_1 = 0.0794169052387116,$	$b_2 = b_3 = 0,$
$b_4 = 0.320063598496390,$	$b_5 = 0.179217292937057,$	$b_6 = -0.2872484367615202,$
$b_7 = 0.573172758378662,$	$b_8 = 0.135377881710699,$	$b_9 = 0$
$\hat{b}_1 = 0.148854176113754,$	$\hat{b}_2 = \hat{b}_3 = 0,$	$\hat{b}_4 = 0.291009331941132,$
$\hat{b}_5 = 0.229278395578701,$	$\hat{b}_6 = -0.1155397766857130,$	$\hat{b}_7 = 0.429687174664803,$
$\hat{b}_8 = 0.0167106983873234,$	$\hat{b}_9 = 0.064345053530889,$	
$a_{21} = 0.173146279530013,$	$a_{31} = 0.0863111204651556,$	$a_{32} = 0.077309649426606,$
$a_{41} = 0.061357788709411,$	$a_{42} = 0,$	$a_{43} = 0.184073366128232,$
$a_{51} = 0.178735636864969,$	$a_{52} = 0,$	$a_{53} = -0.430121641642955,$
$a_{54} = 0.703888882419215,$	$a_{61} = -0.3492563988707026,$	$a_{62} = 0,$
$a_{63} = 4.2286674995349015,$	$a_{64} = -5.131590895887595,$	$a_{65} = 2.155104563890663,$
$a_{71} = -0.004184382566843,$	$a_{72} = 0,$	$a_{73} = 1.062724280290705,$
$a_{74} = -1.188530484293243,$	$a_{75} = 0.8944565948851806,$	$a_{76} = 0.045649127892262,$
$a_{81} = -0.518393300452978,$	$a_{82} = 0,$	$a_{83} = 4.607278279969559,$
$a_{84} = -5.004120306973807,$	$a_{85} = 1.510536380616834,$	$a_{86} = -0.399249451366671,$
$a_{87} = 0.803948398207063,$	$a_{9j} = b_j, j = 1, 2, \cdots, 8.$	

Interpreting Table 1, we observe that DLMP6(5) was 151% and 116% more expensive than NEW6(5) for the first and second run, respectively. The norm of the principal truncation error coefficients was $\|T^{(7)}\|_2 \approx 2.64 \cdot 10^{-4}$, which is much larger than the corresponding value $\|T^{(7)}\|_2 \approx 4.37 \cdot 10^{-5}$ for DLMP6(5). The interval of absolute stability for the new pair was $(-4.24, 0]$ while for for DLMP6(5) it was $(-4.21, 0]$.

In conclusion, no extra property seemed to hold. The pair given in Table 2 does not possess any interesting properties. It is difficult to believe a special performance could be obtained after seeing its traditional characteristics.

3. Numerical Tests

We tested the following pairs chosen from the family studied above.
1. The DLMP6(5) pair, given in [15].
2. NEW6(5), presented here.

DLMP6(5) is the best representative of conventional RK pairs. Everything else presented until now is hardly more efficient [10]. Both pairs were run for tolerances of $10^{-5}, 10^{-6}, \cdots, 10^{-11}$, and the efficiency measures (2) were recorded for each one. We set NEW6(5) as the reference pair. Then we divided each efficiency measure of DLMP6(5) with the corresponding efficiency measure of NEW6(5). Numbers greater than 1 indicate that NEW6(5) is more efficient. Thus, we can interpret the number 1.1 as DLMP6(5) being $0.1 = 10\%$ more expensive than NEW6(5) while an entry of 2 means that DLMP6(5) is 100% more expensive (i.e., has twice the cost for achieving the same accuracy).

The problems we tested were as follows.

1. *The Kepler problem*

This problem is explained above. We ran it for five different eccentricities (i.e., $ecc = 0, 0.2, 0.4, 0.6, 0.8$), while we recorded the efficiency measures using the endpoint errors for $x_{end} = 10\pi$ and $x_{end} = 20\pi$.

The efficiency measure ratios of DLMP6(5) vs. NEW6(5) for Kepler are presented in Tables 3 and 4.

Table 3. Efficiency measure ratios of DLMP6(5) vs. NEW6(5) for Kepler in $[0, 10\pi]$.

$tol->$ ecc	10^{-5}	10^{-6}	10^{-7}	10^{-8}	10^{-9}	10^{-10}	10^{-11}	Mean
0	1.90	2.36	3.66	3.06	2.46	3.18	3.59	2.89
0.2	1.15	1.11	1.14	1.01	1.07	1.46	2.07	1.29
0.4	1.09	1.10	1.11	1.51	0.80	1.27	1.71	1.23
0.6	1.49	1.49	1.86	1.27	1.18	1.43	1.73	1.49
0.8	1.13	1.17	1.32	1.21	1.36	1.08	2.73	1.43

Table 4. Efficiency measure ratios of DLMP6(5) vs. NEW6(5) for Kepler in $[0, 20\pi]$.

$tol->$ ecc	10^{-5}	10^{-6}	10^{-7}	10^{-8}	10^{-9}	10^{-10}	10^{-11}	Mean
0	1.87	2.34	2.59	2.35	2.67	3.36	3.36	2.65
0.2	1.22	1.27	1.33	1.24	1.29	1.67	2.39	1.49
0.4	1.31	1.55	1.21	0.96	1.08	2.36	2.27	1.54
0.6	1.38	1.32	1.17	1.10	0.98	1.14	1.99	1.30
0.8	1.16	1.24	1.85	1.25	1.08	0.94	1.61	1.30

2. *The perturbed Kepler*

This problem describes the motion of a planet according to Einstein's general relativity theory and the Schwarzschild potential is applied. The equations are:

$$^1y'' = -\frac{^1y}{\sqrt{^1y^2 + {}^2y^2}^3} - (2+\delta)\delta\frac{^1y}{\sqrt{^1y^2 + {}^2y^2}^5},$$

$$^2y'' = -\frac{^2y}{\sqrt{^1y^2 + {}^2y^2}^3} - (2+\delta)\delta\frac{^2y}{\sqrt{^1y^2 + {}^2y^2}^5},$$

and the analytical solution is

$$^1y = \cos(x + \delta x),\ ^2y = \sin(x + \delta x).$$

We transformed this problem into a system of four first-order equations and solved for $x_{end} = 10\pi$ and $x_{end} = 20\pi$. After recording the endpoint errors and the costs, we present the efficiency measures ratios of DLMP6(5) vs. NEW6(5) for perturbed Kepler in Tables 5 and 6.

Table 5. Efficiency measures ratios of DLMP6(5) vs. NEW6(5) for perturbed Kepler in $[0, 10\pi]$.

$tol->$ δ	10^{-5}	10^{-6}	10^{-7}	10^{-8}	10^{-9}	10^{-10}	10^{-11}	Mean
0.01	1.90	2.48	2.39	2.33	3.04	3.64	3.49	2.75
0.02	1.93	2.69	2.19	? 11	2.58	3.65	3.45	2.66
0.03	1.91	2.76	2.14	2.07	2.50	3.45	3.47	2.61
0.04	1.87	2.63	2.18	2.12	2.53	3.28	3.57	2.60
0.05	1.87	2.40	2.32	2.30	2.47	3.24	3.72	2.62

Table 6. Efficiency measures ratios of DLMP6(5) vs. NEW6(5) for perturbed Kepler in $[0, 20\pi]$.

$tol->$ δ	10^{-5}	10^{-6}	10^{-7}	10^{-8}	10^{-9}	10^{-10}	10^{-11}	Mean
0.01	1.88	2.44	2.35	2.18	2.43	3.11	3.34	2.53
0.02	1.86	2.49	2.29	2.14	2.38	3.09	3.36	2.52
0.03	1.85	2.44	2.33	2.17	2.43	3.17	3.39	2.54
0.04	1.83	2.38	2.36	2.17	2.44	3.21	3.43	2.55
0.05	1.82	2.32	2.37	2.16	2.43	3.19	3.44	2.53

3. *The Arenstorf orbit*

Another interesting orbit describes the stable movement of a spacecraft around Earth and Moon ([22], pg. 129).

$$^1y'' = {}^1y + 2 \cdot {}^2y' - \zeta' \cdot \frac{{}^1y+\zeta}{P_1} - \zeta \cdot \frac{{}^1y-\zeta'}{P_2},$$

$$^2y'' = {}^2y + 2 \cdot {}^1y' - \zeta' \cdot \frac{{}^2y}{P_1} - \zeta \cdot \frac{{}^2y}{P_2},$$

with

$$P_1 = \sqrt{({}^1y+\zeta)^2 + {}^2y^2}^3, P_2 = \sqrt{({}^1y-\zeta')^2 + {}^2y^2}^3,$$
$$\zeta = 0.012277471, \zeta' = 0.987722529,$$

initial values

$$^1y(0) = 0.994, \ {}^1y'(0) = 0, \ {}^2y(0) = 0, \ {}^2y'(0) = -2.00158510637908252,$$

and with $x_A = 17.0652165601579625589$ the solution is periodic.

We also transformed this problem to a system of four first-order equations and solved it to x_A and $2x_A$. After recording the endpoint errors and the costs we present the efficiency measures ratios of DLMP6(5) vs. NEW6(5) for Arenstorf in Table 7.

Table 7. Efficiency measure ratios of DLMP6(5) vs. NEW6(5) for Arenstorf.

$tol->$ x_{end}	10^{-5}	10^{-6}	10^{-7}	10^{-8}	10^{-9}	10^{-10}	10^{-11}	Mean
x_A	1.13	1.42	1.89	1.34	0.90	1.51	1.71	1.41
$2x_A$	0.96	1.82	1.64	1.07	1.09	1.62	1.58	1.40

4. *The Pleiades*

Finally, we considered the problem "Pleiades" as given in ([22], pg. 245).

$$^iy'' = \sum_{i \neq j} \frac{\mu_j({}^jy - {}^iy)}{\rho_{ij}}, \ {}^iz'' = \sum_{i \neq j} \frac{\mu_j({}^jz - {}^iz)}{\rho_{ij}},$$

with

$$\rho_{ij} = \sqrt{({}^iy - {}^jy)^2 + ({}^iz - {}^jz)^2}^3, i,j = 1, \cdots, 7.$$

The initial values are

$$^1y(0) = 3, \ {}^2y(0) = 3, \ {}^3y(0) = -1, \ {}^4y(0) = -3, \ {}^5y(0) = 2, \ {}^6y(0) = -2, \ {}^7y(0) = 2,$$

$$^1z(0) = 3, \ {}^2z(0) = -3, \ {}^3z(0) = 2, \ {}^4z(0) = 0, \ {}^5z(0) = 0, \ {}^6z(0) = -4, \ {}^7z(0) = 4,$$

$^1y'(0) = 0$, $^2y'(0) = 0$, $^3y'(0) = 0$, $^4y'(0) = 0$, $^5y'(0) = 0$, $^6y'(0) = 1.75$, $^7y'(0) = -1.5$,
$^1z'(0) = 0$, $^2z'(0) = 0$, $^3z'(0) = 0$, $^4z'(0) = -1.25$, $^5z'(0) = 1$, $^6z'(0) = 0$, $^7z'(0) = 0$,

We again transformed this problem to a system of fourteen first-order equations and solved it to $x_{end} = 3$ and 4. We recorded the endpoint errors after we estimated the solution there by a very accurate integration using Mathematica and quadruple precision. The efficiency measure ratios of DLMP6(5) vs. NEW6(5) for Pleiades can be found in Table 8.

Table 8. Efficiency measures ratios of DLMP6(5) vs. NEW6(5) for Pleiades.

$\underbrace{\frac{tol->}{x_{end}}}$	10^{-5}	10^{-6}	10^{-7}	10^{-8}	10^{-9}	10^{-10}	10^{-11}	Mean
3	1.12	1.02	0.97	1.03	0.89	1.10	1.63	1.11
4	1.13	1.03	0.97	0.96	0.94	1.15	1.64	1.12

We estimated 168 (i.e., 12 problems times 7 tolerances times two end points) efficiency measures for each pair. In average we observed a ratio of 1.98, meaning that DLMP6(5) is about 98% more expensive! This is quite remarkable since a great deal of effort has been put over the years towards achieving 10–20% efficiency [23,24]. In reverse, this means that about $\log_{10} 1.98^6 \approx 1.8$ digits were gained on average at the same costs.

4. Conclusions

This paper is concerned with training the coefficients of a Runge–Kutta pair for addressing a certain kind of problem. We concentrated on problems with Kepler-type orbits and an extensively studied family of Runge–Kutta pairs of orders six and five. After optimizing the free parameters (coefficients) in a couple of runs on Kepler orbits, we concluded to a certain pair. This pair was found to outperform other representatives from this family in a wide range of relevant problems.

Author Contributions: All authors contributed equally. All authors have read and agreed to the published version of the manuscript.

Funding: This research received no external funding.

Institutional Review Board Statement: Not applicable.

Informed Consent Statement: Not applicable.

Data Availability Statement: Not applicable.

Conflicts of Interest: The authors declare no conflicts of interest.

Appendix A

The following Mathematica package implements the algorithm producing the coefficients of the method for double precision. In the input we provide the free coefficients c_2, c_4, c_5, c_6, c_7 and $\hat{b}_9$. In the output we get four vectors, namely $b, \hat{b}, c$ and the matrix A.

```
NEW65[cc2_, cc4_, cc5_, cc6_, cc7_, bbb9_] :=
Module[{b, a, c, bb, vandh, vandl, ac, ac2, cc, ii, ba, cond, soh, b1, b4, b5, b6,
b7, b8, bb1, bb4, bb5, bb6, bb7, bb8, bb9, c2, c3, c4, c5, c6, c7, a21, a31,
a32, a41, a43, a51, a53, a54, a61, a63, a64, a65, a71, a73, a74, a75, a76,
a81, a83, a84, a85, a86, a87, so3, so5, so1, so6, so7, so8},
c2 = Rationalize[cc2, 10^-16]; c4 = Rationalize[cc4, 10^-16];
c5 = Rationalize[cc5, 10^-16]; c6 = Rationalize[cc6, 10^-16];
c7 = Rationalize[cc7, 10^-16]; bb9 = Rationalize[bbb9, 10^-16];
b={b1,0,0,b4,b5,b6,b7,b8,0};
a={{0,0,0,0,0,0,0,0,0},
{a21,0,0,0,0,0,0,0,0},
```

```
            {a31,a32,0,0,0,0,0,0,0},
            {a41,0,a43,0,0,0,0,0,0},
            {a51,0,a53,a54,0,0,0,0,0},
            {a61,0,a63,a64,a65,0,0,0,0},
            {a71,0,a73,a74,a75,a76,0,0,0},
            {a81,0,a83,a84,a85,a86,a87,0,0},
            {b1,0,0,b4,b5,b6,b7,b8,0}};
            c={0,c2,c3,c4,c5,c6,c7,1,1};
            bb={bb1,0,0,bb4,bb5,bb6,bb7,bb8,bb9};
            vandh={b.c==1/2,b.c^2==1/3,b.c^3==1/4,b.c^4==1/5,b.c^5==1/6};
            vandl={bb.c==1/2,bb.c^2==1/3,bb.c^3==1/4,bb.c^4==1/5};
            ac=a.c-c^2/2;
            ac2=a.c^2-c^3/3; cc=DiagonalMatrix[c]; ii=IdentityMatrix[9];
            ba=b.(a+cc-1*ii);
            cond=
            {b.(cc-1*ii).a.(cc-c4*ii).(cc-c5*ii).c-Integrate[(x-1)*Integrate[(x-c5)*(x-c4)*x,
            {x,0,x}],{x,0,1}],
            b.(cc-ii).a.(cc-c4*ii).(cc-c5*ii).c-Integrate[(x-1)*Integrate[(x-c4)*(x-c5)*x,
            {x,0,x}],{x,0,1}] /.{a43->0,a53->0,a63->0,a73->0},
            bb.a.(cc-c5*ii).(cc-c4*ii).c-Integrate[Integrate[(x-c5)*(x-c4)*x,{x,0,x}],
            {x,0,1}]};
            (* start procedure *)
            soh=Solve[vandh,{b4,b5,b6,b7,b8}];
            b4=Together[soh[[1,1,2]]];
            b5=Together[soh[[1,2,2]]];
            b6=Together[soh[[1,3,2]]];
            b7=Together[soh[[1,4,2]]];
            b8=Together[soh[[1,5,2]]];                                      (* OK b *)
            sol=Solve[Join[{(bb.a)[[3]]==0},vandl],{bb4,bb5,bb6,bb7,bb8}];
            bb4=Together[sol[[1,1,2]]];
            bb5=Together[sol[[1,2,2]]];
            bb6=Together[sol[[1,3,2]]];
            bb7=Together[sol[[1,4,2]]];
            bb8=Together[sol[[1,5,2]]];                                     (* OK bb *)
            c3=2/3*c4; a43=c4^2/(2*c3); a32=c3^2/(2*c2);
            so5=Solve[{ac[[5]]==0,ac2[[5]]==0},{a53,a54}];
            a53=Together[so5[[1,1,2]]];a54=Together[so5[[1,2,2]]];    (* after upper left *)
            a87=Together[Solve[{ba[[7]]==0},{a87}][[1,1,2]]];
            a76=Together[Solve[{cond[[2]]==0},{a76}][[1,1,2]]];
            a86=Together[Solve[{ba[[6]]==0},{a86}][[1,1,2]]];
            ac=Together[ac]; ac2=Together[ac2];
            ba=Together[ba]; cond=Together[cond];                     (* OK down right *)
            so3=Solve[{ba[[3]]==0,cond[[1]]==0,cond[[3]]==0},{a63,a73,a83}];
            a63=Together[so3[[1,1,2]]];
            a73=Together[so3[[1,2,2]]];
            a83=Together[so3[[1,3,2]]];                               (* OK 3nd column *)
            so6=Solve[{ac[[6]]==0,ac2[[6]]==0},{a64,a65}];
            a64=Together[so6[[1,1,2]]];a65=Together[so6[[1,2,2]]];
            so7=Solve[{ac[[7]]==0,ac2[[7]]==0},{a74,a75}];
            a74=Together[so7[[1,1,2]]];a75=Together[so7[[1,2,2]]];
            so8=Solve[{ac[[8]]==0,ac2[[8]]==0},{a84,a85}];
            a84=Together[so8[[1,1,2]]];a85=Together[so8[[1,2,2]]];    (* OK ai4, ai5 *)
            b1=1-b4-b5-b6-b7-b8;
            bb1=1-bb4-bb5-bb6-bb7-bb8;
            a21=c2;
            a31=c3-a32;
            a41=c4-a43;
            a51=c5-a53-a54;
            a61=c6-a63-a64-a65;
```

```
a71=c7-a73-a74-a75-a76;
a81=1-a83-a84-a85-a86-a87;
Return[SetAccuracy[{b, bb, c, a}, 16] // Chop]]
```

References

1. Butcher, J.C. On Runge-Kutta processes of high order. *J. Austral. Math. Soc.* **1964**, *4*, 179–194. [CrossRef]
2. Butcher, J.C. *Numerical Methods for Ordinary Differential Equations*; John Wiley & Sons: Chichester, UK, 2003.
3. Tsitouras, C.; Papakostas, S.N. Cheap Error Estimation for Runge-Kutta pairs. *SIAM J. Sci. Comput.* **1999**, *20*, 2067–2088. [CrossRef]
4. Runge, C. Ueber die numerische Auflöung von Differentialgleichungen. *Math. Ann.* **1895**, *46*, 167–178. [CrossRef]
5. Kutta, W. Beitrag zur naherungsweisen Integration von Differentialgleichungen. *Z. Math. Phys.* **1901**, *46*, 435–453.
6. Fehlberg, E. Klassische Runge-Kutta-Formeln fiinfter und siebenter 0rdnung mit Schrittweiten-Kontrolle. *Computing* **1969**, *4*, 93–106. [CrossRef]
7. Fehlberg, E. Klassische Runge-Kutta-Formeln vierter und niedrigererrdnung mit Schrittweiten-Kontrolle und ihre Anwendung auf Warmeleitungsprobleme. *Computing* **1970**, *6*, 61–71. [CrossRef]
8. Dormand, J.R.; Prince, P.J. A family of embedded Runge-Kutta formulae. *J. Comput. Appl. Math.* **1980**, *6*, 19–26. [CrossRef]
9. Prince, P.J.; Dormand, J.R. High order embedded Runge-Kutta formulae. *J. Comput. Appl. Math.* **1981**, *7*, 67–75. [CrossRef]
10. Tsitouras, C. A parameter study of explicit Runge-Kutta pairs of orders 6(5). *Appl. Math. Lett.* **1998**, *11*, 65–69. [CrossRef]
11. Famelis, I.T.; Papakostas, S.N.; Tsitouras, C. Symbolic derivation of Runge-Kutta order conditions. *J. Symbolic Comput.* **2004**, *37*, 311–327. [CrossRef]
12. Tsitouras, C. Runge-Kutta pairs of orders 5(4) satisfying only the first column simplifying assumption. *Comput. Math. Appl.* **2011**, *62*, 770–775. [CrossRef]
13. Medvedev, M.A.; Simos, T.E.; Tsitouras, C. Fitted modifications of Runge-Kutta pairs of orders 6(5). *Math. Meth. Appl. Sci.* **2018**, *41*, 6184–6194. [CrossRef]
14. Tsitouras, C. Optimized explicit Runge-Kutta pair of orders 9(8). *Appl. Numer. Math.* **2001**, *38*, 121–134. [CrossRef]
15. Dormand, J.R.; Lockyer, M.A.; McGorrigan, N.E.; Prince, P.J. Global error estimation with Runge-Kutta triples. *Comput. Math. Appl.* **1989**, *18*, 835–846. [CrossRef]
16. Verner, J.H. Some Runge-Kutta formula pairs. *SIAM J. Numer. Anal.* **1991**, *28*, 496–511. [CrossRef]
17. Simos, T.E.; Tsitouras, C. Evolutionary derivation of Runge-Kutta pairs for addressing inhomogeneous linear problems. *Numer. Algor.* **2020**. [CrossRef]
18. Wolfram Research, Inc. *Mathematica, Version 11.1*; Wolfram Research, Inc.: Champaign, IL, USA, 2017.
19. Tsitouras, C. Neural Networks With Multidimensional Transfer Functions. *IEEE Trans. Neural Netw.* **2002**, *13*, 222–228. [CrossRef]
20. Storn, R.; Price, K. Differential evolution - a simple and efficient heuristic for global optimization over continuous spaces. *J. Glob. Optim.* **1997**, *11*, 341–359. [CrossRef]
21. Liu, C.; Hsu, C.W.; Tsitouras, C.; Simos, T.E. Hybrid Numerov-type methods with coefficients trained to perform better on classical orbits. *Bull. Malays. Math. Sci. Soc.* **2019**, *42*, 2119–2134. [CrossRef]
22. Hairer, E.; Nørsett, S.P.; Wanner, G. *Solving Ordinary Differential Equations I, Nonstiff Problems*, 2nd ed.; Springer: Berlin, Germany, 1993.
23. Papageorgiou, G.; Papakostas, S.N.; Tsitouras, C. A general family of explicit Runge-Kutta pairs of orders 6(5). *SIAM J. Numer. Anal.* **1996**, *33*, 917–936.
24. Papakostas, S.N.; Tsitouras, C. High phase-lag order Runge-Kutta and Nyström pairs. *SIAM J. Sci. Comput.* **1999**, *21*, 747–763. [CrossRef]

Article

Human Networks and Toxic Relationships

Nazaria Solferino [1] and Maria Elisabetta Tessitore [2,*]

[1] Economics Department, University of Calabria UNICA, Via Ponte Pietro Bucci 1C, Arcavacata di Rende, 86133 Cosenza, Italy; nazaria.solferino@unical.it
[2] Economics Department, University of Rome Tor Vergata, Via Columbia 2, 00133 Rome, Italy
* Correspondence: tessitore@economia.uniroma2.it

Abstract: We devise a theoretical model to shed light on the dynamics leading to toxic relationships. We investigate what intervention policy people could advocate to protect themselves and to reduce suffocating addiction in order to escape from physical or psychological abuses either inside family or at work. Assuming that the toxic partner's behavior is exogenous and that the main source of addiction is income or wealth we find that an asymptotically stable equilibrium with positive love is always possible. The existence of a third unconditionally reciprocating part as a benchmark, i.e., presence of another partner, support from family, friends, private organizations in helping victims, plays an important role in reducing the toxic partner's appeal. Analyzing our model, we outline the conditions for the best policy to heal from a toxic relationship.

Keywords: dynamical systems; stability; economics; relationships; networks

JEL Classification: C62; D11; D91

Citation: Solferino, N.; Tessitore, M.E. Human Networks and Toxic Relationships. *Mathematics* **2021**, *9*, 2258. https://doi.org/10.3390/math9182258

Academic Editor: David Carfì

Received: 27 July 2021
Accepted: 9 September 2021
Published: 14 September 2021

Publisher's Note: MDPI stays neutral with regard to jurisdictional claims in published maps and institutional affiliations.

Copyright: © 2021 by the authors. Licensee MDPI, Basel, Switzerland. This article is an open access article distributed under the terms and conditions of the Creative Commons Attribution (CC BY) license (https://creativecommons.org/licenses/by/4.0/).

1. Introduction

In this paper, we aim to give an additional contribution to the literature in Economics of Love devising a modified version of the model in [1]. We analyse the dynamics leading to toxic relationships, i.e., we focus our attention on situations where love is transformed into a negative dependence and the relationship produces a dangerous addiction.

Moreover, we investigate what intervention policy people could advocate to protect themselves and to reduce suffocating addiction in order to escape the trap of physical or psychological abuse either in family or at work. The dynamics of couples' relationships are analyzed through a system of differential equations representing the laws of motions of the amount of love that two individuals put in a relationship which also depends on any source of partner's appeal (financial, physical, intellectual, co-parenthood, etc.).

In our work, the appeal is assumed to change over time proportionally to both the effect of the other partner's love and to a variable representing the main source of addiction (for instance, wealth, status, physical appearance, etc.). The aim of our analysis is to build a model which takes into account the case where toxic relationships are at work, i.e., when one partner chooses to stay in a relationship despite the low or null amount of love received, for the sole reason that their partner's appeal makes it harder for them to terminate the relationship.

In 1995, Dr. Lillian Glass defines a toxic relationship as any relationship [between people who] do not support each other, where there's conflict and one seeks to undermine the other, where there's competition, where there's disrespect and a lack of cohesiveness [2].

By toxic relationship, we mean a relationship disorder characterized by a disparity, a non-egalitarian situation in which one of the two partners is dependent on the other one, triggering a mechanism of dominance and subjection. In these relationships one partner puts into the relationship much more effort than the other one, who, sometimes, could even put no effort at all into it. In an healthy relationship partners can still cut out their spaces, maintaining a capacity for self-determination and taking benefit from reciprocity. In a toxic relationship the emotional dependance enters into play, making the partner our exclusive interlocutor, so that being happy and enthusiastic depends exclusively on the other person, just like drug addiction. In order to avoid the abandonment and the consequent lack of affection, the addicted partner cancels himself or herself out, while the counterpart exploits the relationship to feel admired and to exercise control. A toxic relationship implies psychological, and at times physical, violence, and can develop into a tragic eposide of murder. The majority of the victims of these murders are women

Another typical example of toxic relationship is bullying at a workplace, very often put into action by the boss. The unwillingness to call out such behaviour by the victims and spectators results in to favoring it. The reason for this behaviour is obviously the fear of being involved, of retaliation of some kind or even of losing the job.

In our work, we focus on the conditions which make a toxic relationshio to arise. Due to the exploited parter's addiction, the abusing parter's behaviour seems appealing regardless low affection. In Section 2 we rewiev the literature on this topic. In Section 3 we give an analytical definition of a toxic relationship and we solve an intertemporal dynamic model, where the toxic partner's behaviour is assumed to be exogenous. Assuming that the main source of addiction is income or wealth, we find that an asymptotically stable equilibrium with positive love is always possibile for a high enough level of appeal if subsidies that reduce addiction are introduced. In Section 4, we compare two alternative policies that can be adopted to heal from addiction. One policy consists in healing through a subsidy that can reduce the toxic partner's appeal. The alternative policy is to heal through a third, unconditionally reciprocating, part as a benchmark which represents an alternative, but less attractive, to the partner's love. This third part plays an important role in reducing the toxic partner's appeal. It substantially mimics not only the real presence of another partner but also the support from family, friends and overall private organizations in helping victims of domestic abuses recover their life fully. It may also represent private organizations that offer economic and psychological support as well as legal counselling to victims of bullying at workplace and placement offices which effectively help to find another job. Section 5 contains our discussion and future implications and research.

2. Literature Rewiev

A very particular branch of economics literature, only recently developed, is the Economics of Love. It is focused on the household's well-being, marriage and long-term relationships alongside their effects on economic growth (for an exhaustive survey on this literature see [3,4]).

The first work in this new field of Economics appeared in the early 1970s with the theory of marriage by Becker [5]. According to it, all individuals want to find a partner with whom they will maximise their own well-being. The equilibrium in this marriage market is reached when no one can change partner or become single and when nobody can experience a higher well–being (referred to the consumption of household commodities).

Beckers empirical analysis shows that the gain from marriage is positively dependant on income, on relative difference in wage rates and on the level of intangible variables such as education and beauty. Moreover, individuals choose partners with similar traits such as height, race, social background, etc. Including among the factors which can affect marriages also love (defined as a situation where the utility of one individual depends on the commodity consumption of their partner as well as their own), Becker [6] finds that love raises the likelihood of two people to marry because their well-being is likely to be higher.

After these pioneering works, many other analyses have been focused on understanding how households operate. Outcomes of interest concern consumption, savings, labor supply and other uses of time, household formation and dissolution, demand for health and other forms of human capital, fertility and children outcomes, demand for environmental quality, migration, and household produced goods ([3,4]).

Many papers also investigated the determinants of long-lasting relationships and their effects on economic development. Among them, Brines and Joyner [7] conducted an empirical study on the stability of marriage and cohabiting couples in the United States. They found that inequality in employment and income among the cohabiting couple increased the chances of separation, although the effect was not symmetric since inequality had a larger impact when the female partner earned more than the male partner. Grossbard [4] studied family as a complex decision unit where partners with potentially different objectives made decisions about consumption, work and fertility. He noticed that couples marry and divorce depending upon their ability to coordinate these activities.

More recently Johnson et al. [8] applied a unique longitudinal approach to study the long-term outcomes of relationships among 3405 couples. This paper was concerned on predictors of relationship longevity, from measures of conflict frequency, types of behaviours experienced during times of conflict, satisfaction with the relationship and whether partners believed their relationships would last or not. The German study's findings showed that complacency is perhaps the most significant trap to avoid: a relationship where partners tried not to fall into that same-old routine can be vital and fulfilling for the years to come.

While there are quite a lot of studies on marriage and cohabiting couples see Motz [9] and Houston [10], there are only few papers which study the economic dynamics of romance from a theoretical point of view.

Rinaldi (1998) proposed a mathematical model based on a linear dynamical system where three aspects of love dynamics are taken into account: the forgetting process (oblivion), the pleasure of being loved (return), and the reaction to the appeal of the partner (instinct). The results of the model showed that the equilibrium turns out to be positive if the appeals of the two individuals are positive. Sprott extended those results and discussed various models of love and happiness, like the model of romance between Romeo and Juliet and the one about triangular relationship to analyse how a third part could affect the stability of a relationship, see Sprott J.C. [11].

Wauer et al. [12] studied human romantic relationships via system dynamics methodology where a non-linear modelling was proposed and analysed, showing that there are short-termed and long-termed fluctuations of personal feelings due to, for instance, biological cycles and varying stresses from the daily job. The variability is expected to be more limited for couples of cautious individuals. In Regan [13] individuals behave in order to optimize their net benefit from a given relationship. The desire to maximize their rewards, to minimize their costs and the inequity of the benefits to contributions among the individuals will cause unhappiness in a relationship. It clearly depends on the role of expectations [14] and on the level of effort that is given to the relationship. This commitment then determines whether or not the relationship will be maintained [15]. Ref. [16] added to the initial model of Rinaldi [1] a crossed interactions among partners to analyse the effects and synergies of learning and adapting to live together. According to the results of this model the system is asymptotically stable if the ratio of appeals is greater than the reciprocal of the ratio of mutual intensiveness coefficient.

3. Basic Model of a Toxic Relationship

In this section, we devise a modified version of the model described in [1] where the level of love an individual puts in a relationship varies over time, depending both on oblivion, on the partner's love and on the perception one has of the appeal of the partner.

We denote by 1, 2 the submitted and the toxic partner respectively.

We assume for simplicity that the partner 2's appeal perceived by partner 1, A_1, decreases at the same rate of love x_1 (i.e., oblivion's rate is the same), it increases as individual 1 loves more, and it decreases as fast as the difference between the amount of love partner 2 puts into in the relationship, $\overline{x_2}$, and the desired amount of love that partner 1 would expect from partner 2, $\hat{x}_2$.

We also assume that A_1 depends on a constant factor M_2 of appeal i.e., income, personality, physical appearance, etc.

We study the stability of the following system of dynamic equations:

$$\begin{cases} \dot{x}_1(t) = -\alpha x_1(t) + \beta \overline{x_2} + \gamma_1 A_1(t) \\ \dot{A}_1(t) = -\alpha A_1(t) + k[x_1(t) + (\overline{x_2} - \hat{x}_2)] + M_2 \end{cases} \quad (1)$$

where

(i) $x_1(t)$ is the love, which consists of both passion and intimacy individual 1 has for the partner 2 at time t.

(ii) α refers to the forgetting coefficient and measures how quickly the state of love will decrease, exponentially, in the absence of the partner.

(iii) β refers to the response of each partner to the love they receive from the other partner

(iv) $\overline{x_2}$ is the love the partner 2 puts in the relationship. We assume it is an exogenous variable of the system and it remains constant over time, so that $0 \leq \overline{x_2} < x_1(t)$, $\forall t \geq 0$.

(v) $A_1(t)$ is the appeal factor, It is the partner 1's perception of partner 2 at a time t. It is a subjective variable and depends on the perception of the partner at time t. It represents the measure of the partner's power of attracting or arousing interest. This is affected by partner 2 possessing specific characteristics (physical, intellectual, financial etc) that partner 1 is especially sensitive to.

(vi) γ_1 refers to the response coefficients of the appeal of the other partner.

(vii) k measures the sensitivity of an individual with respect to the excessive unreciprocated love given to the partner.

(viii) $\hat{x}_2$ is the minimum level of desired love by individual 1

(ix) M_2 measures the source of partner 2's appeal, it represents the measure of wealth, beauty, etc. For simplicity we assume M_2 to be constant over time.

We assume that parameters $\alpha, \beta, k, \gamma_1 \in (0,1]$ and $\overline{x_2}, \hat{x}_2 \in [0,1]$

Definition 1. *If there exists a minimum level of desired love $\hat{x}_2$ for individual 1 with $\overline{x_2} \leq \hat{x}_2$ and if $x_1 > 0$ then we say that the relationship between 1 and 2 is a toxic relationship.*

In a toxic relationship, individual 1 loves partner 2 even if the partner 2 does not reciprocate (neither at the minimum possible level normally requested $\hat{x}_2$), since the second partner only provides $\overline{x_2}$ and $\overline{x_2} < \hat{x}_2$. This happens because attraction A_1 of partner 1 towards partner 2 is very high.

We are going to prove that system (1) has a steady state stable equilibrium.

Proposition 1. *Assume $\sqrt{k\gamma_1} < \alpha < \beta$ and $M_2 \geq k\hat{x}_2$, then state steady (x_1^*, A_1^*)*

$$x_1^* = \frac{\alpha \beta \overline{x_2} + k\gamma_1(\overline{x_2} - \hat{x}_2)}{\alpha^2 - k\gamma_1} + \frac{\gamma_1 M_2}{\alpha^2 - k\gamma_1}$$

$$A_1^* = \frac{\beta k \overline{x_2} + \alpha k(\overline{x_2} - \hat{x}_2)}{\alpha^2 - k\gamma_1} + \frac{\alpha M_2}{\alpha^2 - k\gamma_1}$$

is an asympotically stable equilibrium for system (1).

Proof. Let A be the coefficient matrix of the system

$$A = \begin{pmatrix} -\alpha & \gamma_1 \\ k & -\alpha \end{pmatrix}.$$

since $\det A > 0$ and $tr A < 0$ the conclusion follows. □

Remark 1. *Notice that in the steady state equilibrium, the love for the partner is always positive and it grows as the depreciation rate decreases with respect to the sensitivity towards the partner's appeal.*

If partner 1 has $\hat{x}_2 = 1$ and partner 2 provides $\overline{x_2} = 0$, the first partner still loves the second one since

$$x_1^* = -\frac{k\gamma_1}{\alpha^2 - k\gamma_1} + \frac{\gamma_1 M_2}{\alpha^2 - k\gamma_1}$$

We notice that if the amount of love partner 2 puts in the relationship is equal to the desired love of partner 1, i.e., $\overline{x_2} = \hat{x}_2$, then

$$x_1^* = \frac{\alpha \beta \overline{x_2}}{\alpha^2 - k\gamma_1} + \frac{\gamma_1 M_2}{\alpha^2 - k\gamma_1}$$

and

$$A_1^* = \frac{\beta k \overline{x_2}}{\alpha^2 - k\gamma_1} + \frac{\alpha M_2}{\alpha^2 - k\gamma_1}$$

This means that the first partner's love is always positive if the second partner's perceived appeal overcomes the negative impact of the unreciprocated love.

In particular, if $\overline{x_2} = \hat{x}_2 = 0$, then

$$x_1^* = \frac{\gamma_1 M_2}{\alpha^2 - k\gamma_1}$$

and

$$A_1^* = \frac{\alpha M_2}{\alpha^2 - k\gamma_1}$$

So we see that the partner 1 still loves partner 2 only depending upon the factor M_2 which represents wealth, or other benefits.

If individual 1 starts loving individual 2 at time $t = 0$, then 1 will love 2 forever. This is true unless the love desired by 1 $\hat{x}_2$ attains a specific value

Proposition 2. *If partner 1 has an amount of desired love*

$$\hat{x}_2 = \frac{(\alpha\beta + \gamma_1 k)\overline{x_2} + \gamma_1 M_2}{k\gamma_1}$$

then partner 1 stops loving partner 2.

Proof. From the previous Proposition we see that $x_1^* = 0$ with this choice of $\hat{x}_2$. □

Definition 2. *Individual 1 overcomes a toxic relationship, i.e., 1 is healed, if $x_1^* = 0$.*

Remark 2. *Hence we see that from the above Proposition, individual 1 is healed only if the love they desire equals a specific amount.*

In practice, this is hard to achieve because it is not straightforward for a person to select a specific value of love to put in a relationship. This is why in the next Section we investigate if there are other ways to get out of such a relationship.

4. Healing

In this section, we look for conditions to help the submitted partner 1 to heal from toxicity, since in the previous Section this condition could be attained only if the submitted partner has a specific value of desired love $\hat{x}_2$.

We are going to consider two possible ways: the first one is by reducing the toxic partner's appeal 2 via a subsidy $S > 0$, while the second one is going to be the presence of a third partner denoted by 3.

We begin introducing a subsidy $S = sM_2$. This represents a payment from the government or another organization to the abused partner to cover personal living expenses they might incur when leaving the relationship, such as rent. Here s is the factor of proportionality chosen by the government.

In system (1) we introduce the subsidy S in the dynamic of A_1

$$\begin{cases} \dot{x}_1(t) = -\alpha x_1(t) + \beta \overline{x_2} + \gamma_1 A_1(t) \\ \dot{A}_1(t) = -\alpha A_1(t) + k[x_1(t) + (\overline{x_2} - \hat{x}_2)] + M_2(1-s) \end{cases} \quad (2)$$

Proposition 3. *The subsidy $S = sM_2$ with*

$$s = \frac{\alpha \beta \overline{x_2} + k\gamma_1(\overline{x_2} - \hat{x}_2)}{\gamma_1 M_2} + 1$$

is healing individual 1.

Proof. It is easy to see that in this case the steady state x_{1s}^* of system (2) is

$$x_{1s}^* = \frac{\alpha \beta \overline{x_2} + k\gamma_1(\overline{x_2} - \hat{x}_2)}{\alpha^2 - k\gamma_1} + \frac{\gamma_1 M_2(1-s)}{\alpha^2 - k\gamma_1}$$

hence the result follows from the above assumptions. □

Remark 3. *Notice that*

$$x_{1s}^* = x_1^* - \frac{\gamma_1 M_2}{\alpha^2 - k\gamma_1} s$$

so the subsidy reduces the love of partner one towards partner two.

Another way to heal might be the presence of a third person, denoted by 3, we want to see if 1 can heal from the second partner. System (1) becomes

$$\begin{cases} \dot{x}_1(t) = -\alpha x_1(t) + \beta(\overline{x_2} - x_3) + \gamma_1 A_1(t) \\ \dot{A}_1(t) = -\alpha A_1(t) + k[x_1(t) + (\overline{x_2} - \hat{x}_2) - x_3] + M_2 - M_3 \end{cases} \quad (3)$$

where x_3 is the amount of love of individual 3 towards individual 1 and M_3 with $M_3 < M_2$ is the appeal of the third partner.

Proposition 4. *If x_3 is such that*

$$x_3 = \overline{x_2} + \frac{\gamma_1[(M_2 - M_3) - k\hat{x}_2]}{\alpha \beta + k\gamma_1}$$

then 3 is healing individual 1.

Proof. It is enough to see that in this case the steady state x_{13}^* of system (3) is

$$x_{13}^* = \frac{\alpha \beta(\overline{x_2} - x_3) + k\gamma_1[(\overline{x_2} - \hat{x}_2) - x_3]}{\alpha^2 - k\gamma_1} + \frac{\gamma_1(M_2 - M_3)}{\alpha^2 - k\gamma_1}$$

□

Remark 4. *Notice that*

$$x_{13}^* = x_1^* - \frac{\alpha \beta + k\gamma_1}{\alpha^2 - k\gamma_1} x_3 - \frac{\gamma_1}{\alpha^2 - k\gamma_1} M_3.$$

Hence, the third partner reduces the love of partner one towards partner two, similarly to the subsidy's role in the previous case.

If in addition to partner 3 offering a certain fixed amount of love $\overline{x}_3$ to partner 1 there is also a subsidy $\overline{S} = \overline{s} M_2$, then proceeding as before we are going to consider the system

$$\begin{cases} \dot{x}_1(t) = -\alpha x_1(t) + \beta(\overline{x_2} - \overline{x}_3) + \gamma_1 A_1(t) \\ \dot{A}_1(t) = -\alpha A_1(t) + k[x_1(t) + (\overline{x_2} - \hat{x}_2) - \overline{x}_3] + M_2(1 - \overline{s}) - M_3 \end{cases} \quad (4)$$

Proposition 5. *The subsidy* $\overline{S} = \overline{s} M_2$ *with*

$$\overline{s} = \frac{\alpha \beta(\overline{x_2} - \overline{x}_3) + k\gamma_1[(\overline{x_2} - \hat{x}_2) - \overline{x}_3]}{\gamma_1 M_2} + 1 - \frac{M_3}{M_2}$$

is healing individual 1.

Proof.

$$x^*_{1\,3\overline{s}} = \frac{\alpha \beta(\overline{x_2} - \overline{x}_3) + k\gamma_1[(\overline{x_2} - \hat{x}_2) - \overline{x}_3]}{\alpha^2 - k\gamma_1} + \gamma_1 \frac{M_2(1 - \overline{s}) - M_3}{\alpha^2 - k\gamma_1}$$

and the result follows.

Remark 5. *Notice that in the previous case we found that if individual 1 loves 2 without a correspondence, then the only way to get $x_1 = 0$ is by introducing a subsidy that counterbalances the addiction due to income M_2.*

Instead, when there is also a third partner there is no need to take $s > 1$ because the love term x_3 also acts as a counterweight. This results in a lower minimum subsidy required to heal partner 1 since

$$\overline{s} = s - \frac{(\alpha \beta + k\gamma_1)\overline{x}_3 + \gamma_1 M_3}{\gamma_1 M_2}$$

5. Discussion

A toxic relationship can be defined as a relationship characterized by one partner displaying behaviours that are emotionally and often physically damaging the other partner.

A healthy relationship involves mutual caring, respect, compassion and a strong interest in the partner's happiness. In the couple both individuals share control and decision-making. On the contrary, a toxic relationship is characterized by insecurity, self-centeredness, dominance and control.

When two individuals have a toxic relationship, we usually look at the toxic partner's behaviour. We must also observe the individual who is the recipient of the toxic behaviour. In fact, according to psychologists, the reasons that push adults into remaining in toxic reationships, which will almost inevitably damage them emotionally or physically, need to be thoroughly investigated. We think that this often happens because addiction may play a very important role: the partner's appeal grows over time regardless of the amount of love the they invest in the relationship.

In this paper, we approach these issues from a theoretical point of view with the purpose of devising an analytical model which can highlight the main points of this problem and can shed light on useful policy solutions. To this purpose we use the model of Rinaldi [1], adding the possibility of the toxic partner's appeal evolving dynamically according to a specific law of motion. Our model assumes the law's dependence on oblivion, on the excess of love with respect to the partner and on a constant parameter that measures the values of the source of addiction(for instance income or wealth, etc.). Our model shows that in the most simple case, where the partner's behaviour is given (exogenous) and hopelessly toxic, there is an asympotically stable equilibrium for high values of addiction, with a submitted partner always in love.

Nevertheless, an opportune measure of correction based on subsidies can be introduced. On the other hand, the lack of government help is often one of the main reasons for the low levels of immediately reported domestic abuses. For instance, according to

GROVIO(Group of Experts on Action against Violence against Women and Domestic Violence and EstremeConseguences) of the European Council, about 80% of abuse in Italy happens at home, and there are not enough dormitories to host over 5000 women who have left their houses to escape abusive partners. Alongside dedicated laws, penalties and high compensation for the monetary, biological and moral damage, public funds are essential. Furthermore, dedicated public funds play a key role in reducing any dependence on employers or co-workers, and in incentivizing reports from victims. Nevertheless, union organizations offering cheap or free legal help, supporting in searching for other jobs and reintegration are very useful.

To take this problem into account , we look for an alternative policy and we study how the results of our theorethical model change when an alternative third part enters the scene and competes for the submitted parter's love with the toxic partner. In this case lower or zero subsidies can be necessary as the third part works like a substitute to decrease the toxic dependance. Anyway a mix of policy intervention based both on subsidies and on help from third part can be fashioned. Therefore, when a policy based only on subsidies is not sufficient, other factors can be useful to rescue from toxicity.

Often, subsidies are not high enough or people need also to preserve their dignity,security, counselling, etc. In our model for instance a high source of addiction may also come from a very low self esteem which can otherwise be raised offering victims other opportunities like alternative jobs or legal/counseling support. This is why we believe that the best solutions relies in a mix of policies where alonside with the government, private organizations offer support to the victims of abuse as well placement offices in finding new jobs.

With this work we aimed to give a contribution to the literature on Economics of Love and in particular we hope to incentive more theoretical and empirical studies on relationships and to devise better policy solutions. In particular we think that a mix of policies, directly or indirectly created to fight this phenomenon based on monetary help and supportive institutions and organizations could be very effective.

A future development of this paper would be to consider people with low self esteem who are most subject to this kind of addiction and where psychoterapy for couples is strongly needed. In the extreme cases when toxicity externates in physical violence also objective policy solutions are likely to be necessary.

An interesting follow-up investigation we would like pursue is the study of the all-too-common instances of bullying at the workplace. In these instances, too often abuse and harassment are considered normal events, so that the workers who suffer them prefer to remain silent. This occurs especially when the victim's job position is precarious and when the employer can affect the victim's financial condition on a whim. Istat data for Italy tell us that 9 out of 100 women, during their working life, have suffered harassment or blackmail with a sexual background at work (1 million 403 thousand), but that only 20% talk about it with someone (usually office colleagues) and only 0.7% complain, for fear of retaliation, shame, or for a distorted sense of guilt, slander. The company is damaged by these occurrances as well as the workers as the effects are a lower productivity, increased risk of accidents and conflict. The inevitable repercussions then fall on the health service (treatments, drugs) and on the social security system (illnesses, injuries, etc.).

Author Contributions: Both authors equally contributed in every aspect of the writing of this article. Both authors have read and agreed to the published version of the manuscript.

Funding: This research received no external funding.

Institutional Review Board Statement: Not applicable.

Informed Consent Statement: Not applicable.

Data Availability Statement: Not applicable.

Conflicts of Interest: The authors declare no conflict of interest.

References

1. Rinaldi, S. Love dynamics. *Appl. Math. Comput.* **1998**, *95*, 181–192.
2. Glass, L. *Toxic People*; Your Total Image Publsihing. 1995. Available online: https://www.drlillianglass.com/wp-content/uploads/2015/06/Toxic-People_ebook.pdf (accessed on 8 September 2021).
3. Browning, M.; Chiappori, P.A.; Weiss, Y. *Economics of the Family*; Cambridge University Press: Cambridge, UK, 2014.
4. Grossbard, S. *The Economics of Marriage*; The International Library of Critical Writings in Economics Series; San Diego State University: San Diego, CA, USA, 2015.
5. Becker, G.S. A theory of marriage: Part I. *J. Political Econ.* **1973**, *81*, 813–846. [CrossRef]
6. Becker, G.S. *A Theory of Marriage in Economics of the Family: Marriage, Children, and Human Capital*; University of Chicago Press: Chicago, IL, USA, 1974; pp. 299–351.
7. Brines, J.; Joyner, K. The ties that bind: principles of cohesion in cohabitation and marriage. *Am. Sociol. Rev.* **1999**, *64*, 333–355. [CrossRef]
8. Johnson, M.D.; Horne, R.M.; Hardy, N.R.; Anderson, J.R. Temporality of couple conflict and relationship perceptions. *J. Fam. Psychol.* **2018**, *32*, 445–455. [CrossRef] [PubMed]
9. Motz, A. *Toxic Couples: The Psychology of Domestic Violence*; Routledge: Oxfordshire, UK, 2014.
10. Houston, M.J. *The Psychology of Abusive/Predatory Relationships*; iUniverse: Bloomington, Indiana, 2012.
11. Sprott, C. *Dynamics of Love and Happiness*; Stenberg, R.J., Barnas, M.L., Eds.; Chaos and Complex Systems Seminar in Madison: Madison, WI, USA, 2001.
12. Wauer, J.; Schwarzer, D.; Cai, G.Q.; Lin, Y.K. Dynamical models of love with time-varying fluctuations. *Appl. Math. Comput.* **2007**, *188*, 1535–1448. [CrossRef]
13. Regan, P.C. *The Mating Game: A Primer on Love, Sex, and Marriage*; Sage Publications: London , UK, 2008.
14. Thibaut, J.W.; Kelley, H.H. *The Social Psychology of Groups*; Routledge: London, UK, 2007.
15. Rusbult, C.E. A longitudinal test of the investment model: The development (and deterioration) of satisfaction and commitment in heterosexual involvements. *J. Personal. Soc. Psychol.* **1983**, *45*, 101–117. [CrossRef]
16. Satsangi, A.; Sinha, K. Dynamics of Love and Happiness: A Mathematical Analysis. *Mod. Educ. Comput. Sci.* **2012**, *5*, 31–37. [CrossRef]

Article

Evolutionary Derivation of Runge–Kutta Pairs of Orders 5(4) Specially Tuned for Problems with Periodic Solutions

Vladislav N. Kovalnogov [1], Ruslan V. Fedorov [1], Andrey V. Chukalin [1], Theodore E. Simos [1,2,3,4,5,6,*] and Charalampos Tsitouras [7,8]

1. Laboratory of Inter-Disciplinary Problems of Energy Production, Ulyanovsk State Technical University, 32 Severny Venetz Street, 432027 Ulyanovsk, Russia; kvn@ulstu.ru (V.N.K.); r.fedorov@ulstu.ru (R.V.F.); chukalin.andrej@mail.ru (A.V.C.)
2. College of Applied Mathematics, Chengdu University of Information Technology, Chengdu 610225, China
3. Department of Medical Research, China Medical University Hospital, China Medical University, Taichung City 40402, Taiwan
4. Data Recovery Key Laboratory of Sichuan Province, Neijiang Normal University, Neijiang 641100, China
5. Section of Mathematics, Department of Civil Engineering, Democritus University of Thrace, 67100 Xanthi, Greece
6. Department of Mathematics, University of Western Macedonia, 50100 Kozani, Greece
7. General Department, Euripus Campus, National & Kapodistrian University of Athens, 34400 Athens, Greece; tsitourasc@uoa.gr
8. Administration of Businesses and Organizations Department, Hellenic Open University, 26335 Patras, Greece
* Correspondence: tsimos.conf@gmail.com

Abstract: The purpose of the present work is to construct a new Runge–Kutta pair of orders five and four to outperform the state-of-the-art in these kind of methods when addressing problems with periodic solutions. We consider the family of such pairs that the celebrated Dormand–Prince pair also belongs. The chosen family comes with coefficients that all depend on five free parameters. These latter parameters are tuned in a way to furnish a new method that performs best on a couple of oscillators. Then, we observe that this trained pair outperforms other well known methods in the relevant literature in a standard set of problems with periodic solutions. This is remarkable since no special property holds such as high phase-lag order or an extended interval of periodicity.

Keywords: initial value problem; oscillatory problems; Runge–Kutta; differential evolution

MSC: 65L05; 65L06; 90C26; 90C30

1. Introduction

The Initial Value Problem (IVP) is

$$y' = f(x,y), y(x_0) = y_0 \qquad (1)$$

with $x_0 \in \mathbb{R}$ and the vectors $y, y' \in \mathbb{R}^m$. The function f is defined as $f : \mathbb{R} \times \mathbb{R}^m \to \mathbb{R}^m$.

Runge–Kutta (RK) pairs are perhaps the most used numerical methods for addressing (1). They usually presented in a so-called Butcher tableau [1,2] as given below.

$$\begin{array}{c|c} c & A \\ \hline & b \\ & \hat{b} \end{array}$$

In this type of tableau, we have $b^T, \hat{b}^T, c \in \mathbb{R}^s$ while $A \in \mathbb{R}^{s \times s}$. Then, the method shares s stages and in case that A is strictly lower triangular, it is evaluated explicitly. The numerical approximations of the solution step from $(x_n, y_n) \in \mathbb{R}^{1+m}$ to $x_{n+1} = x_n + h_n$

by producing two numerical estimations for $y(x_{n+1})$. Namely, $y_{n+1} \in \mathbb{R}^m$ and $\hat{y}_{n+1} \in \mathbb{R}^m$, given by

$$y_{n+1} = y_n + h_n \sum_{i=1}^{s} b_i f_i,$$

and

$$\hat{y}_{n+1} = y_n + h_n \sum_{i=1}^{s} \hat{b}_i f_i,$$

with

$$f_i = f(x_n + c_i h_n, y_n + h_n \sum_{j=1}^{i-1} a_{ij} f_j),$$

for $i = 1, 2, \cdots, s$. These two approximations $y_{n+1} \in \mathbb{R}^m$ and $\hat{y}_{n+1} \in \mathbb{R}^m$ are of algebraic orders p and $q < p$, respectively. This means that when expanding them in Taylor series, they attain orders $O(h^p)$ and $O(h^q)$, respectively, with h being the proper step–length. Then, a local error estimation

$$\epsilon_n = h_n^{p-q-1} \cdot \|y_{n+1} - \hat{y}_{n+1}\|_\infty,$$

is formed in every step and is combined in an algorithm for changing the steplength.

$$h_{n+1} = 0.8 \cdot h_n \cdot \left(\frac{t}{\epsilon_n}\right)^{1/p},$$

with t a small positive number which is set by the user and is named tolerance. The safety factor 0.8 is in common use in such formulas and offers increased reliability to the results. Whenever $\epsilon_n < t$, we use the above formula for defining the length of the next step forward. In reverse, when $\epsilon_n \geq t$ we again use it without advancing the solution in this case and using instead the value h_{n+1} as a new trial step h_n. Information in the issue can be found with details in [3]. As an abbreviation these methods are named RKp(q) airs.

Carl David Tolmé Runge [4] and Martin Wilhelm Kutta [5] introduced the methods bearing their names almost in the turning of the 19th century. For almost 60 years the these methods were implemented with constant step sizes. Richardson extrapolation appeared in the meantime [6] and was used in a kind of step control through doubling and halving [7]. Runge–Kutta pairs appeared 60 years ago. The first series of well-known Runge–Kutta pairs of orders 5(4), 6(5), and 8(7) were presented by Fehlberg [8,9]. In the early 1980s, Dormand and Prince gave their celebrated pairs [10,11].

Non-stiff problems having the form (1) are well suited for being efficiently solved by Runge–Kutta pairs. There is a number of different pairs sharing various orders. We may explain this by the accuracy on demand. Thus, the lesser the accuracy required, the lesser order pairs are chosen. Otherwise, for stringent accuracies at quadruple precision, a high order pair has to be preferred.

Here, we concentrate on RK5(4) pairs which are the first choice when middle tolerances are used. Our special interest is in problems of the form (1) with periodic/oscillatory solutions. In the following, we focus on producing a RK5(4) pair that best address the latter type of problems.

The paper is organized in sections as follows.

1. Introduction
2. Theory of Runge–Kutta pairs for orders 5(4)
3. Training the coefficients
4. Numerical tests
5. Conclusions

2. Theory of Runge–Kutta Pairs for Orders 5(4)

Runge–Kutta pairs of orders five and four are perhaps the most used ones. The coefficients of these pairs have to satisfy 25 order conditions when the almost obligatory

$$A \cdot e = c, \; e = [1, 1, \cdots, 1] \in \mathbb{R}^s \tag{2}$$

holds. Namely, 17 order conditions for the higher order formula and another 8 conditions for the fourth order formula. For a seven stages (i.e., $s = 7$) pair with an FSAL (First Stage As Last) property there are 28 coefficients after considering (2). Over the years, various techniques for solving this system have been presented. The solutions form different families. Dormand and Prince presented such a family and perhaps the most famous pair of all in [10]. Papakostas and Papageorgiou studied this family extensively [12]. Then, we may choose arbitrarily the coefficients $c_2, c_3, c_4, c_5, \hat{b}_7$ and produce all the rest coefficients explicitly. The particular pair DP5(4) appeared in [10] shares small principal truncation error coefficients and it is implemented in the builtin function ode45 of MATLAB [13].

We now proceed presenting explicit formulas for the remaining coefficients that only depend on the five free parameters.

$$b_3 = \frac{c_4(5 - 10c_5) + 5c_5 - 3}{60(c_3 - 1)c_3(c_3 - c_4)(c_3 - c_5)}, \; b_4 = \frac{5c_3(2c_5 - 1) - 5c_5 + 3}{60(c_4 - 1)c_4(c_3 - c_4)(c_4 - c_5)},$$

$$b_5 = \frac{5c_3(2c_4 - 1) - 5c_4 + 3}{60(c_5 - 1)c_5(c_3 - c_5)(c_5 - c_4)},$$

$$b_6 = \frac{5c_3(c_4(6c_5 - 4) - 4c_5 + 3) - 20c_4c_5 + 15c_4 + 15c_5 - 12}{60(c_3 - 1)(c_4 - 1)(c_5 - 1)},$$

$$\hat{b}_3 = \frac{\left(\dfrac{\left(\begin{array}{c} 10(6\hat{b}_7 - 1)c_3^2 c_4 \\ +c_3(-8\hat{b}_7(7c_4 + 1) \\ +8c_4 + 1) + 2(8\hat{b}_7 - 1)c_4 \end{array} \right) \left(\begin{array}{c} 5c_3(c_4(6c_5 - 4) - 4c_5 + 3) \\ -20c_4c_5 + 15c_4 + 15c_5 - 12 \end{array} \right)}{5(c_3 - 1)\left(\begin{array}{c} 10c_3^2 c_4 \\ -c_3(8c_4 + 1) + 2c_4 \end{array} \right)} - 12\hat{b}_7(c_4 - 1)(c_5 - 1) + 2c_4(3c_5 - 2) - 4c_5 + 3 \right)}{12c_3(c_3 - c_4)(c_3 - c_5)},$$

$$\hat{b}_4 = \frac{\left(-\dfrac{\left(\begin{array}{c} 10(6\hat{b}_7 - 1)c_3^2 c_4 \\ +c_3(-8\hat{b}_7(7c_4 + 1) + 8c_4 + 1) \\ +2(8\hat{b}_7 - 1)c_4 \end{array} \right) \left(\begin{array}{c} 5c_3(c_4(6c_5 - 4) - 4c_5 + 3) \\ -20c_4c_5 + 15c_4 + 15c_5 - 12 \end{array} \right)}{5(c_4 - 1)\left(\begin{array}{c} 10c_3^2 c_4 \\ -c_3(8c_4 + 1) + 2c_4 \end{array} \right)} + 12\hat{b}_7(c_3 - 1)(c_5 - 1) - 2c_3(3c_5 - 2) + 4c_5 - 3 \right)}{12c_4(c_3 - c_4)(c_4 - c_5)},$$

$$\hat{b}_5 = \frac{\left(\left\{ \dfrac{\left(\begin{array}{c} 10(6\hat{b}_7 - 1)c_3^2 c_4 \\ +c_3(-8\hat{b}_7(7c_4 + 1) + 8c_4 + 1) \\ +2(8\hat{b}_7 - 1)c_4 \end{array} \right) \left(\begin{array}{c} 5c_3(c_4(6c_5 - 4) - 4c_5 + 3) \\ -20c_4c_5 + 15c_4 + 15c_5 - 12 \end{array} \right)}{5(c_5 - 1)\left(\begin{array}{c} 10c_3^2 c_4 \\ -c_3(8c_4 + 1) + 2c_4 \end{array} \right)} \right\} - 12\hat{b}_7(c_3 - 1)(c_4 - 1) + 2c_3(3c_4 - 2) - 4c_4 + 3 \right)}{12c_5(c_3 - c_5)(c_4 - c_5)},$$

$$\hat{b}_6 = -\frac{\left\{ \begin{array}{c} \left(10(6\hat{b}_7 - 1)c_3^2 c_4 + c_3(-8\hat{b}_7(7c_4 + 1) + 8c_4 + 1) + 2(8\hat{b}_7 - 1)c_4 \right) \cdot \\ (5c_3(c_4(6c_5 - 4) - 4c_5 + 3) - 20c_4c_5 + 15c_4 + 15c_5 - 12) \end{array} \right\}}{60(c_3 - 1)(c_4 - 1)(c_5 - 1)(10c_3^2 c_4 - c_3(8c_4 + 1) + 2c_4)},$$

$$a_{3,2} = \frac{c_3^2}{2c_2}, a_{4,2} = \frac{c_4^2(3c_3 - 2c_4)}{2c_2c_3}, a_{4,3} = \frac{c_4^2(c_4 - c_3)}{c_3^2},$$

$$a_{5,2} = \frac{c_5\left(15c_3^2c_4(2c_5 - 1) + c_3(c_4(6 - 20c_5^2) + (3 - 5c_5)c_5) + 2c_4c_5(5c_5 - 3)\right)}{2c_2c_3(5c_3(2c_4 - 1) - 5c_4 + 3)},$$

$$a_{5,3} = -\frac{c_5(c_3 - c_5)\left(10c_3^2c_4(2c_5 - 1) + c_3\left(\begin{array}{c}-5c_4^2(4c_5 - 3)\\+c_4(4 - 15c_5) + 2c_5\end{array}\right) + 2c_4^2(5c_5 - 3)\right)}{2c_3^2(c_3 - c_4)(5c_3(2c_4 - 1) - 5c_4 + 3)},$$

$$a_{5,4} = \frac{(5c_3 - 2)c_5(c_3 - c_5)(c_4 - c_5)}{2c_4(c_3 - c_4)(5c_3(2c_4 - 1) - 5c_4 + 3)},$$

$$a_{6,2} = \frac{15c_3^2c_4(2c_5 - 1) + c_3(c_4(16 - 30c_5) - 5c_5 + 3) + 2c_4(5c_5 - 3)}{2c_2c_3(5c_3(c_4(6c_5 - 4) - 4c_5 + 3) - 20c_4c_5 + 15c_4 + 15c_5 - 12)},$$

$$a_{6,3} = -\frac{(c_3 - 1) \cdot \left(\begin{array}{c}-c_3^2(5c_4^2(4c_5 - 3) + 20c_4c_5^2 + c_4 - 2)\\+c_3(c_4^2(25c_5 - 16) + c_4(40c_5^2 - 45c_5 + 16) - 2(5c_5^2 - 7c_5 + 3))\\10c_3^3c_4(2c_5 - 1) + 2c_4^2(3 - 5c_5)c_5\end{array}\right)}{2c_3^2(c_3 - c_4)(c_3 - c_5)(5c_3(c_4(6c_5 - 4) - 4c_5 + 3) - 20c_4c_5 + 15c_4 + 15c_5 - 12)},$$

$$a_{6,4} = \frac{(c_3 - 1)(c_4 - 1)\left(5c_3(c_4 - 4c_5^2 + 5c_5 - 2) - 2(c_4 - 5c_5^2 + 7c_5 - 3)\right)}{2c_4(c_3 - c_4)(c_4 - c_5)(5c_3(c_4(6c_5 - 4) - 4c_5 + 3) - 20c_4c_5 + 15c_4 + 15c_5 - 12)},$$

$$a_{6,5} = \frac{(c_3 - 1)(c_4 - 1)(c_5 - 1)(5c_3(2c_4 - 1) - 5c_4 + 3)}{c_5(c_3 - c_5)(c_4 - c_5)(5c_3(c_4(6c_5 - 4) - 4c_5 + 3) - 20c_4c_5 + 15c_4 + 15c_5 - 12)},$$

$$b_1 = 1 - b_3 - b_4 - b_5 - b_6, \hat{b}_1 = 1 - \hat{b}_3 - \hat{b}_4 - \hat{b}_5 - \hat{b}_6 - \hat{b}_7,$$

$$a_{21} = c_2, a_{31} = c_3 - a_{32}, a_{41} = c_4 - a_{42} - a_{43},$$

$$a_{51} = c_5 - a_{52} - a_{53} - a_{54}, a_{61} = c_6 - a_{62} - a_{63} - a_{64} - a_{65},$$

and finally the FSAL property holds

$$a_{7j} = b_j, j = 1, 2, \cdots, 6.$$

This means that although $s = 7$, the method wastes only six stages per step and the seventh stage is reused as first stage of the next step.

The question raising now is how to choose the free parameters. Traditionally, the method developers try to minimize some norm for the principal term of the local truncation error, i.e., the terms of h^6 in the residual of Taylor error expansions corresponding to the fifth order method of the underlying RK pair. Another choice is to increase the phase-lag order. This means that we try to reduce the gap in the angle among the numerical and the theoretical solution in a free oscillator [14]. The latter approach is well suited for usage in problems with periodic solutions.

3. Training the Coefficients

We intent to derive a particular RK5(4) pair that belongs to the family discussed above. The resulting pair has to perform best on harmonic oscillators and other problems with periodic solutions. For achieving this, we will first try to find a pair that performs best on a couple of harmonic oscillators. Then, we will check if this performance expands to other problems with periodic solutions.

Thus, we concentrate on the harmonic oscillator

$$y'' = -\mu^2 y, \; y(0) = 1, \; y'(0) = 0, x \in [0, 10\pi],$$

with theoretical solution $y(x) = \cos \mu x$. This problem can be transformed to a first-order system,

$$\begin{bmatrix} y_1' \\ y_2' \end{bmatrix} = \begin{bmatrix} 0 & 1 \\ -\mu^2 & 0 \end{bmatrix} \begin{bmatrix} y_1 \\ y_2 \end{bmatrix}, \ y_1(0) = 1, y_2(0) = 0, x \in [0, 10\pi],$$

and then solved it numerically by a RK5(4) pair picked from the family of solutions we are concerned here. We use tolerance $t = 10^{-11}$ and $\mu = 3$ and $\mu = 7$. The choice of μ is tailored by the numerical tests we will present below. The values selected are best placed when $\mu \in [0, 10]$. Notice that the above selection of μ is for the training phase. It is hoped that the resulted method will furnish better results for every μ.

We record the number k_1 and k_2 of stages (i.e., function evaluations) needed and the global errors g_1 and g_2 observed over the grid (mesh) in the interval of integration, respectively (i.e for both selections of μ). Then, we form two efficiency measures

$$u_j = k_j \cdot g_j^{1/5}, \ j = 1, 2 \tag{3}$$

in the sense that higher values mean lower efficiency. These measures were introduced in [15] for comparing pairs of the same order.

Now we may set as fitness function the sum $u_1 + u_2$ which is meant to be minimized. Thus, the fitness function consists of two runs of an Initial Value Problem. The value $u_1 + u_2$ changes according to the selection of the free parameters c_2, c_3, c_4, c_5, and $\hat{b}_7$. We actually do not care at this stage for $\hat{b}_7$, as this coefficient actually affects only the tolerance. Indeed we may choose

$$\tilde{b}_7 = \lambda \cdot \hat{b}_7, \lambda \neq 0,$$

and set a new $\tilde{b} = \lambda \hat{b} + (1 - \lambda)b$, as the new fourth order formula. Then, the tolerance simply becomes λt.

This idea was originally appeared in [16]. Here, for the minimization of $u_1 + u_2$ we tried Differential Evolution [17]. We have already got positive results using this approach for methods in integrating of orbits [18,19]. In these latter works, we trained the coefficients of the methods on a Kepler orbit. Then we observed very pleasant results over a set of Kepler orbits as long as on other known orbital problems.

DE is an iterative procedure and in every iteration, named generation g, we work with a "population" of individuals $\left(c_2^{(g)}, c_3^{(g)}, c_4^{(g)}, c_5^{(g)}, \hat{b}_7^{(g)}\right)_i, i = 1, 2, \cdots, P$ with P the population size. An initial population $\left(c_2^{(0)}, c_3^{(0)}, c_4^{(0)}, c_5^{(0)}, \hat{b}_7^{(0)}\right)_i, i = 1, 2, \cdots, P$ is randomly created in the first step of the method. We have also set as fitness function the measure $u_1 + u_2$ obtained after two runs of harmonic oscillator. The fitness function is then evaluated for each individual in the initial population. In each generation (iteration) g, a three-phase sequential scheme updates all of the individuals involved. These phases are Differentiation, Crossover, and Selection. For further details in the issue see in [20]. We used MATLAB Software DeMat [21] for implementing the latter technique.

The optimization furnished five values for the parameters. The result is rather robust, i.e., we get almost the same optimal value for u even for neighboring parameters. Thus, we present the selected parameters in 6 significant decimal digits below,

$$c_2 = \frac{6618}{21991}, \ c_3 = \frac{3679}{11497}, \ c_4 = \frac{25691}{30789}, \ c_5 = \frac{5444}{5589}, \ \hat{b}_7 = \frac{11}{400}.$$

The resulting pair is presented in Table 1.

Table 1. Coefficients of NEW5(4) pair, accurate for double precision computations.

0							
$\frac{6618}{21991}$	$\frac{6618}{21991}$						
$\frac{3679}{11497}$	$\frac{105068699}{701077884}$	$\frac{87461119}{514086615}$					
$\frac{25691}{30789}$	$-\frac{156758655}{1553593837}$	$-\frac{1971428717}{769326967}$	$\frac{1150666171}{328963002}$				
$\frac{5444}{5589}$	$-\frac{492306695}{897757177}$	$-\frac{4668023671}{453052236}$	$\frac{11886685592}{971735195}$	$-\frac{563000739}{1384986010}$			
1	$-\frac{1277080003}{2297156422}$	$-\frac{19858667372}{1842147371}$	$\frac{12595531818}{990040061}$	$-\frac{479293713}{1359193574}$	$\frac{43409699}{1295767884}$		
1	$\frac{118291366}{1206413123}$	0	$\frac{224782023}{473511539}$	$\frac{563088416}{949003535}$	$-\frac{735589742}{998947995}$	$\frac{326830465}{573133003}$	
5th-order	$\frac{118291366}{1206413123}$	0	$\frac{224782023}{473511539}$	$\frac{563088416}{949003535}$	$-\frac{735589742}{998947995}$	$\frac{326830465}{573133003}$	
4th-order	$\frac{34973117}{364942645}$	0	$\frac{660068138}{1367732753}$	$\frac{376526469}{703576622}$	$-\frac{319022417}{656211193}$	$\frac{219368109}{635728846}$	$\frac{11}{400}$

For the above selection of free parameters, we got

$$u_1^{\text{NEW54}} = 88.37, \ u_2^{\text{NEW54}} = 284.89,$$

while for DP5(4) we observed

$$u_1^{\text{DP54}} = 279.28, \ u_2^{\text{DP54}} = 797.55$$

i.e.,

$$\frac{u_1^{\text{DP54}}}{u_1^{\text{NEW54}}} + \frac{u_2^{\text{DP54}}}{u_2^{\text{NEW54}}} = \frac{279.28}{88.37} + \frac{797.55}{284.89} \approx 3.16 + 2.80 = 5.96,$$

meaning that DP5(4) is 216% (interpreting number 3.16) and 180% (interpreting number 2.80), respectively, more expensive for delivering the same accuracy in the two oscillators chosen above.

The Euclidean norm of the principal truncation error coefficients for the new pair is $\|T^{(6)}\|_2 \approx 2.82 \times 10^{-4}$ which is a little smaller than the corresponding value $\|T^{(6)}\|_2 \approx 3.99 \times 10^{-4}$ for DP5(4). The absolute stability interval is $(-3.55, 0]$ which is rather in normal magnitude. No extra phase-lag order is observed as $bA^4c = \frac{13128101}{9439496880} \neq \frac{1}{840}$. See in [14] for details on phase-lag property.

In conclusion, it seems that no extra property is present. The new pair appeared in Table 1 does not possess something interesting. It is hard to believe its special performance after seeing its traditional characteristics.

Other authors have also tried recently to train coefficients of RK methods [22]. However, in that later paper, only second- and third-order methods are considered [4,5] with constant step sizes and over single problems (e.g., Van der Pol). The learning algorithm given there remains to be tested on current and stiffer cases. Our proposal for Differential evolution comes after several papers through the years [16].

4. Numerical Tests

We tested the following two pairs chosen from the family studied above.
1. DP5(4) pair given in [10].
2. NEW5(4) pair given here in Table 1.

DP5(4) has proven over the years to be perhaps the best pair of orders five and four. Other pairs also exist but the difference with DP5(4) is very small. We do not consider pairs that exploit the knowledge of frequency since this property is not considered here.

All the pairs were run for tolerances $10^{-5}, 10^{-6}, \cdots, 10^{-11}$, and the efficiency measures of the form (3) were recorded. Notice that actually all the problems are transformed in systems of first order equations.

The problems we tested are the following.

1–5. *The model problem*

$$y''(x) = -\mu^2 y(x), \ y(0) = 1, y'(0) = 0, x \in [0, 10\pi],$$

with theoretical solution $y(x) = \cos(\mu x)$. This problem was run for five different selections of μ. Thus, when we use $\mu = 1$ the problem is numbered as 1st problem. Then we choose $\mu = 3$ and the problem is numbered as 2nd problem. In consequence when $\mu = 5$ the problem is numbered as 3rd problem, when $\mu = 7$ the problem is numbered as 4th problem, and when $\mu = 9$ the problem is numbered as 5th problem.

6. *The inhomogeneous problem*

$$y''(x) = -100 y(x) + 99 \sin x, y(0) = 1, y'(0) = 11, x \in [0, 10\pi],$$

with theoretical solution $y(x) = \cos(10x) + \sin(10x) + \sin x$.

7. *The Bessel equation*

The well-known Bessel equation

$$y''(x) = -y(x) \cdot \frac{1 + 400x^2}{4x^2},$$

is verified by a theoretical solution of the form [14]

$$y(x) = J_0(10x) \cdot \sqrt{x},$$

with J_0 the zeroth order Bessel function of the first kind. This equation in also integrated in the interval $[0, 10\pi]$.

8. *The Duffing equation*

Next, we choose the equation

$$\begin{aligned} y''(x) &= \frac{1}{500} \cdot \cos(1.01x) - y(x) - y(x)^3, \\ y(0) &= 0.2004267280699011, y'(0) = 0, \end{aligned}$$

with an approximate analytical solution given in [23],

$$y(x) \approx \left\{ \begin{array}{l} 6 \cdot 10^{-16} \cos(11.11x) + 4.609 \cdot 10^{-13} \cos(9.09x) \\ +3.743495 \cdot 10^{-10} \cos(7.07x) + 3.040149839 \cdot 10^{-7} \cos(5.05x) \\ +2.469461432611 \cdot 10^{-4} \cos(3.03x) 0.2001794775368452 \cos(1.01x) \end{array} \right\}$$

We again solved the above equation in the interval $[0, 10\pi]$.

9. *semi-Linear system.*

The nonlinear problem proposed by Franco and Gomez [24] follows.

$$\begin{aligned} y''(t) &= \begin{pmatrix} -199 & -198 \\ 99 & 98 \end{pmatrix} \cdot y(x) + \begin{pmatrix} (y_1 + y_2)^2 + \sin^2(10x) - 1 \\ (y_1 + 2y_2)^2 - 10^{-6} \sin^2(x) \end{pmatrix}, \\ x &\in [0, 10\pi], \end{aligned}$$

with theoretical solution

$$y(t) = \begin{pmatrix} 2\cos(10x) - 10^{-3} \sin(x) \\ -\cos(10x) + 10^{-3} \sin(x) \end{pmatrix}.$$

10. *Van der Pol oscillator.*

The equation we solved is

$$y'' = 0.1 \cdot (1 - y(x)^2)y'(x) - y(x), \ y(0) = -0.2, \ y'(0) = 0, \ x \in [0, 10\pi],$$

and no analytical solution is known. Thus, the error at grid was estimated using an eighth-order pair from [25] at tolerance 10^{-14}.

We calculated seventy (i.e., 7 tolerances times 10 problems) efficiency measures for each pair. We set NEW54 as the reference pair. Then, we divide each efficiency measure of DP5(4) with the corresponding efficiency measure of NEW5(4). The results are recorded in Table 2. The two underlined numbers correspond to the ratios found in the phase of training above as the training was done for problems 2 and 4 and tolerance 10^{-11}. Numbers greater than 1 are in favor of the second pair. $\hat{b}_7$ was chosen so that the total function evaluations spend for both pairs over all 70 runs is almost equal. The rightmost column shows the mean over all tolerances for each problem. The overall average observed ratio is 1.85 meaning that DP5(4) is about 85% more expensive. This is quite remarkable since much effort has been put over the years for achieving even 10–20% of efficiency [25]. In reverse, this means that about $\log_{10} 1.85^5 \approx 1.34$ digits were gained in average at the same costs [15].

Table 2. Efficiency measures ratios of DP5(4) vs. NEW5(4) over the interval $[0, 10\pi]$.

	Tolerances							
Problem	10^{-5}	10^{-6}	10^{-7}	10^{-8}	10^{-9}	10^{-10}	10^{-11}	Mean
1	1.33	1.45	1.60	1.76	1.93	2.12	2.65	1.83
2	1.36	1.48	1.63	1.79	1.96	2.17	<u>3.16</u>	1.94
3	1.37	1.50	1.64	1.80	1.98	2.20	2.74	1.89
4	1.38	1.51	1.65	1.81	1.99	2.22	<u>2.80</u>	1.91
5	1.39	1.51	1.66	1.82	1.99	2.23	2.24	1.83
6	1.41	1.54	1.68	1.85	2.02	2.35	1.75	1.80
7	1.32	1.44	1.57	1.72	1.89	2.08	2.67	1.81
8	1.14	1.4	1.65	1.93	2.19	2.38	2.40	1.87
9	1.52	1.67	1.84	2.00	2.17	2.54	1.98	1.96
10	1.25	1.36	1.49	1.62	1.77	1.94	2.24	1.67

Because of the problems used for training, it is obvious that we expect better results when there is a larger linear part and a smaller nonlinear part. However, NEW5(4) outperformed DP5(4) even in the clearly nonlinear problems. We also mention that we got more or less similar results for longer integrations. Especially the results for the interval $[0, 20\pi]$ are shown in Table 3. The overall average observed is 1.84 and the results slightly differ from those of the previous Table.

As a final test, we included a more challenging problem which appears frequently in similar works [14,23], namely, the hyperbolic PDE,

$$\frac{\partial u}{\partial x} = \frac{\partial u}{\partial r}, \ u(x,0) = 0, \ u(0,r) = \sin \pi^2 r^2,$$
$$0 \leq r \leq 1, \ x \geq 0,$$

is discretized by symmetric differences (with $\Delta r = 1/50$) to the system of ODEs

$$\begin{bmatrix} y'_1 \\ y'_2 \\ \vdots \\ y'_{50} \end{bmatrix} = \frac{1}{2} \cdot \frac{1}{(1/50)} \begin{bmatrix} 0 & -1 & & & & \\ 1 & 0 & -1 & & & \\ & & \ddots & & & \\ & & & 1 & 0 & -1 \\ & & & -1 & 4 & -3 \end{bmatrix} \cdot \begin{bmatrix} y_1 \\ y_2 \\ \vdots \\ y_{50} \end{bmatrix}.$$

The 500th zero of the 20th component in the above problem is reached for

$$x_{500} = 33.50999699533,$$

which is found by a very accurate integration at stringent tolerances. We integrated the methods to that point. The results presented as stages vs. error in a semi-log form and are given in Figure 1.

Table 3. Efficiency measures ratios of DP5(4) vs. NEW5(4) over the interval $[0, 20\pi]$.

	Tolerances							
Problem	10^{-5}	10^{-6}	10^{-7}	10^{-8}	10^{-9}	10^{-10}	10^{-11}	Mean
1	1.33	1.45	1.60	1.75	1.92	2.11	2.64	1.83
2	1.36	1.49	1.63	1.78	1.96	2.16	3.17	1.94
3	1.37	1.50	1.64	1.80	1.97	2.18	2.58	1.86
4	1.38	1.51	1.65	1.81	1.98	2.19	2.79	1.90
5	1.39	1.51	1.66	1.82	1.99	2.23	2.42	1.86
6	1.41	1.54	1.68	1.85	2.03	2.36	1.80	1.81
7	1.32	1.44	1.57	1.72	1.89	2.07	2.65	1.81
8	1.08	1.36	1.66	1.98	2.33	2.58	2.58	1.94
9	1.52	1.67	1.84	2.00	2.17	2.44	1.73	1.91
10	1.24	1.28	1.34	1.44	1.58	1.75	2.17	1.54

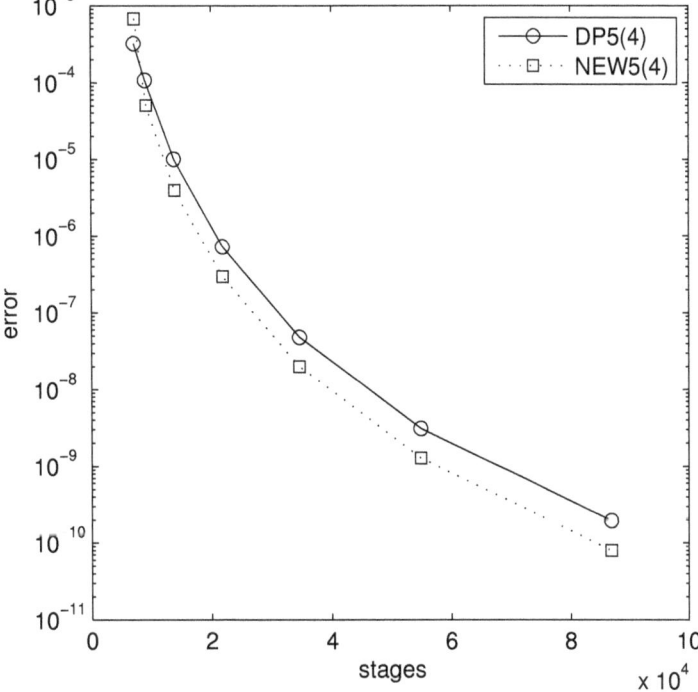

Figure 1. Results of DP5(4) vs. NEW5(4) for the Hyperbolic PDE.

The results are very promising. Some future research may use optimization on a wider range of tolerances and model problems. Perhaps a pair spending a parameter for fulfilling the phase-lag property and then trained for periodic problems would furnish even more interesting results. Of course, application of this technique on other classes of problems is also possible, e.g., orbits.

5. Conclusions

We proposed the proper training the coefficients of Runge–Kutta pairs of orders five and four in order to perform best on problems with oscillatory solutions. We actually chose a couple of harmonic oscillators, an interval and a tolerance and tried to achieve an outstanding performance there. Thus, we concluded to a new pair which is found to outperform other representatives from this family in a wide range of relevant problems. This pair is supposed to be better than classical DP5(4) for problems with periodic solutions. If there are limitations remain to be clarified by applications in the future research.

Author Contributions: All authors have contributed equally. All authors have read and agreed to the published version of the manuscript.

Funding: The research was supported by a Mega Grant from the Government of the Russian Federation within the framework of the federal project No. 075-15-2021-584.

Institutional Review Board Statement: Not applicable.

Informed Consent Statement: Not applicable.

Data Availability Statement: Not applicable.

Conflicts of Interest: The authors declare no conflict of interest.

References

1. Butcher, J.C. On Runge-Kutta processes of high order. *J. Austral. Math. Soc.* **1964**, *4*, 179–194. [CrossRef]
2. Butcher, J.C. *Numerical Methods for Ordinary Differential Equations*; John Wiley & Sons: Chichester, UK, 2003.
3. Shampine, L.F.; Watts, H.A. The Art of Writing a runge-kutta Cosde. II. *Appl. Math. Comput.* **1979**, *5*, 93–121.
4. Runge, C. Ueber die numerische Auflöung von Differentialgleichungen. *Math. Ann.* **1895**, *46*, 167–178. [CrossRef]
5. Kutta, W. Beitrag zur naherungsweisen Integration von Differentialgleichungen. *Z. Math. Phys.* **1901**, *46*, 435–453
6. Richardson, L.F. The deferred approach to the limit. Part I.—Single lattice. *Philos. Trans. R. Soc. Lond. Ser. A* **1927**, *226*, 299–349.
7. Shampine, L.F. Local Error Estimation by Doubling. *Computing* **1985**, *34*, 179–190. [CrossRef]
8. Fehlberg, E. Klassische Runge-Kutta-Formeln fünfter und siebenter 0rdnung mit Schrittweiten-Kontrolle. *Computing* **1969**, *4*, 93–106. [CrossRef]
9. Fehlberg, E. Klassische Runge-Kutta-Formeln vierter und niedrigererrdnung mit Schrittweiten-Kontrolle und ihre Anwendung auf Warmeleitungsprobleme. *Computing* **1970**, *6*, 61–71. [CrossRef]
10. Dormand, J.R.; Prince, P.J. A family of embedded Runge-Kutta formulae. *J. Comput. Appl. Math.* **1980**, *6*, 19–26. [CrossRef]
11. Prince, P.J.; Dormand, J.R. High order embedded Runge-Kutta formulae. *J. Comput. Appl. Math.* **1981**, *7*, 67–75. [CrossRef]
12. Papakostas, S.N.; Papageorgiou, G. A family of fifth order Runge-Kutta pairs. *Math. Comput.* **1996**, *65*, 1165–1181. [CrossRef]
13. Shampine, L.F.; Reichelt, M.W. The MATLAB ODE Suite. *SIAM J. Sci. Comput.* **1997**, *18*, 1–22. [CrossRef]
14. Papageorgiou, G.; Tsitouras, C.; Papakostas, S.N. Runge-Kutta pairs for periodic initial value problems. *Computing* **1993**, *51*, 151–163. [CrossRef]
15. Shampine, L.F. Some practical Runge-Kutta formulas. *Math. Comput.* **1986**, *46*, 135–150. [CrossRef]
16. Tsitouras, C. Neural Networks With Multidimensional Transfer Functions. *IEEE Trans. Neural Netw.* **2002**, *13*, 222–228. [CrossRef]
17. Storn, R.; Price, K. Differential evolution—A simple and efficient heuristic for global optimization over continuous spaces. *J. Glob. Optim.* **1997**, *11*, 341–359. [CrossRef]
18. Tsitouras, C.; Famelis, I.T. Using neural networks for the derivation of Runge–Kutta–Nyström pairs for integration of orbits. *New Astron.* **2012**, *17*, 469–473 [CrossRef]
19. Shen, Y.C.; Lin, C.L.; Simos, T.E.; Tsitouras, C. Runge–Kutta Pairs of Orders 6 (5) with Coefficients Trained to Perform Best on Classical Orbits. *Mathematics* **2021**, *9*, 1342. [CrossRef]
20. Famelis, I.T.; Alexandridis, A.; Tsitouras, C. High Accuracy Hybrid DE-PSO Algorithm for the construction of Runge–Kutta pairs. *Enginr. Optim.* **2017**, *50*, 1364–1379.
21. DeMat. Available online: https://www.swmath.org/software/24853 (accessed on 23 August 2021).
22. Guo, Y.; Dietrich, F.; Bertalan, T.; Doncevic, D.T.; Dahmen, M.; Kevrekidis, I.G. Personalized Algorithm Generation: A Case Study in Meta-Learning ODE Integrators. *arXiv* **2021**, arXiv:2105.01303v1.

23. Simos, T.E.; Tsitouras, C.; Famelis, I.T. Explicit Numerov Type Methods with Constant Coefficients: A Review. *Appl. Comput. Math.* **2017**, *16*, 89–113.
24. Franco, J.M.; Gomez, I. Trigonometrically fitted nonlinear two-step methods for solving second order oscillatory IVPs. *Appl. Math. Comput.* **2014**, *232*, 643–657. [CrossRef]
25. Papakostas, S.N.; Tsitouras, C. High phase-lag order Runge-Kutta and Nyström pairs. *SIAM J. Sci. Comput.* **1999**, *21*, 747–763. [CrossRef]

Article

SEIR Mathematical Model of Convalescent Plasma Transfusion to Reduce COVID-19 Disease Transmission

Hennie Husniah [1], Ruhanda Ruhanda [1,2], Asep K. Supriatna [3,*] and Md. H. A. Biswas [4]

1. Department of Industrial Engineering, Faculty of Engineering, Universitas Langlangbuana, Bandung 40261, Indonesia; h.husniah@unla.ac.id (H.H.); ruhanda@unla.ac.id (R.R.)
2. Indonesia Red Cross, Bandung 40135, Indonesia
3. Department of Mathematics, Faculty of Mathematics and Natural Sciences, Universitas Padjadjaran, Sumedang 45363, Indonesia
4. Mathematics Discipline, Khulna University, Khulna 9208, Bangladesh; mhabiswas@math.ku.ac.bd
* Correspondence: a.k.supriatna@unpad.ac.id

Abstract: In some diseases, due to the restrictive availability of vaccines on the market (e.g., during the early emergence of a new disease that may cause a pandemic such as COVID-19), the use of plasma transfusion is among the available options for handling such a disease. In this study, we developed an SEIR mathematical model of disease transmission dynamics, considering the use of convalescent plasma transfusion (CPT). In this model, we assumed that the effect of CPT increases patient survival or, equivalently, leads to a reduction in the length of stay during an infectious period. We attempted to answer the question of what the effects are of different rates of CPT applications in decreasing the number of infectives at the population level. Herein, we analyzed the model using standard procedures in mathematical epidemiology, i.e., finding the trivial and non-trivial equilibrium points of the system including their stability and their relation to basic and effective reproduction numbers. We showed that, in general, the effects of the application of CPT resulted in a lower peak of infection cases and other epidemiological measures. As a consequence, in the presence of CPT, lowering the height of an infective peak can be regarded as an increase in the number of remaining healthy individuals; thus, the use of CPT may decrease the burden of COVID-19 transmission.

Keywords: SEIR ODE model; COVID-19 transmission; convalescent plasma transfusion (CPT)

Citation: Husniah, H.; Ruhanda, R.; Supriatna, A.K.; Biswas, M.H.A. SEIR Mathematical Model of Convalescent Plasma Transfusion to Reduce COVID-19 Disease Transmission. *Mathematics* **2021**, *9*, 2857. https://doi.org/10.3390/math9222857

Academic Editor: Arsen Palestini

Received: 13 October 2021
Accepted: 3 November 2021
Published: 10 November 2021

Publisher's Note: MDPI stays neutral with regard to jurisdictional claims in published maps and institutional affiliations.

Copyright: © 2021 by the authors. Licensee MDPI, Basel, Switzerland. This article is an open access article distributed under the terms and conditions of the Creative Commons Attribution (CC BY) license (https://creativecommons.org/licenses/by/4.0/).

1. Introduction

The WHO officially declared the COVID-19 pandemic more than a year ago, i.e., on 11 March 2020 [1]. COVID-19 is caused by the SARS-CoV-2 virus, which is thought to have originated in Wuhan, China. At the time of writing this paper, over 247,434,286 cases have been reported across 223 countries with a total of 5,014,576 people having died [2]. Since the announcement of the pandemic, almost every country has made a concerted effort to control the virus, but the number of COVID-19 infections is still climbing in many parts of the world. Although more than a year has passed, there remain some unwanted effects of the pandemic impacting almost every facet of human life. In terms of health, economy, and other human aspects, COVID-19 is still considered a very dangerous new disease. After more than a year since its first appearance, COVID-19 is still reoccurring in many parts of the world for multiple reasons including mutation of the virus into different variants. This is one of the reasons why most infected countries are failing in battling the disease.

Some works in the literature have shown that convalescent plasma transfusion (CPT) is currently being used as an alternative medical treatment method for COVID-19 patients. This treatment has been successfully implemented and has resulted, in particular, in increasing the number of survivors from the disease and reducing the number of deaths in moderate and severe cases. Convalescent plasma transfusion involves the use of blood plasma to assist COVID-19 patients with the process of recovery. Blood plasma is taken from people who have recovered from COVID-19 and who have antibodies against COVID-19 in their blood. Since there is currently no approved treatment for COVID-19, the US Food and Drug Administration has approved convalescent plasma therapy for people with COVID-19 [3]. Before blood can be transfused to a patient, it must be processed to produce plasma and antibodies through the removal of blood cells. Upon transfusion, this plasma has the ability to boost the attack rate of the body of its recipient against the virus. This treatment is commonly referred to as CPT [4,5]. It has been documented that many governments have already advocated for the use of this method to combat COVID-19. Among the governments that have implemented CPT in their countries are Indonesia, the United States, the United Kingdom, Australia, and India [6–8].

CPT is not a new concept. For more than a century, CPT has been used as a passive immunization strategy in the prevention and treatment of epidemic infections [9]. The first documented use of CPT dates back to at least 1918–1920, when it was used to treat Spanish influenza A (H1N1) pneumonia, but it could be even older [10]. This method is being used as a potential therapy for patients infected with COVID-19 [11]. Several studies have also shown that convalescent plasma can reduce the risk of mortality in a patient receiving CPT treatment [12,13]. Many works have shown that the result is a reduction in a patient's mortality risk as well as an increase in viral clearance [14].

Despite its increasing popularity as an alternative clinical treatment for COVID-19 patients, a recent finding [14] pointed out that "most clinical studies, in particular case reports and case series, were of poor quality. Only 1 RCT [randomized controlled trials] was of high quality". Hence, the authors argued that "future research is necessary to fill the knowledge gap regarding prevention and treatment for patients with COVID-19 with CP while other therapeutics are being developed". Currently, medical and epidemiological studies use not only clinical methods but include other forms or approaches such as mathematical modeling. The other shortcomings of studies on CPT are that, to date, the impacts of CPT applications on the population have remained unclear. The present study had the objective of filling in this gap via a mathematical approach in the hope that new insight could be gained regarding the effect of CPT applications, especially at the population level.

Only a few mathematical modeling papers (e.g., [15,16]) have addressed this issue mathematically. The authors of [16] performed preliminary work on this issue and presented mathematical models not specific to COVID-19 but that take the form of general discrete time SIR and SEIR models [16]. In the present paper, a mathematical modeling approach was used to answer an important question on the effect of convalescent plasma transfusion on the reduction of COVID-19 transmission at the population level. The assumptions used in the development of the model were taken from the literature, showing that the majority of patients who received CPT recovered and had lower mortality rates than patients who were not treated using CPT transfusion. In the developed model, we assumed that the effect of CPT would be to increase the rate of recovery. A continuous SEIR epidemic model was used to describe the transmission of COVID-19. The SEIR model can appear in the form of discrete models [17,18], but we used the continuous form here, since this is the most often used version in the literature.

2. Materials and Methods

The tool used to conduct the research was a mathematical model, i.e., a system of differential equations representing the transmission dynamics of COVID-19. The mathematical model was obtained through the process of mathematical modeling to convert the transmission mechanisms and problems therein into mathematical concepts and mathematical problems. In this case, the main concepts were a system of differential equations and related problems on how to determine and understand solutions to the problems at hand (the detailed method can be found in [19–21]). The following section presents the mathematical modeling process used for the remaining discussion.

Mathematical Model

Let us consider a human population, which, due to the circulation of COVID-19, is divided into four sub-classes/sub-populations, namely, the susceptible (S), the exposed (E), the infective (I), and the recovered, who are assumed to be immune (R). For all variables in the model (i.e., $X = S, E, I, R, N$), the notation $X(t)$ means the number of individuals in X class at time t.

Suppose that the health authority responsible for the population administers a CPT intervention to cure infected people. We may raise the question of, in this case, how and to what extent does the presence of CPT affect the dynamics of the system. What is the main contribution of CPT at the population level? There are several scenarios regarding how CPT is administered depending on the real situation such as a constant versus proportional rate of CPT administration. Herein, we analyzed the continuous SEIR model in the presence of CPT using a standard procedure in mathematical epidemiology, i.e., finding the trivial and non-trivial equilibrium points of the system including their stability. A schematic diagram of disease transmission is shown in Figure 1a. The detailed route from compartment I to compartment R is as shown in Figure 1b with various possible numerical responses $f(I(t),R(t))$ as outlined in Table 1.

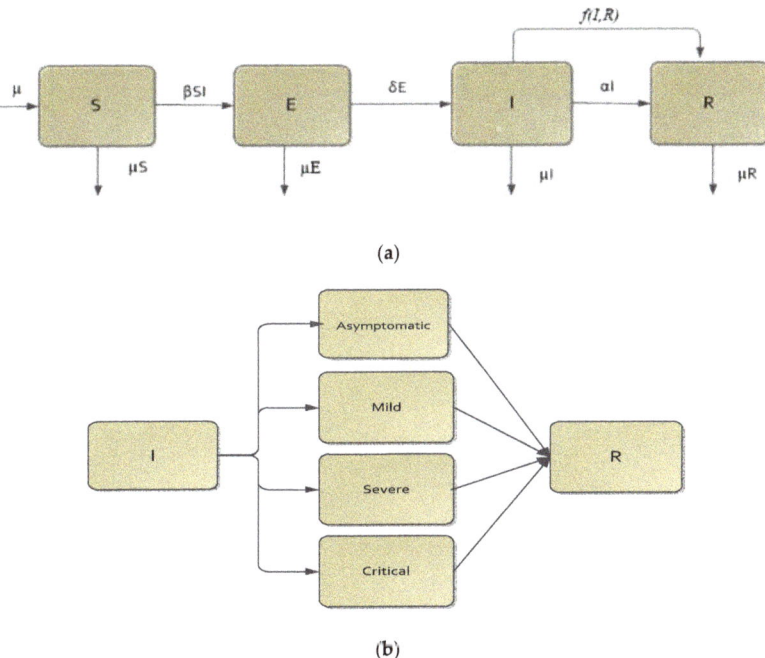

Figure 1. Progression diagram of SEIR transmission with CPT effect $f(I(t),R(t))$ (**a**) and four possible severity levels of COVID-19 infected patients (**b**).

The notations used in the schematic diagram above are:

β	Transmission rate;
δ	Transition rate from exposed class to infective class;
α	Recovery rate;
μ	Demographic rate (birth and death);
$f(I,R)$	Functional form, which together with ε, acts as the CPT intervention rate.

Table 1. Different possible scenarios of CPT implementation.

Number	CPT Scenario	Numerical Response $f(I(t),R(t))$
1	Proportional rate to infectives	$\varepsilon I(t)$
2	Proportional rate to recovered	$\varepsilon R(t)$
3	Mass action rate (Lotka–Volterra)	$\varepsilon I(t)R(t)$
4	Constant rate	ε
5	Saturating rate (Michaelis–Menten)	$\frac{\varepsilon R(t)}{r+R(t)}$
6	Maximum service limitation	$\min(\varepsilon I(t), \text{Maxserv})$
7	Maximum service limitation	$\min(\varepsilon R(t), \text{Maxserv})$
8	Maximum service limitation	$\min(\varepsilon I(t)R(t), \text{Maxserv})$
9	Maximum service limitation	$\min(\frac{\varepsilon R(t)}{r+R(t)}, \text{Maxserv})$

Maxserv is the maximum rate of CPT intervention that a health authority could afford.

To introduce CPT into the SEIR system, we assumed that the CPT rate was a function of both the infective and recovered, most likely proportional to them, say with functional form $f(I(t),R(t))$. We called this function a numerical response. The exact form of the numerical response may vary depending on the assumption being used. For example, it may only depend on $I(t)$ when the disease has already developed and many infected peoples have already recovered, being the source of the convalescent plasma (CP). We may assume that the blood source of the CP is abundant. Other examples are presented in Table 1. By assuming a normalized population with $N(t) = S(t) + E(t) + I(t) + R(t)$, the general mathematical model of CPT in SEIR transmission is given by Equations (1)–(4):

$$\frac{dS}{dt} = \mu - \beta S(t) I(t) - \mu S(t) \qquad (1)$$

$$\frac{dE}{dt} = \beta S(t) I(t) - \delta E(t) - \mu E(t) \qquad (2)$$

$$\frac{dI}{dt} = \delta E(t) - \alpha I(t) - \mu I(t) - f(I(t), R(t)) \qquad (3)$$

$$\frac{dR}{dt} = \alpha I(t) - \mu R(t) + f(I(t), R(t)) \qquad (4)$$

In the subsequent section, we analyze the model by showing its steady-state solutions, their stability, and their relation to the basic reproduction number, which is central in mathematical epidemiology studies. Furthermore, we show that the use of CPT may decrease the burden of COVID-19 transmission such as resulting in a lower peak of infection cases and a higher number of persons who remain susceptible. In this paper, a detailed analysis was conducted for one of the numerical responses, i.e., the CPT rate proportional to the number of infectives, reflecting an abundance of sources for the CP. The equilibrium solution of the model was investigated analytically, while the transient solution was explored numerically.

3. Results and Discussions

As mentioned earlier, herein, we considered the simplest case in which we assumed that the availability of the CP was abundant. This might not be realistic but was used as the first attempt to answer the abovementioned question. Once we obtained the answer, we explored it in more realistic cases. Since we assumed that the CP was widely available, a health authority may apply a CPT rate proportional to the number of infected people. We did not differentiate between mild, severe, and critical patients. Thus, in the presence of CPT, the rate of recovery due to the fact of this intervention also increased proportionally to the number of those infected given CPT. The following section discusses the SEIR model by considering the simplest numerical response, and other forms of numerical response are explored in the numerical examples section.

3.1. The SEIR Continuous Model with CPT Proportional to Infective Class

The modification of Equations (1)–(4), by considering the introduction of CPT proportional to the infective class, yields the following equations:

$$\frac{dS}{dt} = \mu - \beta S(t)I(t) - \mu S(t) \quad (5)$$

$$\frac{dE}{dt} = \beta S(t)I(t) - \delta E(t) - \mu E(t) \quad (6)$$

$$\frac{dI}{dt} = \delta E(t) - \alpha I(t) - \mu I(t) - \varepsilon I(t) \quad (7)$$

$$\frac{dR}{dt} = \alpha I(t) - \mu R(t) + \varepsilon I(t) \quad (8)$$

An endemic-free or non-endemic equilibrium always exists for any parameters of the model. However, we show that there is a threshold that determines the existence of an endemic equilibrium, say $\mathcal{T}^\varepsilon$, so that the endemic equilibrium exists only if $\mathcal{T}^\varepsilon$ is above a certain value; otherwise, an endemic equilibrium does not exist. We sum up this property in the following theorem.

Theorem 1. *In the SEIR model (Equations (5)–(8)), the following properties hold:*

(a) *A non-endemic equilibrium always exists, given by* $(S_0^*, E_0^*, I_0^*, R_0^*) = (1, 0, 0, 0)$;

(b) *The endemic equilibrium is given by* $(S_e^*, E_e^*, I_e^*, R_e^*)$ *with:*

$S_e^* = \frac{\delta\alpha + \delta\varepsilon + \delta\mu + \mu\alpha + \mu\varepsilon + \mu^2}{\beta\delta}$,

$E_e^* = \frac{(\mu\delta + \mu\alpha + \delta\alpha + \delta\varepsilon + \mu\varepsilon + \mu^2 - \beta\delta)\mu}{(\delta + \mu)\beta\delta}$,

$I_e^* = -\frac{(\mu\delta + \mu\alpha + \delta\alpha + \delta\varepsilon + \mu\varepsilon + \mu^2 - \beta\delta)\mu}{(\delta\alpha + \delta\varepsilon + \delta\mu + \mu\alpha + \mu\varepsilon + \mu^2)\beta}$,

$R_e^* = -\frac{(\mu\delta + \mu\alpha + \delta\alpha + \delta\varepsilon + \mu\varepsilon + \mu^2 - \beta\delta)(\alpha + \varepsilon)}{(\delta\alpha + \delta\varepsilon + \delta\mu + \mu\alpha + \mu\varepsilon + \mu^2)\beta}$.

(c) *There is a threshold,* $\mathcal{T}^\varepsilon$, *such that an endemic equilibrium exists only if* $\mathcal{T}^\varepsilon > 1$; *otherwise, an endemic equilibrium does not exist.*

Proof of Theorem 1. By solving Equations (5)–(8) simultaneously under steady-state conditions (i.e., when all LHSs of the equations are equal to zero), the system has two equilibria, i.e., $(S_0^*, E_0^*, I_0^*, R_0^*)$ and $(S_e^*, E_e^*, I_e^*, R_e^*)$, with $(S_0^*, E_0^*, I_0^*, R_0^*) = (1, 0, 0, 0)$ and:

$S_e^* = \frac{\delta\alpha + \delta\varepsilon + \delta\mu + \mu\alpha + \mu\varepsilon + \mu^2}{\beta\delta}$,

$E_e^* = \frac{(\mu\delta + \mu\alpha + \delta\alpha + \delta\varepsilon + \mu\varepsilon + \mu^2 - \beta\delta)\mu}{(\delta + \mu)\beta\delta}$,

$I_e^* = -\frac{(\mu\delta + \mu\alpha + \delta\alpha + \delta\varepsilon + \mu\varepsilon + \mu^2 - \beta\delta)\mu}{(\delta\alpha + \delta\varepsilon + \delta\mu + \mu\alpha + \mu\varepsilon + \mu^2)\beta}$,

$R_e^* = -\frac{(\mu\delta + \mu\alpha + \delta\alpha + \delta\varepsilon + \mu\varepsilon + \mu^2 - \beta\delta)(\alpha + \varepsilon)}{(\delta\alpha + \delta\varepsilon + \delta\mu + \mu\alpha + \mu\varepsilon + \mu^2)\beta}$.

(a) $(S_0^*, E_0^*, I_0^*, R_0^*) = (1, 0, 0, 0)$ is a non-endemic equilibrium, since all of the infected classes (E and I) are zero;

(b) $(S_e^*, E_e^*, I_e^*, R_e^*)$ could be an endemic equilibrium, since all of the infected classes (E and I) could be positive for some parameter choices;

(c) To prove this part of the theorem, we looked for a threshold number, so that $S_e^* \geq 0$, $I_e^* > 0$, $E_e^* > 0$, and $R_e^* \geq 0$. Note that by using some algebraic manipulation, it is easy to show that the components of the equilibrium can be re-written in the following forms: $S_e^* = \frac{1}{\mathcal{T}^\varepsilon}$, $I_e^* = (\mathcal{T}^\varepsilon - 1)\frac{\mu}{\beta}$, $E_e^* = (\mathcal{T}^\varepsilon - 1)\frac{\mu}{\beta} + \frac{(\alpha + \mu + \varepsilon)}{\delta}$, and $R_e^* = $

$1 - S_e^* - E_e^* - I_e^* = (\mathcal{T}^\varepsilon - 1)\frac{\alpha+\varepsilon}{\beta}$, with $\mathcal{T}^\varepsilon = \frac{\beta\delta}{(\alpha+\mu+\varepsilon)(\delta+\mu)}$. Hence, it is clear that if $\mathcal{T}^\varepsilon = \frac{\beta\delta}{(\alpha+\mu+\varepsilon)(\delta+\mu)} > 0$, then $I_e^* > 0$ and $E_e^* > 0$. □

Note that when $\varepsilon = 0$ (i.e., when there is no CPT intervention), then $\mathcal{T}^0 = \frac{\beta\delta}{(\alpha+\mu)(\delta+\mu)}$. Thus, the condition that should be satisfied in order for an endemic equilibrium to exist is $\mathcal{T}^0 = \frac{\beta\delta}{(\alpha+\mu)(\delta+\mu)} > 1$. This can be written as $\mathcal{T}^0 = \beta \frac{1}{(\alpha+\mu)} \delta \frac{1}{(\delta+\mu)} > 1$ and can be read verbally as the multiplication of four epidemiological factors, namely, (the rate of infection)·(the length of stay within the infectious period)·(the rate of transition from exposed class to infectious class)·(the length of stay within the incubation period). We called $\mathcal{T}^0$ the basic threshold number and $\mathcal{T}^\varepsilon$ the effective threshold number. Thus, it is clear that $\mathcal{T}^0 > \mathcal{T}^\varepsilon$.

To provide a deeper interpretation of this threshold, let us consider a clinical intervention. In the health context, any intentional action designed to obtain an outcome is called a clinical intervention. If, in the absence of clinical intervention, we have $\mathcal{T}^0 > 1$ (hence, an endemic equilibrium exists), then we could apply a clinical intervention (such as CPT), so that it is possible to reduce the threshold to be less than 1 by changing $\mathcal{T}^0$ to $\mathcal{T}^\varepsilon$ for a certain choice of $\varepsilon > 0$, resulting in $\mathcal{T}^\varepsilon < 1$ (removing the endemic equilibrium from the system). This is the basic idea behind controlling/eliminating contagious diseases from a mathematical point of view. Finding this kind of threshold is vital in the study of mathematical epidemiology. In the modern literature, this threshold is usually called the basic reproduction number (sometimes the basic reproduction/reproductive ratio). It is not easy to find this number for more complex transmissions of a disease. There are some good and rigorous literature studies regarding this concept, such as [19,22–24] and [25] (pp. 285–319), that provide a more systematic way of constructing the basic reproduction number. We prove, by standard theory, that the $\mathcal{T}^0$ and $\mathcal{T}^\varepsilon$ mentioned above are indeed the basic reproduction number and the effective reproduction number, respectively. We begin by defining the basic reproduction number.

The basic reproduction number of an infection is the expected number of cases produced by one case in a population where all the individuals are susceptible to infection. The authors of [19] (p. 4) defined the basic reproduction number, with the symbol $\mathcal{R}_0$, as the expected number of secondary cases per primary case in a "virgin" population. In the same book, they showed that $\mathcal{R}_0 := \lim_{n\to\infty} \|K^n\|^{1/n}$ [19] (p. 75), where K is the next-generation matrix defined therein. According to the authors, this is a natural definition of the basic reproduction number from which its value can be computed. However, there is another way to compute the basic reproduction number other than from this definition. In fact, there are some methods that are easier to use to obtain the basic reproduction number. As an example, the following method is suggested in [24]. The authors looked at an epidemic multi-compartment model $\frac{dx_i}{dt} = f_i(x) = \mathcal{F}_i(x) - \mathcal{V}_i(x)$, $i = 1,\ldots,n$ (as in Equations (5)–(8) above). They showed that the function $f_i(x)$ can be decomposed into the rate of appearance of new infections in the ith compartment, $\mathcal{F}_i(x)$, and the rate of transfer of individuals from/into the ith compartment, $\mathcal{V}_i(x)$. Furthermore, they defined F and V to be the Jacobian matrix evaluated at the non-endemic equilibrium and showed that the basic reproduction number can be calculated as the spectral radius $\mathcal{R}_0 = \rho(FV^{-1})$. The following theorem provides the reproduction numbers of the SEIR model (Equations (5)–(8)).

Theorem 2. *The SEIR model (Equations (5)–(8)) has the following reproduction numbers:*

(a) *The effective reproduction number* $\mathcal{R}_0^\varepsilon = \frac{\beta\delta}{(\alpha+\mu+\varepsilon)(\delta+\mu)}$;
(b) *The basic reproduction number* $\mathcal{R}_0 = \frac{\beta\delta}{(\alpha+\mu)(\delta+\mu)}$.

In addition, the following hold:
$\mathcal{R}_0^\varepsilon = \mathcal{T}^\varepsilon$ *and* $\mathcal{R}_0 = \mathcal{T}^0$.

Proof of Theorem 2.

(a) Following the method in [24], with reference to Equations (5)–(8), we have the rate of appearance of new infections vector $\mathcal{F}(x)$ and the rate of transfer of individuals vector $\mathcal{V}(x)$:

$$\mathcal{F} = \begin{pmatrix} 0 \\ \beta SI \\ 0 \\ 0 \end{pmatrix} \text{ and } \mathcal{V} = \begin{pmatrix} \beta SI + \mu S - \mu \\ \delta E + \mu E \\ -\delta E + \alpha I + \mu I + \varepsilon I \\ -\alpha I + \mu R - \varepsilon I \end{pmatrix}.$$

Note that there are only two sub-classes that involve infected persons (i.e., E and I), meaning we have F and V as 2 × 2 matrices. Here, we count a new infection as only occurring in E with the rate βSI and do not count the rate δE in I as a new infection, since it is only the transition from E to I. Next, from the two vectors, we obtain two matrices: $F = \begin{pmatrix} 0 & \beta \\ 0 & 0 \end{pmatrix}$ and $V = \begin{pmatrix} \delta + \mu & 0 \\ -\delta & \alpha + \mu + \varepsilon \end{pmatrix}$. Consequently, $V^{-1} = \begin{pmatrix} \frac{1}{\delta+\mu} & 0 \\ \frac{\delta}{(\delta+\mu)(\alpha+\mu+\varepsilon)} & \frac{1}{\alpha+\mu+\varepsilon} \end{pmatrix}$ and $FV^{-1} = \begin{pmatrix} \frac{\beta\delta}{(\delta+\mu)(\alpha+\mu+\varepsilon)} & \frac{\beta}{\alpha+\mu+\varepsilon} \\ 0 & 0 \end{pmatrix}$, which gives rise to the effective reproduction number $\mathcal{R}_0^\varepsilon = \rho(FV^{-1}) = \frac{\beta\delta}{(\alpha+\mu+\varepsilon)(\delta+\mu)}$.

(b) It is clear from (a) that when $\varepsilon = 0$, then $\mathcal{R}_0^{\varepsilon=0} = \rho(FV^{-1}) = \frac{\beta\delta}{(\alpha+\mu)(\delta+\mu)}$, which is the basic reproduction number of the model in Equations (5)–(8).

(c) In addition, comparing the results to Theorem 1, obviously, we have $\mathcal{R}_0^\varepsilon = \mathcal{T}^\varepsilon$, and consequently $\mathcal{R}_0 = \mathcal{T}^0$, which completes the proof. □

Theorem 3. *The SEIR model in Equations (5)–(8) always has a trivial equilibrium $(S_0^*, E_0^*, I_0^*, R_0^*)$, while the non-trivial equilibrium $(S_e^*, E_e^*, I_e^*, R_e^*)$ exists only if the effective reproduction number is greater than 1, i.e., $\mathcal{R}_0^\varepsilon = \frac{\beta\delta}{(\alpha+\mu+\varepsilon)(\delta+\mu)} > 1$.*

Proof of Theorem 3. It is obvious as a consequence of Theorems 1 and 2. □

Up to this point, we concluded that the threshold we found earlier (i.e., $\mathcal{T}^\varepsilon$) is actually equivalent to the "true" effective reproduction number, $\mathcal{R}_0^\varepsilon$ (Theorem 2(c)). Here, we could actually find another threshold that has the same threshold value as $\mathcal{R}_0^\varepsilon$. Remember that in the derivation of the basic reproduction number, we noticed that there are only two sub-classes involving infected persons, i.e., E and I. Then, we have F and V as 2 × 2 matrices. Here, we count new infections only in E with the rate βSI and do not count the rate δE in I as a new infection, since it is only the transition from E to I. However, if we count new infections in E with the rate βSI and do count the rate δE in I as a new infection, then we have:

$$\mathcal{F} = \begin{pmatrix} 0 \\ \beta SI \\ \delta E \\ 0 \end{pmatrix} \text{ and } \mathcal{V} = \begin{pmatrix} \beta SI + \mu S - \mu \\ \delta E + \mu E \\ \alpha I + \mu I + \varepsilon I \\ -\alpha I + \mu R - \varepsilon I \end{pmatrix},$$

Then we will have:

$$F = \begin{pmatrix} 0 & \beta \\ \delta & 0 \end{pmatrix}$$

and:

$$V = \begin{pmatrix} \delta + \mu & 0 \\ 0 & \alpha + \mu + \varepsilon \end{pmatrix}$$

giving:

$$V^{-1} = \begin{pmatrix} \frac{1}{\delta+\mu} & 0 \\ 0 & \frac{1}{\alpha+\mu+\varepsilon} \end{pmatrix}.$$

Hence, we obtain:
$$FV^{-1} = \begin{pmatrix} 0 & \frac{\beta}{\alpha+\mu+\varepsilon} \\ \frac{\delta}{\delta+\mu} & 0 \end{pmatrix}$$
which implies that:
$$\rho(FV^{-1}) = \sqrt{\frac{\beta\delta}{(\alpha+\mu+\varepsilon)(\delta+\mu)}}.$$

Note that the last expression is actually the square root of the reproduction number, so that by referring to [24], we have an alternative threshold, $\mathcal{A}^\varepsilon = \rho(FV^{-1}) = \sqrt{\mathcal{R}_0^\varepsilon}$, which is not a reproduction number but has the same threshold value, i.e., 1.

Theorem 4. *The non-endemic equilibrium $(S_0^*, E_0^*, I_0^*, R_0^*)$ of Equations (5)–(8) is asymptotically stable whenever $\mathcal{R}_0^\varepsilon = \frac{\beta\delta}{(\alpha+\mu+\varepsilon)(\delta+\mu)} < 1$ and unstable otherwise.*

Proof of Theorem 4. Let us consider the non-endemic equilibrium $(S_0^*, E_0^*, I_0^*, R_0^*) = (1, 0, 0, 0)$. The Jacobian matrix at this point is given by: $\begin{bmatrix} -\mu & 0 & -\beta & 0 \\ 0 & -\delta-\mu & \beta & 0 \\ 0 & \delta & -\alpha-\mu & -\varepsilon \\ 0 & 0 & \alpha & \varepsilon-\mu \end{bmatrix}$,

which has the polynomial characteristics: $a_4\lambda^4 + a_3\lambda^3 + a_2\lambda^2 + a_1\lambda + a_0 = 0$ with:

$a_4 = 1;$

$a_3 = (4\mu + \delta + \alpha - \varepsilon);$

$a_2 = \mu(\delta + 3\mu + \alpha - \varepsilon) + \delta\alpha + 2\mu\delta - \delta\varepsilon + 2\mu\alpha + 3\mu^2 - 2\mu\varepsilon - \beta\delta);$

$a_1 = \mu(\delta\alpha + 2\mu\delta - \delta\varepsilon + 2\mu\alpha + 3\mu^2 - 2\mu\varepsilon - \beta\delta) + (\mu\delta\alpha - \mu\delta\varepsilon + \mu^2\delta + \mu^2\alpha - \mu^2\varepsilon + \mu^3 + \beta\varepsilon\delta - \beta\mu\delta);$

$a_0 = \mu(\mu\delta\alpha - \mu\delta\varepsilon + \mu^2\delta + \mu^2\alpha - \mu^2\varepsilon + \mu^3 + \beta\varepsilon\delta - \beta\mu\delta).$

Clearly, $a_4 > 0$ and $a_3 > 0$. Furthermore, we have $a_0 > 0$, provided $\mathcal{R}_0^\varepsilon < 1$. The detail of the proof is as follows.

Proof of $a_0 > 0$

We need $\mu(\mu\delta\alpha + \mu\delta\varepsilon + \mu^2\delta + \mu^2\alpha + \mu^2\varepsilon + \mu^3 + \beta\varepsilon\delta - \beta\mu\delta) > 0$, which can be written as follows:

$\mu^2(\delta\varepsilon + \mu\delta + \mu\varepsilon + \mu^2) + (\mu\delta\alpha + \mu^2\alpha + \beta\varepsilon\delta - \beta\mu\delta)\mu > 0$

⇨ $\mu(\delta\varepsilon + \mu\delta + \mu\varepsilon + \mu^2) + (\mu\delta\alpha + \mu^2\alpha + \beta\varepsilon\delta - \beta\mu\delta) > 0$

⇨ $\mu(\delta\varepsilon + \mu\delta + \mu\varepsilon + \mu^2 + \delta\alpha + \mu\alpha) > \beta\delta(\mu - \varepsilon)$

⇨ $\frac{\beta\delta(\mu-\varepsilon)}{\mu(\varepsilon+\mu+\alpha)(\delta+\mu)} < 1$

⇨ $\frac{\beta\delta}{(\varepsilon+\mu+\alpha)(\delta+\mu)} < \frac{\mu}{(\mu-\varepsilon)}.$

Here, we need $\mu > \varepsilon$ to make the inequality consistent, since all of the parameters are non-negative. Note that in this case, $\frac{\mu}{(\mu-\varepsilon)} > 1$; hence, if $\mathcal{R}_0^\varepsilon < 1$, then the inequality $\frac{\beta\delta}{(\varepsilon+\mu+\alpha)(\delta+\mu)} < \frac{\mu}{(\mu-\varepsilon)}$ holds.

Proof of $a_1 > 0$

Note that a_1 can be written in the form of $a_1 = a_{11} + a_0$ with $a_{11} = \mu(\delta\alpha + 2\mu\delta + \delta\varepsilon + 2\mu\alpha + 3\mu^2 + 2\mu\varepsilon - \beta\delta)$. We also note that $a_{11} - a_0 = 2\mu^3 + \delta\mu^2 + \mu^2\varepsilon + \mu^2\alpha$ is positive, so that $a_{11} > 0$, since we proved earlier that $a_0 > 0$. Furthermore, since both $a_{11} > 0$ and $a_0 > 0$, then, consequently, $a_1 > 0$.

Proof of $a_2 > 0$

Note that $a_2 = a_{21} + a_{11}/\mu$ with $a_{21} = \mu(\delta + 3\mu + \alpha + \varepsilon)$ is clearly positive. Since $a_{11} > 0$, then $a_2 > 0$. Therefore, we proved that all of the coefficients of the polynomial characteristics are positive. Consequently, from the Descartes rule of signs, all roots have negative real parts. This proves the stability of the disease-free equilibrium whenever $\mathcal{R}_0^\varepsilon < 1$. □

Theorem 5. *If the endemic equilibrium* $(S_e^*, E_e^*, I_e^*, R_e^*)$ *of Equations (5)–(8) exists (i.e., whenever* $\mathcal{R}_0^\varepsilon = \frac{\beta\delta}{(\alpha+\mu+\varepsilon)(\delta+\mu)} > 1$), *then it is asymptotically stable.*

Proof of Theorem 5. The proof is analogous as before. □

Assuming that in the absence of CPT, the system has a large basic reproduction number (otherwise, the administration of CPT will not make sense), then when CPT is administered, we could compute the ratio of the effective reproduction number to the basic reproduction number as:

$$\mathcal{R}_0^\varepsilon : \mathcal{R}_0 = \frac{\beta\delta}{(\alpha+\mu+\varepsilon)(\delta+\mu)} : \frac{\beta\delta}{(\alpha+\mu)(\delta+\mu)} = \frac{(\alpha+\mu)}{(\alpha+\mu+\varepsilon)} < 1$$

Hence, clearly, $\mathcal{R}_0^\varepsilon : \mathcal{R}_0$. Consequently, we have the following theorem.

Theorem 6. *For the SEIR model in Equations (5)–(8), we have:*

$S_e^* = \frac{1}{\mathcal{R}_0^\varepsilon} > \frac{1}{\mathcal{R}_0} = S_0^*$ *and* $I_e^* = (\mathcal{R}_0^\varepsilon - 1)\frac{\mu}{\beta} < (\mathcal{R}_0 - 1)\frac{\mu}{\beta} = I_0^*$ *with the difference*

$S_e^* - S_0^* = \frac{\varepsilon(\delta+\mu)}{\delta\beta}$ *and* $I_0^* - I_\varepsilon^* = \frac{\delta\mu\varepsilon}{(\delta+\mu)(\alpha+\mu)(\mu+\alpha+\varepsilon)}$.

Proof of Theorem 6. The proof is obvious. □

Analysis for the case of the rate of CPT proportional to the number of recovered class can be conducted analogously. We do not present the results explicitly, since all proofs are similar to the one presented here. In the next section, we carried out several simulations to assess the impact of CPT both to the transient solution and to the equilibrium solution. The simulation was conducted by implementing the Runge–Kutta numerical scheme to determine the numerical solution of the system, and the results are presented numerically.

3.2. Numerical Examples

In this section, we present numerical examples to show the behavior of the SEIR model with and without the presence of convalescent plasma transfusion. The results, in general, support the analysis of the SEIR equilibrium solutions presented in the earlier section. For the numerical examples, we used the CPT parameters in Table 2 and the other parameters written in the respective resulting figures. The results are summarized in the figures that follow.

Table 2. Parameter values used for different scenarios of CPT implementation.

Number	CPT Scenario	Numerical Response $f(I(t), R(t))$	Used in the Figures	Parameter Values in the Figures
1	Proportional rate to infectives	$\varepsilon I(t)$	7.a	$\varepsilon = 0.05$
2	Proportional rate to recovered	$\varepsilon R(t)$	7.b	$\varepsilon = 0.05$
3	Mass action rate (Lotka–Volterra)	$\varepsilon I(t) R(t)$	7.c	$\varepsilon = 0.05$
4	Constant rate	ε	7.d	$\varepsilon = 0.001$
5	Saturating rate (Michaelis–Menten)	$\frac{\varepsilon R(t)}{r+R(t)}$	7.e	$\varepsilon = 0.001, r = 0$
6	Maximum service limitation	$\min(\varepsilon I(t), \text{Maxserv})$	7.f, 9.a	$\varepsilon = 0.55$, Maxserv = 0.0028
7	Maximum service limitation	$\min(\varepsilon R(t), \text{Maxserv})$	9.b	$\varepsilon = 0.55$, Maxserv = 0.0028
8	Maximum service limitation	$\min(\varepsilon I(t) R(t), \text{Maxserv})$	9.c	$\varepsilon = 0.55$, Maxserv = 0.0028
9	Maximum service limitation	$\min(\frac{\varepsilon R(t)}{r+R(t)}, \text{Maxserv})$	9.d	$\varepsilon = 0.55$, Maxserv = 0.0028

Figure 2 shows a graph of the disease dynamics predicted by the SEIR model for specific parameters (written in the figure caption) with a high basic reproduction number (approximately 2.3). It suggests that, eventually, the disease will endemic to a certain level with a stable number of infectives (approximately 2% of the total population). Figure 3 shows the changes in the graph when CPT is utilized to cure patients. It shows that, for a relatively high rate of CPT intervention, it can reduce the basic reproduction number to the effective reproduction number as low as 0.97, which leads to a stable disease-free equilibrium.

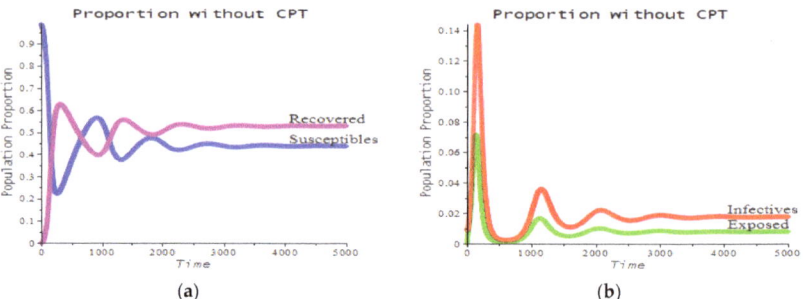

Figure 2. A graph of the SEIR model without CPT showing the susceptible and recovered classes (**a**) and the exposed and infective classes (**b**). The SEIR parameters were $\mu = 1/75$, $\beta = 0.95$, $\delta = 0.90$, and $\alpha = 0.40$, with initial values of $S_0 = 0.99$, $E_0 = 0$, $I_0 = 0.01$, and $R_0 = 0$. The resulting equilibrium was approximately $S = 44\%$, $E = 1\%$, $I = 2\%$, and $R = 53\%$ with the basic reproduction number $\mathcal{R}_0 = 2.265$.

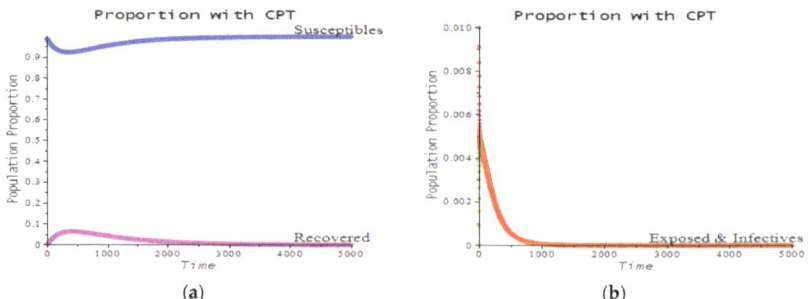

Figure 3. A graph of the SEIR model with CPT, showing the susceptible and recovered classes (**a**) and the exposed and infective classes (**b**). The SEIR parameters were $\mu = 1/75$, $\beta = 0.95$, $\delta = 0.90$, and $\alpha = 0.40$, with initial values of $S_0 = 0.99$, $E_0 = 0$, $I_0 = 0.01$, and $R_0 = 0$. The CPT rate was assumed to be $\varepsilon = 0.55$. The resulting equilibrium was approximately $S = 99\%$, $R = 0.05\%$, and the remaining E and I were nearly zero. In this case, the resulting effective reproduction number was $\mathcal{R}_0 = 0.97$ (less than 1).

Figure 3 also suggests that early application of CPT significantly reduces the risk of disease outbreak. In the early transmission of COVID-19, this was clearly not the case, since COVID-19 is a new and emerging disease; hence, the availability of CP was almost null in the beginning. The figure also suggests a practical consequence of creating a convalescent plasma bank. Now, looking closer at the graph in Figure 2, during the first 200 time steps, we have the graph in Figure 4. It can be seen that there were already many recovered patients; hence, the availability of CP stock may be justified. Suppose that at time $t = 200$, the health authority begins to apply CPT as a curative method, then we have Figure 5, which shows that CPT significantly drove the disease cases down to zero, eventually. This is among the promising findings suggested by the SEIR model.

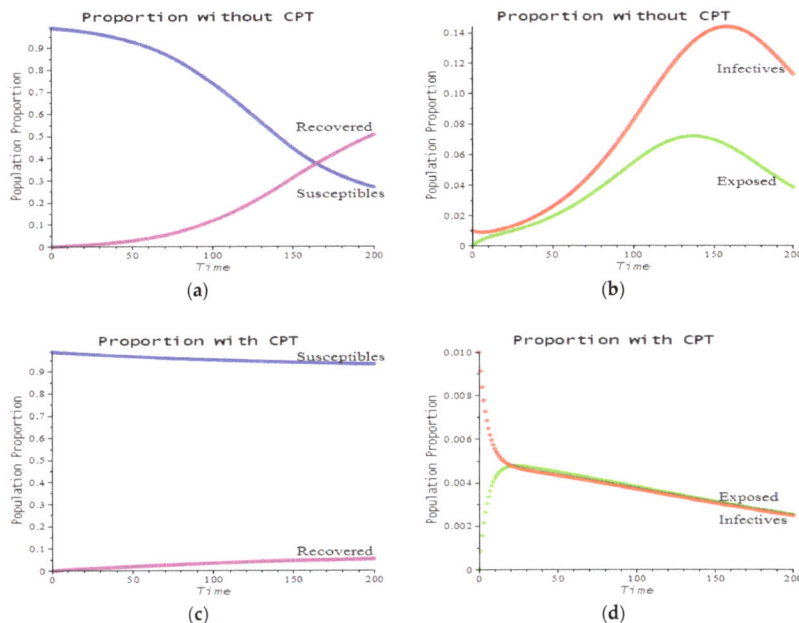

Figure 4. A graph of the SEIR model without CPT (top figures) showing the susceptible and recovered classes (**a**) and the exposed and infective classes (**b**) as in Figure 2 but with a shorter time horizon. (**c**,**d**) With CPT. The bottom figures show similar graphs for the SEIR model with CPT as in Figure 3 but with a shorter time horizon.

Figure 5 shows a graph of the SEIR model as in Figure 2, assuming that in the beginning (i.e., during the time interval (0,200)), the health authority takes the "do nothing" decision in controlling the disease (blue and red circles), and then, at time $t = 200$, begins to implement CPT with a relatively high rate of implementation (approximately half of the infectives are given CPT, proportional to the number of infectives with $\varepsilon = 0.55$). The black dots reveal that the intervention quickly pulls the number of infectives to zero (b) while, at the same time, pushes the number of susceptibles upward (a).

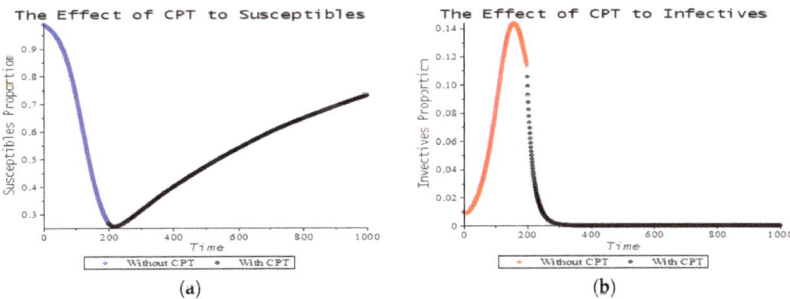

Figure 5. Graphs of the SEIR model assuming the "do nothing" decision during the time interval (0,200), followed by the implementation of CPT with the rate proportional to the number of infectives. The graph in (**a**) shows the dynamics of the susceptibles, while the graph in (**b**) shows the dynamics of the infectives.

Figure 6 shows the effects of different rates of CPT on decreasing the number of infectives (hence, the height of the infective peak). Here, we assumed a scenario in which CPT is conducted with the rate proportional to the infectives (implicitly assuming an abundance of CP bloods). Figure 7 shows the effect of different scenarios (see Table 1) on the decrease in the infective numbers over time. All of the figures assumed that there was no limit for the health authority to set CPT rates, except in Figure 7f, in which it was assumed that the maximum CPT rate was the Maxserv (response function number 6 in Table 2).

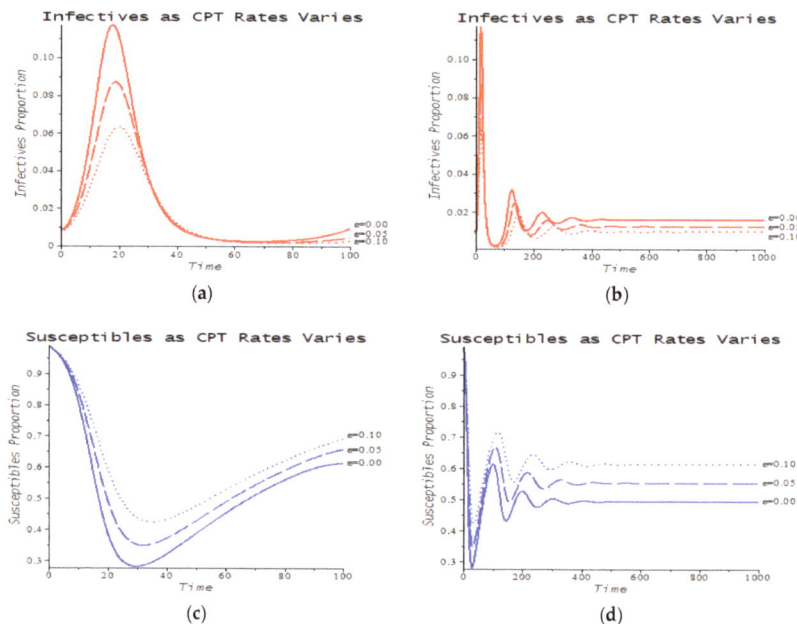

Figure 6. Graphs showing the effects of different rates of CPT on decreasing the number of infectives (i.e., lowering the height of the infective peaks) (**a**,**b**) and, consequently, increasing the number of remaining susceptibles (**c**,**d**). The other parameters were the same as in Figure 2.

In Figure 7f, if the Maxserv is unbounded, then the result is the same as in Figure 3b, which is unlikely in reality. Figure 8 shows examples of the Maxserv graphs used in Figure 7. The effect of various Maxserv response functions on the numbers of infectives and the exposed population is shown in Figure 9.

In all of the numerical simulations above, we assumed that the effect of CPT was on increasing patient survival. The recent findings reported in [26] support the assumption we used in this paper. They carried out a meta-analytical approach to collect and analyze the daily survival data from all controlled studies that reported Kaplan–Meier survival plots. The authors showed that CPT contributes to improving the symptomatology and viral clearance. Furthermore, they pointed out that the aggregate Kaplan–Meier survival plot in their study revealed a good agreement pattern among all different studies in which CPT was generally associated with greater patient survival [26].

The historical evidence shows the promising results of applying the therapeutic treatment of CPT for critical patients infected by contagious diseases such as COVID-19. A more recent study provided strong evidence that if the convalescent plasma is transfused into patients within three days of the onset of illness, a 41% lower risk of death compared to patients transfused four or more days after onset of illness is demonstrated [26,27]. This remarkable result highlights an important role for the timely use of convalescent plasma transfusion. We discussed all such situations in terms of mathematical modeling with real data collected from a secondary source in the numerical analysis.

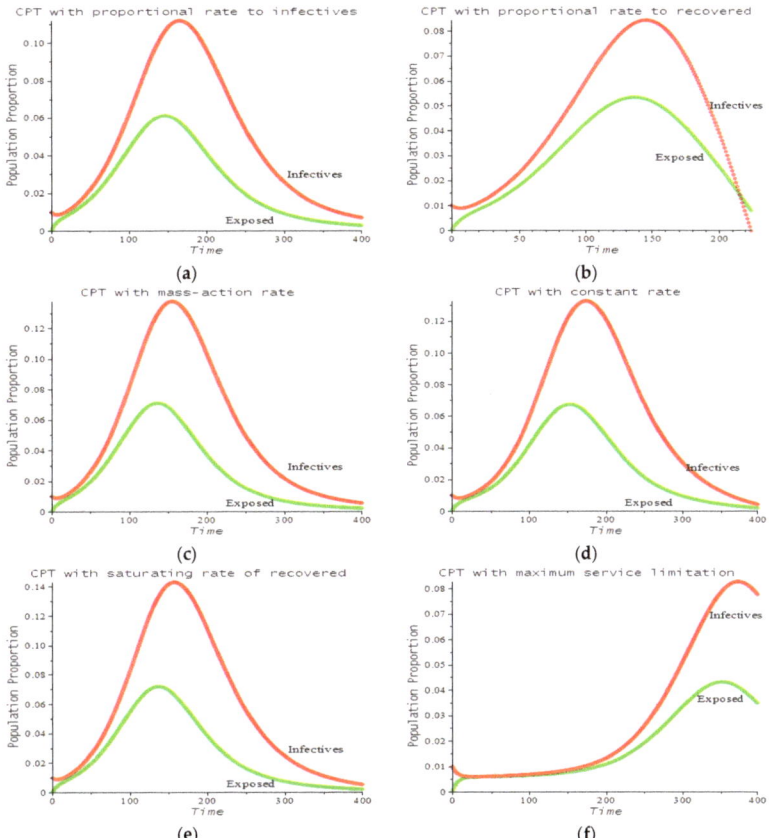

Figure 7. Plots of the effect of various CPT scenarios on the dynamics of the infective (red) and exposed (green) classes, with the assumption that the CPT intervention was carried out from the beginning of the pandemic. The scenarios and parameters were the same as in Table 2. The response functions and the parameters in the response functions for the graphs in (**a**–**f**) are presented in Table 2. See also Figure 2 as the reference for the other epidemiological parameters. Note that if Maxserv is unbounded, then the result is the same as Figure 3b.

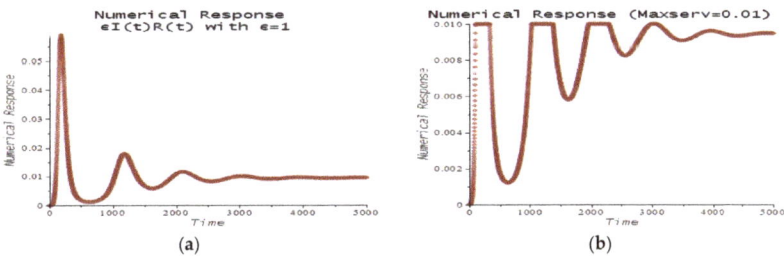

Figure 8. The graph in (**a**) shows a plot the of mass action term of $\varepsilon I(t)R(t)$ in Figure 7c. The graph in (**b**) shows a plot of the numerical response $\min(\varepsilon I(t)R(t), \text{Maxserv})$ used in Figure 7f with $\varepsilon = 1$ and Maxserv = 0.01.

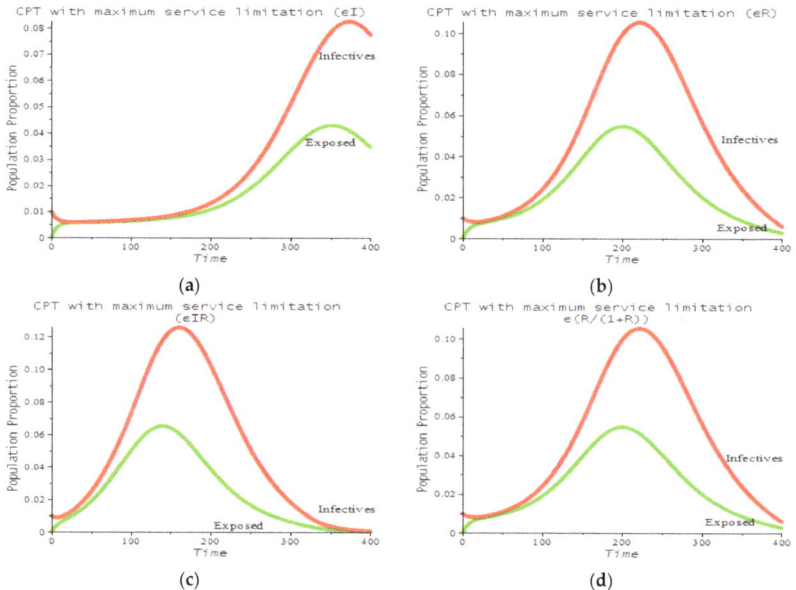

Figure 9. Plots of the effect of various Maxserv CPT scenarios on the dynamics of infective (red) and exposed (green) classes, with the assumption that the CPT intervention is conducted from the beginning of the pandemic. The scenarios and parameters for the graphs in (**a**–**d**) are as in Table 2.

In this research, a standard analytical evaluation, from proving the existence of equilibria, their local stability, and their relationships with the reproduction numbers, was only carried out for the model with the response function for the CPT rate proportional to the number of infected class. The numerical simulations showed the consistency of other forms of the response functions with the findings in real phenomena such as reported in [26,27]. However, to obtain more prudent results, it is necessary to undertake a complete mathematical analysis of all proposed response functions that will presumably provide more in-depth insight and better implementation. Well-posedness of solutions and the threshold criteria for the global stability of equilibria should certainly be sought [28]. On the contrary, the numerical solutions presented in this paper were obtained by the RK45, although according to the current findings [29,30], there is a better scheme to produce a dynamically consistent numerical solution. Other future research could focus on the application of optimal control theory for disease prevention and control based on different nonlinear response functions for the therapeutic rate of CPT. In particular, a study concentrating on applying a wider class of control variables to formulate an optimal control problem in order to find better control and preventive strategies in CPT implementation would be beneficial as found in [31].

4. Conclusions

We presented a continuous SEIR epidemic model considering the effect of an intervention using convalescent plasma transfusion (CPT) to the infected class. We analyzed the model using the standard procedure and found the trivial and non-trivial equilibrium points of the system including their stability and relation to the basic reproduction number. In general, the effect of the application of CPT on the individual level resulted in a shorter time of infection and a higher survival rate for infected individuals that received CPT. Furthermore, we showed that at the population level, it could also decrease the peak of the outbreak as well as the length of the epidemic period. In this case, the decrease in the infection peak indicated the good effect of the use of CPT, which may eventually decrease the burden of COVID-19 transmission. The model presented here is still simple in terms of biological and epidemiological complexity; hence, further refinement of the model is still needed to obtain a more realistic model and a more accurate prediction.

In this paper, we proposed various functional forms/numerical responses that could be used to model the CPT rate, but not all were evaluated analytically. These numerical responses can be considered as a parametric viewpoint of control strategy. Hence, analytical investigation regarding the use of these various functional forms is also worthy to explore the robustness of the results presented here and to generate some possible epidemiological precautions not explored in the current paper. The model in this paper also only assumed a single strain or variant. In reality, viruses are always changing and mutating, and this could cause a new strain or variant. How would the results here be affected by such phenomena? Another question important for future research involves finding optimal CPT strategies that minimize both the number of infections and the related costs of CPT implementation. Our future research will focus on the application of optimal control theory for disease prevention and control based on different nonlinear response functions for the therapeutic rate of CPT. In particular, we will concentrate on applying a wider class of control variables to formulate an optimal control problem in order to find better control and preventive strategies for implementation of CPT.

Author Contributions: Conceptualization, H.H. and A.K.S.; methodology, H.H., A.K.S. and M.H.A.B.; software, A.K.S.; validation, H.H. and R.R.; formal analysis, A.K.S.; investigation, R.R.; resources, R.R.; data curation, R.R.; writing—original draft preparation, H.H.; writing—review and editing, H.H. and M.H.A.B.; visualization, A.K.S.; supervision, A.K.S.; project administration, H.H.; funding acquisition, H.H. All authors have read and agreed to the published version of the manuscript.

Funding: This research was funded by the Indonesian Government through the scheme "Penelitian Kompetitif Nasional dan Penelitian Dasar", contract number 1207/UN6.3.1/PT.00/2021.

Institutional Review Board Statement: Not applicable.

Conflicts of Interest: The authors declare no conflict of interest.

References

1. WHO. WHO Announces COVID-19 Outbreak a Pandemic. Available online: https://www.euro.who.int/en/health-topics/health-emergencies/coronavirus-covid-19/news/news/2020/3/who-announces-covid-19-outbreak-a-pandemic (accessed on 10 September 2021).
2. Worldometer 2020. Available online: https://www.worldometers.info/coronavirus/ (accessed on 1 November 2021).
3. FDA. FDA Issues Emergency Use Authorization for Convalescent Plasma as Potential Promising COVID–19 Treatment, Another Achievement in Administration's Fight against Pandemic. Available online: https://www.fda.gov/news-events/press-announcements/fda-issues-emergency-use-authorization-convalescent-plasma-potential-promising-covid-19-treatment (accessed on 7 December 2020).
4. Mayo Clinic. Patient Care & Health Information: Tests & Procedures: Convalescent Plasma Therapy. Available online: https://www.mayoclinic.org/tests-procedures/convalescent-plasma-therapy/about/pac-20486340 (accessed on 7 December 2020).
5. Klassen, S.A.; Senefeld, J.W.; Johnson, P.W.; Carter, R.E.; Wiggins, C.C.; Shoham, S.; Grossman, B.J.; Henderson, J.P.; Musser, J.; Salazar, E.; et al. The Effect of Convalescent Plasma Therapy on Mortality among Patients With COVID-19: Systematic Review and Meta-Analysis. *Mayo Clin. Proc.* **2021**, *96*, 1262–1275. Available online: https://www.mayoclinicproceedings.org/article/S0025-6196(21)00140-3/fulltext (accessed on 18 October 2021). [CrossRef] [PubMed]
6. CNN Indonesia. 4 RS di RI Yang Mulai Terapi Plasma Darah Obati Pasien Corona (in Bahasa Indonesia). Available online: https://www.cnnindonesia.com/teknologi/20200908163921-199-544140/4-rs-di-ri-yang-mulai-terapi-plasma-darah-obati-pasien-corona (accessed on 7 December 2020).
7. Lewin, E. Australian COVID-19 Trials Add Convalescent Plasma as a Treatment. NewGP 30 July 2020. Available online: https://www1.racgp.org.au/newsgp/clinical/australian-covid-19-trials-add-convalescent-plasma (accessed on 1 November 2021).
8. Agarwal, A.; Mukherjee, A.; Kumar, G.; Chatterjee, P.; Bhatnagar, T.; Malhotra, P.; on behalf of the PLACID Trial Collaborators. Convalescent plasma in the management of moderate COVID-19 in adults in India: Open label phase II multicentre randomised controlled trial (PLACID Trial). *BMJ* **2020**, *371*, 371. [CrossRef] [PubMed]
9. Garroud, O.; Heshmati, F.; Pozzetto, B.; Lefrere, F.; Girot, R.; Saillol, A. Plasma therapy against infectious pathogens, as of yesterday, today and tomorrow. *Transfus. Clin. Biol.* **2016**, *23*, 39–44. [CrossRef] [PubMed]
10. Marson, P.; Cozza, A.; De Silvestro, G. The true historical origin of convalescent plasma therapy. *Transfus. Apheresis Sci.* **2020**, *59*, 102847. [CrossRef] [PubMed]

11. Cao, H.; Shi, Y. Convalescent plasma: Possible therapy for novel coronavirus disease 2019. *Transfusion* **2020**, *60*, 1078–1083. [CrossRef] [PubMed]
12. Salazar, E.; Perez, K.K.; Ashraf, M.; Chen, J.; Castillo, B.; Christensen, P.A.; Eubank, T.; Bernard, D.W.; Eagar, T.N.; Long, S.W.; et al. Treatment of Coronavirus Disease 2019 (COVID-19) patients with convalescent plasma. *Amer. J. Pathol.* **2020**, *190*, 1680–1690. [CrossRef] [PubMed]
13. Salazar, E.; Christensen, P.A.; Graviss, E.A.; Nguyen, D.T.; Castillo, B.; Chen, J.; Lopez, B.V.; Eagar, T.N.; Yi, X.; Zhao, P.; et al. Significantly decreased mortality in a large cohort of Coronavirus Disease 2019 (COVID-19) patients transfused early with convalescent plasma containing high-titer Anti-Severe Acute Respiratory Syndrome Coronavirus 2 (SARS-CoV-2) spike protein IgG. *Am. J. Pathol.* **2020**, *191*, 90–107. [CrossRef] [PubMed]
14. Peng, H.T.; Rhind, S.G.; Beckett, A. Convalescent plasma for the prevention and treatment of COVID-19: A systematic review and quantitative analysis. *JMIR Public Health Surveill.* **2021**, *7*, e25500. [CrossRef] [PubMed]
15. Huo, X.; Sun, X.; Bragazzi, N.L.; Wu, J. Effectiveness and feasibility of convalescent blood transfusion to reduce COVID-19 fatality ratio. *Roy. Soc. Open Sci.* **2020**, *8*, 202248. [CrossRef] [PubMed]
16. Supriatna, A.K.; Husniah, H. Can convalescent plasma transfusion reduce the COVID-19 transmission? In Proceedings of the 2nd African International Conference on Industrial Engineering and Operations Management, IEOM, Harare, Zimbabwe, 7–10 December 2020; pp. 3116–3124.
17. Nykamp, D.Q.; Morrissey, D.P. A Discrete SIR Infectious Disease Model. From Math Insight. Available online: http://mathinsight.org/discrete_sir_infectious_disease_model (accessed on 30 September 2021).
18. Switkes, J. A Modified Discrete SIR Model. *Coll. Math. J.* **2003**, *3*, 399–402. [CrossRef]
19. Diekmann, O.; Heesterbeek, J.A.P. *Mathematical Epidemiology of Infectious Diseases: Model Building, Analysis and Interpretation*, 1st ed.; Wiley: New York, NY, USA, 2000.
20. Anderson, R.M.; May, R.M.; Anderson, B. *Infectious Diseases of Humans: Dynamics and Control*, Revised ed.; Oxford University Press: London, UK, 1992.
21. Brauer, F.; van den Driessche, P.; Wu, J. *Mathematical Epidemiology*; Springer: Berlin/Heidelberg, Germany, 2008.
22. Diekmann, O.; Heesterbeek, J.A.P.; Metz, J.A.J. On the definition and the computation of the basic reproduction ratio R 0 in models for infectious diseases in heterogeneous populations. *J. Math. Biol.* **1990**, *28*, 365–382. [CrossRef] [PubMed]
23. Diekmann, O.; Heesterbeek, J.A.P.; Roberts, M.G. The construction of next-generation matrices for compartmental epidemic models. *J. R. Soc. Interface* **2010**, *7*, 873–885. [CrossRef] [PubMed]
24. Van den Driessche, P.; Watmough, J. Reproduction numbers and sub-threshold endemic equilibria for compartmental models of disease transmission. *Math Biosci.* **2002**, *180*, 29–48. [CrossRef]
25. Zhao, X.Q. The Theory of Basic Reproduction Ratios. In *Dynamical Systems in Population Biology*; Springer Nature Switzerland AG: Cham, Switzerland, 2003. [CrossRef]
26. Klassen, S.A.; Senefeld, J.W.; Senese, K.A.; Johnson, P.W.; Wiggins, C.C.; Baker, S.E.; van Helmond, N.; Bruno, K.A.; Pirofski, L.; Shoham, S.; et al. Convalescent Plasma Therapy for COVID-19: A Graphical Mosaic of the Worldwide Evidence. *Front. Med.* **2021**, *8*, 684151. [CrossRef] [PubMed]
27. Liu, S.T.H.; Lin, H.M.; Baine, I.; Wajnberg, A.; Gumprecht, J.P.; Rahman, F.; Rodriguez, D.; Tandon, P.; Bassily-Marcus, A.; Bander, J.; et al. Convalescent plasma treatment of severe COVID-19: A propensity score–matched control study. *Nat. Med.* **2020**, *26*, 1708–1713. [CrossRef] [PubMed]
28. Chen, W.; Wu, W.X.; Teng, Z.D. Complete dynamics in a nonlocal dispersal two-strain SIV epidemic model with vaccinations and latent delays. *Appl. Comput. Math.* **2020**, *19*, 360–391.
29. Khalsaraei, M.M.; Shokri, A.; Ramos, H.; Heydari, S. A positive and elementary stable nonstandard explicit scheme for a mathematical model of the influenza disease. *Math. Comput. Simul.* **2021**, *182*, 397–410. [CrossRef]
30. Shokri, A.; Khalsaraei, M.M.; Molayi, M. Dynamically consistent NSFD methods for predator prey system. *J. Appl. Comput. Mech.* **2021**, *7*, 1565–1574. [CrossRef]
31. Biswas, M.H.A.; Paiva, L.T.; de Pinho, M. A SEIR model for control of infectious diseases with constraints. *Math. Biosci. Eng.* **2014**, *11*, 761–784. [CrossRef]

Article

Accidental Degeneracy of an Elliptic Differential Operator: A Clarification in Terms of Ladder Operators

Roberto De Marchis [†], Arsen Palestini [*,†] and Stefano Patrì [†]

MEMOTEF, Faculty of Economics, Sapienza University of Rome, Via del Castro Laurenziano 9, 00161 Rome, Italy; Roberto.Demarchis@uniroma1.it (R.D.M.); Stefano.Patri@uniroma1.it (S.P.)
* Correspondence: Arsen.Palestini@uniroma1.it
† These authors contributed equally to this work.

Abstract: We consider the linear, second-order elliptic, Schrödinger-type differential operator $\mathcal{L} := -\frac{1}{2}\nabla^2 + \frac{r^2}{2}$. Because of its rotational invariance, that is it does not change under $SO(3)$ transformations, the eigenvalue problem $\left[-\frac{1}{2}\nabla^2 + \frac{r^2}{2}\right]f(x,y,z) = \lambda f(x,y,z)$ can be studied more conveniently in spherical polar coordinates. It is already known that the eigenfunctions of the problem depend on three parameters. The so-called *accidental degeneracy* of $\mathcal{L}$ occurs when the eigenvalues of the problem depend on one of such parameters only. We exploited ladder operators to reformulate accidental degeneracy, so as to provide a new way to describe degeneracy in elliptic PDE problems.

Keywords: degeneracy; elliptic PDE; ladder operator; commuting operator; eigenvalues

1. Introduction

In this paper, we intend to treat an elliptic PDE (Among the numerous textbooks on elliptic PDEs, we think that Gilbarg and Trudinger's book [1], first published in 1998 and then again in 2001 and 2015, is the main contribution to acquire the necessary knowledge on this fascinating topic. On the other hand, the main notions to tackle the typical mathematical physics problems can be found in [2], for example.) with a special focus on the property of the *degeneracy* of its spectrum.

To begin with, we consider the following elliptic PDE:

$$\left[-\frac{1}{2}\nabla^2 + \frac{r^2}{2}\right]f(x,y,z) = \lambda f(x,y,z), \tag{1}$$

where $r = \sqrt{x^2 + y^2 + z^2}$, and the function $f(x,y,z)$ belongs to the following Hilbert space:

$$\mathcal{H} = \left\{ f(\cdot) \in L^2(\mathbb{R}^3) \cap C^2(\mathbb{R}^3) \mid \lim_{r \to \infty} f(x,y,z) = 0 \right\}. \tag{2}$$

As is known, ∇^2 is the Laplacian operator:

$$\nabla^2 = \frac{\partial^2}{\partial x^2} + \frac{\partial^2}{\partial y^2} + \frac{\partial^2}{\partial z^2}.$$

The operator $\mathcal{L} := -\frac{1}{2}\nabla^2 + \frac{r^2}{2}$ satisfies the property of rotational invariance, i.e., it is invariant under $SO(3)$ transformations. Addressing the problem (1) in polar coordinates is not difficult, and it is well known that the eigenfuctions in $\mathcal{H}$ depend on three parameters, say, l, m, n, whereas the eigenvalues only depend on n, meaning that $\mathcal{L}$ is a degenerate operator. However, there are different kinds of degeneracy: If the eigenvalues λ_i are independent of m, that is called *natural degeneracy*. If λ_i are independent of l, *accidental*

Citation: De Marchis, R.; Palestini, A.; Patrì, S. Accidental Degeneracy of an Elliptic Differential Operator: A Clarification in Terms of Ladder Operators. *Mathematics* **2021**, *9*, 3005. https://doi.org/10.3390/math9233005

Academic Editor: Andrea Scapellato

Received: 26 October 2021
Accepted: 22 November 2021
Published: 23 November 2021

Publisher's Note: MDPI stays neutral with regard to jurisdictional claims in published maps and institutional affiliations.

Copyright: © 2021 by the authors. Licensee MDPI, Basel, Switzerland. This article is an open access article distributed under the terms and conditions of the Creative Commons Attribution (CC BY) license (https://creativecommons.org/licenses/by/4.0/).

degeneracy occurs. Namely, we focus on accidental degeneracy and on its relationship with ladder operators (a similar procedure applied to spherical hydrogen atom eigenfuctions can be found in [3]).

Recent papers in which the various types of degeneracy are treated are [4–6], just to cite a few.

The paper is organized as follows: In Section 2 the main notions and a selection of useful results on invariance and degeneracy are presented. In Section 3, the ladder operators are introduced and summarized. Section 4 intends to describe the accidental degeneracy of the operator $\mathcal{L}$ in detail. Section 5 features a final discussion and the possible future developments of this theory.

2. Invariance and Degeneracy

We took into account only the linear operators having a discrete spectrum. The following definitions and results, which are well known in the literature, are helpful to characterize our setup and to establish the notation that is used.

Definition 1 (Invariant operator). *A linear operator $\mathbb{O}$, defined on a Hilbert space, is said to be **invariant** under a linear transformation $\mathbb{U}$, defined on the same Hilbert space, if for any eigenvalue λ of $\mathbb{O}$, the corresponding eigenspace $E_\lambda(\mathbb{O})$ is an invariant subspace, i.e., $\forall\, \mathbf{v} \in E_\lambda(\mathbb{O})$, also $\mathbb{U}\mathbf{v} \in E_\lambda(\mathbb{O})$.*

Definition 2 (Commuting operators). *Given two linear operators $\mathbb{O}_1$, $\mathbb{O}_2$ defined on a Hilbert space, they are **commuting** if the commutator is null, that is:*

$$[\mathbb{O}_1, \mathbb{O}_2] = \mathbb{O}_1\mathbb{O}_2 - \mathbb{O}_2\mathbb{O}_1 = 0.$$

Since the operator $\mathcal{L}$ is self-adjoint, it is easy to prove an invariance result, which holds for all linear and self-adjoint operators admitting a complete set of eigenvectors generating the Hilbert space.

Theorem 1 (Invariance theorem). *The linear operator $\mathbb{O}$ is invariant under a linear transformation $\mathbb{U}$ if and only if $[\mathbb{O}, \mathbb{U}] = 0$.*

Proof. If the commutator is zero, we have that, for any eigenvector $\mathbf{v}$ of the operator $\mathbb{O}$:

$$\mathbb{O}\mathbb{U} = \mathbb{U}\mathbb{O} \quad \Longleftrightarrow \quad \mathbb{U}(\mathbb{O}\mathbf{v}) = \mathbb{O}(\mathbb{U}\mathbf{v}),$$

hence $\mathbb{O}(\mathbb{U}\mathbf{v}) = \lambda \mathbb{U}\mathbf{v}$, meaning that $\mathbb{O}$ is invariant. Conversely, if $\mathbb{O}$ is invariant, this means that, by linearity:

$$\mathbb{O}(\mathbb{U}\mathbf{v}) = \lambda(\mathbb{U}\mathbf{v}) = \mathbb{U}(\lambda\mathbf{v}) = \mathbb{U}(\mathbb{O}\mathbf{v}),$$

implying that $[\mathbb{O}, \mathbb{U}] = 0$, because the eigenvectors generate the whole Hilbert space, by assumption. □

It is straightforward to note that the operator $\mathcal{L}$ is invariant under the action of three different linear operators, i.e.:

$$\mathbb{M}_1 = i\left(z\frac{\partial}{\partial y} - y\frac{\partial}{\partial z}\right), \quad \mathbb{M}_2 = i\left(x\frac{\partial}{\partial z} - z\frac{\partial}{\partial x}\right), \quad \mathbb{M}_3 = i\left(y\frac{\partial}{\partial x} - x\frac{\partial}{\partial y}\right), \quad (3)$$

where the imaginary unit i is necessary to guarantee that the operators are self-adjoint (we recall that in the framework of quantum mechanics, the operators $\mathbb{M}_1$, $\mathbb{M}_2$, and $\mathbb{M}_3$ are the components of the pseudo-vector "angular momentum", and the invariance of an operator under the action of all three is called *rotational invariance* or *invariance under the rotation group $SO(3)$*).

Given its rotational invariance, it is more convenient to study the eigenvalue problem by employing the spherical polar coordinates, which depend on the original variables through the following relations:

$$r = \sqrt{x^2 + y^2 + z^2}, \quad \theta = \arccos\left(\frac{z}{\sqrt{x^2 + y^2 + z^2}}\right), \quad \phi = \arctan\left(\frac{y}{x}\right),$$

where $(r, \theta, \phi) \in [0, +\infty) \times [0, \pi] \times [0, 2\pi]$. By using the standard formulas, we also reformulate the Laplacian operator in terms of partial derivatives with respect to the spherical polar coordinates, i.e.:

$$\nabla^2 = \frac{\partial^2}{\partial r^2} + \frac{2}{r}\frac{\partial}{\partial r} + \frac{1}{r^2}\left(\frac{\partial^2}{\partial \theta^2} + \cot\theta\frac{\partial}{\partial \theta} + \frac{1}{\sin^2\theta}\frac{\partial^2}{\partial \phi^2}\right), \quad (4)$$

whereas the operator $\mathbb{M}_3$ becomes $\widetilde{\mathbb{M}}_3 = -i\frac{\partial}{\partial \phi}$.

Plugging the expression (4) into $\mathcal{L}$ yields the following form for the operator:

$$\widetilde{\mathcal{L}} = -\frac{1}{2}\left(\frac{\partial^2}{\partial r^2} + \frac{2}{r}\frac{\partial}{\partial r}\right) + \frac{A(\theta, \phi)}{2r^2} + \frac{r^2}{2}, \quad (5)$$

and consequently, the eigenvalue problem becomes:

$$\left[\frac{\partial^2}{\partial r^2} + \frac{2}{r}\frac{\partial}{\partial r} - \frac{A(\theta, \phi)}{r^2} - r^2 + 2\lambda\right]\psi(r, \theta, \phi) = 0, \quad (6)$$

where $A(\theta, \phi)$ is the following self-adjoint operator (An alternative formulation of the problem (6) takes place when A is a constant, i.e., $A := l(l + q - 2)$, where q is the dimension of the space and l is an integer number. This problem is usually solved numerically. Another kind of degeneracy would occur, and although a deep analysis of such a case deserves future research, it is beyond the scope of our paper.).

$$A(\theta, \phi) = -\frac{\partial^2}{\partial \theta^2} - \cot\theta\frac{\partial}{\partial \theta} - \frac{1}{\sin^2\theta}\frac{\partial^2}{\partial \phi^2}. \quad (7)$$

Based on the change of variables, it is necessary to modify the Hilbert space of the solutions as well:

$$\widetilde{\mathcal{H}} = \Big\{\psi : \mathbb{R}^3 \longrightarrow \mathbb{R} \mid \psi \in C^2(\mathbb{R}^3) \cap L^2(\mathbb{R}^3),$$
$$\psi(r, \theta, \phi + 2\pi) = \psi(r, \theta, \phi), \lim_{r \to \infty} \psi(r, \theta, \phi) = 0\Big\}. \quad (8)$$

The next theorem is very relevant for the subsequent analysis of degeneracy.

Theorem 2. *The following relation holds in spherical polar coordinates:*

$$A(\theta, \phi) = \mathbb{M}_1^2 + \mathbb{M}_2^2 + \mathbb{M}_3^2,$$

where the operators $\mathbb{M}_i$, for $i = 1, 2, 3$, are defined by (3).

Proof. The sum of the squares of the operators defined in (3) reads as:

$$\mathbb{M}_1^2 + \mathbb{M}_2^2 + \mathbb{M}_3^2 = -\left(z\frac{\partial}{\partial y} - y\frac{\partial}{\partial z}\right)^2 - \left(x\frac{\partial}{\partial z} - z\frac{\partial}{\partial x}\right)^2 - \left(y\frac{\partial}{\partial x} - x\frac{\partial}{\partial y}\right)^2$$

$$= \cdots = -x^2\left(\frac{\partial^2}{\partial y^2} + \frac{\partial^2}{\partial z^2}\right) - y^2\left(\frac{\partial^2}{\partial x^2} + \frac{\partial^2}{\partial z^2}\right) - z^2\left(\frac{\partial^2}{\partial x^2} + \frac{\partial^2}{\partial y^2}\right)$$

$$+2\left(xy\frac{\partial}{\partial x}\frac{\partial}{\partial y}+xz\frac{\partial}{\partial x}\frac{\partial}{\partial z}+yz\frac{\partial}{\partial y}\frac{\partial}{\partial z}+x\frac{\partial}{\partial x}+y\frac{\partial}{\partial y}+z\frac{\partial}{\partial z}\right).$$

Now, we recall the well-known identities among partial derivatives:

$$\frac{\partial}{\partial x}=\sin\theta\cos\phi\frac{\partial}{\partial r}+\frac{\cos\theta\cos\phi}{r}\frac{\partial}{\partial\theta}-\frac{\sin\phi}{r\sin\theta}\frac{\partial}{\partial\phi},$$

$$\frac{\partial}{\partial y}=\sin\theta\sin\phi\frac{\partial}{\partial r}+\frac{\cos\theta\sin\phi}{r}\frac{\partial}{\partial\theta}-\frac{\cos\phi}{r\sin\theta}\frac{\partial}{\partial\phi},$$

$$\frac{\partial}{\partial z}=\cos\theta\frac{\partial}{\partial r}-\frac{\sin\theta}{r}\frac{\partial}{\partial\theta}.$$

Applying the above formulas to the latest expression we obtained for the sum of squares yields:

$$\mathbb{M}_1^2+\mathbb{M}_2^2+\mathbb{M}_3^2=\cdots=-\frac{\partial^2}{\partial\theta^2}-\cot\theta\frac{\partial}{\partial\theta}-\frac{1}{\sin^2\theta}\frac{\partial^2}{\partial\phi^2}=A(\theta,\phi).$$

□

Back to the identification of the solution of (6), we can proceed by the separation of the variables. The eigenvalues of $\widetilde{\mathcal{L}}$ are countable; more precisely for all $n\in\mathbb{N}$, they have the form:

$$\lambda_n=n+\frac{3}{2}.$$

The associated eigenfunctions read as:

$$\psi(\cdot)=\psi_{nlm}(r,\theta,\phi)=R_{n\ell}(r)Y_{\ell m}(\theta,\varphi)=\left[N_1\,r^\ell\,e^{-r^2/2}\,\mathfrak{L}_{n/2-\ell/2}^{(\ell+1/2)}(u)\Big|_{u=r^2}\right][N_2\mathcal{Y}_{\ell m}(\theta,\varphi)], \quad (9)$$

where the terms:

$$R(r)\doteq N_1\,r^\ell\,e^{-r^2/2}\,\mathfrak{L}_{n/2-\ell/2}^{(\ell+1/2)}(u)\Big|_{u=r^2}$$

and

$$Y_{\ell m}(\theta,\varphi)=N_2\,\mathcal{Y}_{\ell m}(\theta,\varphi)$$

are respectively called the *radial part* and the *angular part*.

In the expression (9), we have that:

- the coefficient N_1, N_2 are normalization constants, as in every eigenvalue problem, with respect to the norm of the Hilbert space, that is:

$$\int_0^\infty r^2|R(r)|^2\,dr=1 \quad\text{and}\quad \int_0^{2\pi}d\varphi\int_0^\pi |Y_{\ell m}(\theta,\varphi)|^2\sin\theta\,d\theta=1;$$

- n is a nonnegative integer number $n=0,1,2,\ldots$;
- For any fixed value of n, the parameter ℓ takes all the integer values from zero to n such that n and ℓ are both even numbers or both odd numbers, implying that the difference between two subsequent values of ℓ is two;
- For any fixed value of ℓ, the parameter m assumes all integer values between $-\ell$ and ℓ;
- The functions $\mathfrak{L}_{n/2-\ell/2}^{(\ell+1/2)}(u)$ are the so-called *Laguerre polynomials* whose general expression is:

$$\mathfrak{L}_j^{(h)}(u)=\frac{e^u}{u^h}\frac{d^j}{du^j}(u^{j+h}e^{-u});$$

- The functions $\mathcal{Y}_{\ell m}(\theta,\varphi)$ are the *spherical harmonics*:

$$\mathcal{Y}_{\ell m}(\theta,\varphi)=e^{im\varphi}\sin^m\theta\left(\frac{1}{\sin\theta}\frac{d}{d\theta}\right)^{\ell+m}\sin^{2\ell}\theta,$$

for $m > 0$, whereas $\mathcal{Y}^*_{\ell,m}(\theta,\varphi) = (-1)^m \mathcal{Y}_{\ell m}(\theta,\varphi)$ for $m < 0$. They are simultaneous eigenfunctions of the operator $A(\theta,\varphi)$ and of the operator $\widetilde{\mathbb{M}}_3$, in compliance with the following equations:

$$A(\theta,\varphi)\mathcal{Y}_{\ell m}(\theta,\varphi) = \ell(\ell+1)\mathcal{Y}_{\ell m}(\theta,\varphi), \tag{10a}$$

$$\widetilde{\mathbb{M}}_3 \mathcal{Y}_{\ell m}(\theta,\varphi) = m\mathcal{Y}_{\ell m}(\theta,\varphi). \tag{10b}$$

It is well known that the "degeneracy" of an eigenvalue λ of a linear operator is the property for which the eigenspace corresponding to λ has dimension greater than one. Under such a circumstance, we can state that the eigenvalue λ is *degenerate* as well. When the spectrum of a linear operator has a *degeneracy*, a problem usually arises: given a degenerate eigenvalue λ, it is not possible to guarantee that a related eigenvector **v** is selected unambiguously.

From the secular Equations (10a) and (10b), the three simultaneous secular equations:

$$\widetilde{\mathcal{L}}\psi_{n\ell m}(r,\theta,\varphi) = \lambda_n \psi_{n\ell m}(r,\theta,\varphi), \tag{11a}$$

$$A(\theta,\varphi)\psi_{n\ell m}(r,\theta,\varphi) = \ell(\ell+1)\psi_{n\ell m}(r,\theta,\varphi), \tag{11b}$$

$$\widetilde{\mathbb{M}}_3 \psi_{n\ell m}(r,\theta,\varphi) = m\psi_{n\ell m}(r,\theta,\varphi) \tag{11c}$$

follow, and the degeneracy of the spectrum of the operator $\widetilde{\mathcal{L}}$ given in (5) is, in other words, due to the dependence of the eigenfunctions on the given parameters. Namely, the eigenfunctions $\psi_{n\ell m}(r,\theta,\varphi)$ depend on the three parameters n,ℓ,m, whereas the eigenvalues λ_n of the operator $\widetilde{\mathcal{L}}$ in (11a) depend on n only, being independent of the other two parameters ℓ,m. The next result, whose proof is rather straightforward, describes the *commutation property* of the operators.

Theorem 3 (Commutation theorem). *The linear operators $\mathbb{O}_1, \mathbb{O}_2, \ldots, \mathbb{O}_n$ acting on the same Hilbert space are pairwise commuting if and only if there exists a basis of the Hilbert space formed by all simultaneous eigenfunctions of $\mathbb{O}_1, \mathbb{O}_2, \ldots, \mathbb{O}_n$.*

Theorem (3) provides an important connection with the degeneracy of the spectrum of an operator, as the next theorem shows.

Theorem 4 (Degeneracy theorem). *If a linear operator $\mathbb{O}$, acting on a Hilbert space, is invariant under at least two linear transformations $\mathbb{U}_1, \mathbb{U}_2$, acting on the same Hilbert space, which are not pairwise commuting, then the spectrum of the operator $\mathbb{O}$ has a degeneracy.*

Proof. By *reductio ad absurdum*, suppose that the spectrum of the operator $\mathbb{O}$ has no degeneracy. Since $\mathbb{O}$ is invariant under the linear transformation $\mathbb{U}_1$, we can apply Theorem 1, from which the commutation relation $[\mathbb{O},\mathbb{U}_1] = 0$ follows. Hence, there exists a basis of the Hilbert space formed by all simultaneous eigenfunctions $\{y_i^{(1)}\}$ of $\mathbb{O}$ and $\mathbb{U}_1$. For the same reason, there exists a basis of the Hilbert space formed by all simultaneous eigenfunctions $\{y_j^{(2)}\}$ of $\mathbb{O}$ and $\mathbb{U}_2$. Since the spectrum of the operator $\mathbb{O}$ has no degeneracy, it follows that the two sets of eigenfunctions $\{y_i^{(1)}\}$ and $\{y_j^{(2)}\}$ are the same set, but this conclusion is absurd because the operators $\mathbb{U}_1, \mathbb{U}_2$ do not commute with each other, and then, there cannot exist a basis of the Hilbert space formed by all simultaneous eigenfunctions of the non-commuting operators $\mathbb{U}_1, \mathbb{U}_2$. □

At the present stage, based on Theorem 4, we can state that the degeneracy of the spectrum of the operator $\widetilde{\mathcal{L}}$ is not surprising, in that this operator is invariant under the action of the three operators $\mathbb{M}_1, \mathbb{M}_2, \mathbb{M}_3$, which fail to be pairwise commuting.

Definition 3 (Complete set of operators). *If the linear operators of the set $\{\mathbb{O}_1, \mathbb{O}_2, \ldots, \mathbb{O}_n\}$ are all pairwise commuting and there exists no other linear operator commuting with them, except the trivial operators, then the set is called the complete set of operators.*

Each complete set of operators is endowed with the following key property. Provided that an operator has a degenerate spectrum, that is the knowledge of an eigenvalue does not allow selecting its eigenfunction unambiguously in the corresponding eigenspace, such a degeneracy can be removed. Basically, if a certain eigenfunction is also an eigenfunction of all the operators in the complete set with respect to a fixed eigenvalue for every operator simultaneously, then the operator's degeneracy is eliminated. The notion of *ladder operators* is very helpful to outline our procedure.

3. Ladder Operators and the Degeneracy of the Spectrum of Operators

We identify the degeneracy of the spectrum of the operator $\widetilde{\mathcal{L}}$ as a consequence of the existence of a particular kind of operators, called ladder operators. We provide a general definition of ladder operator after proving the following result, which can be indicated as the *shift theorem*.

Theorem 5 (Shift theorem). *Let $\mathbb{O}$ be an operator acting on a Hilbert space, and let $\mathbf{v}$ be an eigenfunction of $\mathbb{O}$ having an eigenvalue λ. If another operator $\mathbb{T}$ satisfies the condition $[\mathbb{O}, \mathbb{T}]\mathbf{v} = \mu \mathbb{T}\mathbf{v}$, where the coefficient μ is a real number, then: either $\mathbb{T}\mathbf{v}$ is the null function or $\mathbb{T}\mathbf{v}$ is another eigenfunction of the operator $\mathbb{O}$ with eigenvalue $\lambda + \mu$.*

Proof. If such an operator $\mathbb{T}$ exists, we have that, by linearity and and since λ is an eigenvalue of $\mathbb{O}$, the above relation becomes:

$$[\mathbb{O}, \mathbb{T}]\mathbf{v} = \mu \mathbb{T}\mathbf{v} \quad \Longleftrightarrow \quad \mathbb{O}\mathbb{T}\mathbf{v} - \mathbb{T}\mathbb{O}\mathbf{v} = \mathbb{O}\mathbb{T}\mathbf{v} - \lambda \mathbb{T}\mathbf{v} = \mu \mathbb{T}\mathbf{v},$$

implying the new eigenvalue equation:

$$\mathbb{O}\mathbb{T}\mathbf{v} = (\lambda + \mu)\mathbb{T}\mathbf{v},$$

meaning that either $\mathbb{T}\mathbf{v} = \mathbf{0}$ or $\lambda + \mu$ is an eigenvalue of $\mathbb{O}$ associated with the eigenfunction $\mathbb{T}\mathbf{v}$, so the proof is complete. □

Definition 4 (Ladder operators). *An operator $\mathbb{T}$ satisfying the hypothesis of the shift theorem is called the ladder operator for the operator $\mathbb{O}$. In particular, $\mathbb{T}$ is a:*
- *Raising operator if $\mu > 0$;*
- *Lowering operator if $\mu < 0$.*

A very interesting case in which Theorem 5 is applied occurs when there exists a complete set of n self-adjoint operators $\mathbb{O}_1, \mathbb{O}_2, \ldots, \mathbb{O}_n$ acting on a Hilbert space such that, by virtue of Theorem 3, there exists a basis of the space formed by all their simultaneous eigenfunctions $\{y_1, y_2, \ldots, y_n\}$.

If there exists an operator $\mathbb{T}$ commuting with the k operators $\mathbb{O}_{i_1}, \mathbb{O}_{i_2}, \ldots, \mathbb{O}_{i_k}$ and satisfying the $n - k$ relations of the shift theorem with the remaining $n - k$ operators $\mathbb{O}_{j_1}, \mathbb{O}_{j_2}, \ldots, \mathbb{O}_{j_{n-k}}$ for some certain eigenfunction $\bar{y}$, the following relations hold:

$$\begin{cases} \mathbb{O}_{i_1}(\mathbb{T}\bar{y}) = \mathbb{T}\mathbb{O}_{i_1}\bar{y} = \mathbb{T}\lambda_{i_1}\bar{y} = \lambda_{i_1}(\mathbb{T}\bar{y}) \\ \mathbb{O}_{i_2}(\mathbb{T}\bar{y}) = \mathbb{T}\mathbb{O}_{i_2}\bar{y} = \mathbb{T}\lambda_{i_2}\bar{y} = \lambda_{i_2}(\mathbb{T}\bar{y}) \\ \quad \vdots \\ \mathbb{O}_{i_k}(\mathbb{T}\bar{y}) = \mathbb{T}\mathbb{O}_{i_k}\bar{y} = \mathbb{T}\lambda_{i_k}\bar{y} = \lambda_{i_k}(\mathbb{T}\bar{y}) \end{cases} \tag{12a}$$

and:

$$[\mathbb{O}_{j_1}, \mathbb{T}]\bar{y} = \mu_{j_1}\mathbb{T}\bar{y}, \quad [\mathbb{O}_{j_2}, \mathbb{T}]\bar{y} = \mu_{j_2}\mathbb{T}\bar{y}, \quad \cdots, \quad [\mathbb{O}_{j_k}, \mathbb{T}]\bar{y} = \mu_{j_k}\mathbb{T}\bar{y}, \tag{12b}$$

from which we obtain that the function $\mathbb{T}\tilde{y}$ is either the null function or a simultaneous eigenfunction of $\mathbb{O}_{i_1}, \mathbb{O}_{i_2}, \ldots, \mathbb{O}_{i_k}$ with respect to the same eigenvalues $\lambda_{i_1}, \lambda_{i_2}, \ldots, \lambda_{i_k}$, respectively. Therefore, by Theorem 5, that function is a simultaneous eigenfunction of $\mathbb{O}_{j_1}, \ldots, \mathbb{O}_{j_{n-k}}$ with respect to the shifted eigenvalues $\lambda_{j_1} + \mu_{j_1}, \ldots, \lambda_{j_{n-k}} + \mu_{j_{n-k}}$.

Remark 1. *The degeneracy of the spectrum of a given operator $\mathbb{O}$ can be clarified (we precisely use the term 'clarification' if it is viewed in terms of ladder operators). Basically, we can consider the complete set of operators as a necessary tool to eliminate the degeneracy of the spectrum of $\mathbb{O}$ and to identify all the operators $\mathbb{T}_1, \ldots, \mathbb{T}_p$ that satisfy the relations (12a) together with the operator $\mathbb{O}$ and the relations (12b) of the shift theorem with the remaining operators of the complete set.*

The operator $\widetilde{\mathcal{L}}$ has a degenerate spectrum because its eigenvalues λ_n given in (11a) are independent of the parameters ℓ and m. Since the operator $\widetilde{\mathcal{L}}$ belongs to the complete set of operators $\{\widetilde{\mathcal{L}}, A(\theta, \varphi), \widetilde{\mathbb{M}}_3\}$, in order to clarify the whole degeneracy in terms of ladder operators, it is sufficient to find the ladder operators $\mathbb{T}_1$ and $\mathbb{T}_2$ commuting with $\widetilde{\mathcal{L}}$. Besides commuting with $\widetilde{\mathcal{L}}$, such operators also satisfy the relations (12b) with the operators $A(\theta, \varphi)$ and $\widetilde{\mathbb{M}}_3$, in such a way that the functions $\mathbb{T}_1 \psi_{n\ell m}(r, \theta, \varphi)$ and $\mathbb{T}_2 \psi_{n\ell m}(r, \theta, \varphi)$ are eigenfunctions of $\widetilde{\mathcal{L}}$ associated with the same eigenvalue λ_n and eigenfunctions of $A(\theta, \varphi)$ and of $\widetilde{\mathbb{M}}_3$ associated with a shifted eigenvalue with respect to ℓ and m, respectively.

Natural Degeneracy of a Spectrum

The first ladder operator $\mathbb{T}_1$ of $\widetilde{\mathcal{L}}$ is already well known in the literature. Namely, it can be easily reconstructed as a combination of the three operators $\mathbb{M}_1$, $\mathbb{M}_2$, and $\mathbb{M}_3$. To be more precise, we take into account the two combinations of the operators $\mathbb{M}_1$ and $\mathbb{M}_2$ that we express in Cartesian and in spherical polar coordinates as follows:

$$\mathbb{T}_1^{(+)} := \mathbb{M}_1 + i\mathbb{M}_2 = i\left(z\frac{\partial}{\partial y} - y\frac{\partial}{\partial z}\right) - \left(x\frac{\partial}{\partial z} - z\frac{\partial}{\partial x}\right) = e^{i\phi}\left(\frac{\partial}{\partial \theta} + \frac{i\cos\theta}{\sin\theta}\frac{\partial}{\partial \phi}\right),$$
$$\mathbb{T}_1^{(-)} := \mathbb{M}_1 - i\mathbb{M}_2 = i\left(z\frac{\partial}{\partial y} - y\frac{\partial}{\partial z}\right) + \left(x\frac{\partial}{\partial z} - z\frac{\partial}{\partial x}\right) = e^{-i\phi}\left(\frac{i\cos\theta}{\sin\theta}\frac{\partial}{\partial \phi} - \frac{\partial}{\partial \theta}\right),$$
(13)

which respectively are the *raising operator* and the *lowering operator*.

Since the two ladder operators $\mathbb{T}_1^{(\pm)}$ satisfy the conditions:

$$[\widetilde{\mathcal{L}}, \mathbb{T}_1^{(\pm)}] = [A(\theta, \varphi), \mathbb{T}_1^{(\pm)}] = 0, \qquad [\widetilde{\mathbb{M}}_3, \mathbb{T}_1^{(\pm)}] = \pm \mathbb{T}_1^{(\pm)},$$

we obtain, according the Equations (12a) and (12b), that the functions $\mathbb{T}_1^{(\pm)} \psi_{n,\ell,m}$ are eigenfunctions of the operators $\widetilde{\mathcal{L}}$ and $A(\theta, \varphi)$ with respect to the same eigenvalues λ_n, $\ell(\ell+1)$, respectively, and eigenfunctions of $\widetilde{\mathbb{M}}_3$ with respect to the shifted eigenvalue $m \pm 1$.

The action of the ladder operators on the functions $\psi_{n,\ell,m}$ is described by the next result.

Theorem 6. *The functions $\mathbb{T}_1^{(+)} \psi_{n,\ell,\ell}$ and $\mathbb{T}_1^{(-)} \psi_{n,\ell,-\ell}$ are identically zero.*

Proof. If we expand the function $\mathbb{T}_1^{(+)} \psi_{n,\ell,\ell}$, we can note that $(1-u^2)^\ell$ is a polynomial having degree 2ℓ in u. Indicating with the constant $\mathcal{K}$ the 2ℓ th derivative of the function w.r.t. u, we obtain the following expression:

$$\mathbb{T}_1^{(+)} \psi_{n,\ell,\ell} = e^{i\phi}\left(\frac{\partial}{\partial \theta} + \frac{i\cos\theta}{\sin\theta}\frac{\partial}{\partial \phi}\right)\left[e^{i\ell\phi} \sin^\ell \theta \left(\frac{1}{\sin\theta}\frac{\partial}{\partial \theta}\right)^{2\ell} \sin^{2\ell}\theta\right]$$

$$= e^{i(\ell+1)\phi}\left\{\frac{\partial}{\partial \theta}\left[\sin^\ell\theta \left(\frac{1}{\sin\theta}\frac{\partial}{\partial \theta}\right)^{2\ell} \sin^{2\ell}\theta\right] - \ell\cos\theta \sin^{\ell-1}\theta \left(\frac{1}{\sin\theta}\frac{\partial}{\partial \theta}\right)^{2\ell} \sin^{2\ell}\theta\right\}.$$

Now, if we posit $\cos\theta = u$ and $\sin\theta = \sqrt{1-u^2}$, the latest expression becomes:

$$e^{i(\ell+1)\phi}\left\{-\sqrt{1-u^2}\left[\frac{d}{du}\left((1-u^2)^{\ell/2}\frac{d^{2\ell}}{du^{2\ell}}(1-u^2)^\ell\right)\right]\right.$$

$$\left. -\ell u(1-u^2)^{(\ell-1)/2}\frac{d^{2\ell}}{du^{2\ell}}(1-u^2)^\ell\right\}$$

$$= \mathcal{K}e^{i(\ell+1)\phi}\left\{-\sqrt{1-u^2}\left[\frac{d}{du}(1-u^2)\ell/2\right] - \ell u(1-u^2)^{(\ell-1)/2}\right\} = 0.$$

□

The pair of ladder operators $\mathbb{T}_1^{(\pm)}$ provides a *clarification* of that part of the degeneracy of the spectrum of $\widetilde{\mathcal{L}}$, which is called *natural degeneracy*. As a matter of fact, the operator $\widetilde{\mathcal{L}}$, depending on the Laplacian operator ∇^2 and the norm r of the vector $\mathbf{r}$, only, has a natural and intrinsic invariance under rotations belonging to the proper rotation group $SO(3)$.

The existence of the ladder operators $\mathbb{T}_1^{(\pm)}$ can be easily deduced from such invariance properties. It is also straightforward to capture the notion that the natural degeneracy of the spectrum of the operator $\widetilde{\mathcal{L}}$ is the independence of its eigenvalues λ_n from the parameter m.

More precisely, because we have the following actions:

$$\mathbb{T}_1^{(-)}\psi_{n,-\ell,-\ell} = \mathbb{T}_1^{(+)}\psi_{n\ell\ell} = 0,$$

we can iterate the action of the lowering operator $\mathbb{T}_1^{(-)}$ so as to obtain:

$$\mathbb{T}_1^{(-)}\psi_{n\ell\ell} = C_{\ell-1}\psi_{n,\ell,\ell-1}, \qquad \mathbb{T}_1^{(-)}\mathbb{T}_1^{(-)}\psi_{n\ell\ell} = C_{\ell-2}\psi_{n,\ell,\ell-2},$$

$$\ldots, \qquad (\mathbb{T}_1^{(-)})^{\ell-1}\psi_{n\ell\ell} = C_{-\ell}\psi_{n,\ell,-\ell},$$

or vice versa, by iterating the action of the raising operator $\mathbb{T}_1^{(+)}$, the sequence:

$$\mathbb{T}_1^{(+)}\psi_{n,\ell,-\ell} = C_{-\ell+1}\psi_{n,\ell,-\ell+1}, \qquad \mathbb{T}_1^{(+)}\mathbb{T}_1^{(+)}\psi_{n,\ell,-\ell} = C_{-\ell+2}\psi_{n,\ell,-\ell+2},$$

$$\ldots, \qquad (\mathbb{T}_1^{(+)})^{\ell-1}\psi_{n,\ell,-\ell} = C_\ell\psi_{n,\ell,+\ell},$$

where the coefficients C_i are coefficients of normalization, that is the actions of the raising and lowering operators $\mathbb{T}_1^{(\pm)}$ on the eigenfunctions $\psi_{n,\ell,m}$ leave the parameters n and ℓ unchanged and modify the parameter m, only.

4. Accidental Degeneracy of the Spectrum of $\widetilde{\mathcal{L}}$

Here, we illustrate the main result, which is absent in the literature so far, to the best of our knowledge. We intend to determine the suitable ladder operators for the degeneracy with respect to the parameter ℓ, which is denoted as accidental degeneracy.

The so-called *accidental degeneracy* of the spectrum of the operator $\widetilde{\mathcal{L}}$ consists of the independence of the eigenvalues λ_n from the parameter ℓ. We explain also this type of degeneracy with the help of ladder operators, denoted by $\mathbb{T}_2^{(\pm)}$. Such ladder operators map an eigenfunction $\psi_{n,\ell,m}(\mathbf{r})$ associated with the eigenvalue λ_n either to the null function or to another eigenfunction, denoted by:

$$\psi_{n,\ell',m'}(\mathbf{r}) = \mathbb{T}_2^{(\pm)}\psi_{n,\ell,m}(\mathbf{r}).$$

The two eigenfunctions belong to the same eigenspace of λ_n, that is the value of n is the same in both of them, whereas the two values of ℓ are different, and the two values of m may be either equal or different.

First of all, we establish the conditions for the functions $\psi_{n,\ell,m}(\mathbf{r})$ and $\mathbb{T}_2^{(\pm)}\psi_{n,\ell,m}(\mathbf{r})$ to be eigenfunctions of $\widetilde{\mathcal{L}}$ associated with the same eigenvalue λ_n. Namely, by virtue of Theorem 1, any ladder operator $\mathbb{T}_2^{(\pm)}$ has to satisfy the following equality:

$$[\widetilde{\mathcal{L}}, \mathbb{T}_2^{(\pm)}] = 0. \tag{14}$$

If $g(r)$ is any function depending on the polar coordinate r only, and the operator:

$$\widetilde{\mathcal{L}}_g := -\frac{1}{2}\nabla^2 + g(r),$$

is defined on the Hilbert space (8), it follows that every operator $\widetilde{\mathcal{L}}_g$ is endowed with rotational invariance. Moreover, there are only two particular circumstances where the operator $\widetilde{\mathcal{L}}_g \equiv \widetilde{\mathcal{L}}$ has a further invariance, which is then "purely accidental" and is responsible for accidental degeneracy. Such cases occur if either $g(r) = \frac{r^2}{2}$ or $g(r) = -\frac{1}{r}$. The latter case was extensively treated in [3], so we focus on the former case.

A synthetic explanation may sound as follows: We know that the eigenfunction $\psi_{n,\ell,m}(\mathbf{r})$ is associated with the eigenvalues $\ell(\ell+1)$, with respect to which $\psi_{n,\ell,m}(\mathbf{r})$ is also an eigenfunction of the operator $A(\theta,\varphi)$ in (7). Furthermore, since the variation of ℓ between two consecutive values is two, this implies that the eigenvalue of $A(\theta,\varphi)$, which is subsequent after $\ell(\ell+1)$, is $(\ell+2)(\ell+3)$. Hence, the raising operator $\mathbb{T}_2^{(+)}$, whose expression is to be identified, must induce the shift $(\ell+2)(\ell+3) - \ell(\ell+1) = 4\ell+6$ on the eigenvalues of $A(\theta,\varphi)$.

In order to do that, by virtue of Theorem 5, the raising operator $\mathbb{T}_2^{(+)}$ has to satisfy the following condition:

$$[A(\theta,\varphi), \mathbb{T}_2^{(+)}]\psi_{n,\tilde{\ell},\tilde{m}}(\mathbf{r}) = (4\ell+6)[\mathbb{T}_2^{(+)}\psi_{n,\tilde{\ell},\tilde{m}}(\mathbf{r})], \tag{15}$$

where $\psi_{n,\tilde{\ell},\tilde{m}}(r)$ is a particular eigenfunction of $A(\theta,\varphi)$. Therefore, we are supposed to identify an operator that verifies both conditions (14) and (15). The underlying degeneracies have different natures. On the one hand, *natural degeneracy* is clarified by the ladder operators $\mathbb{T}_1^{(\pm)}$ given in (13) and obtained as combinations of the angular momentum operators, and this is due to the fact that the ladder operators have to induce a shift of one unit on the parameter m. On the other hand, *accidental degeneracy* has to be clarified by operators $\mathbb{T}_2^{(+)}$, which are obtained from the combinations of the components of a tensor, because such operators have to induce a shift of two units on the parameter ℓ.

The invariance of the operator $\mathcal{L}$ is illustrated by the next result.

Theorem 7. *All the components of the following second-rank tensor:*

$$T_{ij} = -\frac{\partial}{\partial r_i}\frac{\partial}{\partial r_j} + r_i r_j, \qquad \text{for } i,j = 1,2,3, \tag{16}$$

where r_1, r_2, r_3 are the coordinates of $\mathbf{r}$, satisfy the commutation identity $[\mathcal{L}, T_{ij}] = 0$, i.e., $\mathcal{L}$ is invariant under the action of all components.

Proof. We can employ the following property of the commutator, which holds for all A, B, and C:

$$[AB, C] = A[B, C] + [A, C]B.$$

Expanding the quantity $[\mathcal{L}, T_{ij}]$ yields (Some calculations are omitted for the sake of brevity. However, all the calculations are available upon request to the authors.):

$$[\mathcal{L}, T_{ij}] = \left[-\frac{1}{2}\nabla^2 + \frac{r^2}{2}, -\frac{\partial}{\partial r_i}\frac{\partial}{\partial r_j} + r_i r_j\right] = \left[-\frac{1}{2}\nabla^2, r_i r_j\right] + \left[\frac{r^2}{2}, -\frac{\partial}{\partial r_i}\frac{\partial}{\partial r_j}\right]$$

$$= -\frac{1}{2}\sum_{k=1}^{3}\left\{\left[-\frac{1}{2}\nabla^2, r_i r_j\right] + \left[r_k^2, -\frac{\partial}{\partial r_i}\frac{\partial}{\partial r_j}\right]\right\}$$

$$= \cdots = -\frac{1}{2}\left(\frac{\partial}{\partial r_j}r_i + \frac{\partial}{\partial r_i}r_j + r_i\frac{\partial}{\partial r_j} + r_j\frac{\partial}{\partial r_i} - r_j\frac{\partial}{\partial r_i} - r_i\frac{\partial}{\partial r_j} - \frac{\partial}{\partial r_i}r_j - \frac{\partial}{\partial r_j}r_i\right) = 0,$$

meaning that $\mathcal{L}$ is invariant under the action of all nine components T_{ij}. □

The components T_{ij} are the further linear operators that accidentally commute with $\mathcal{L}$, in addition to $\mathbb{M}_1$, $\mathbb{M}_2$ and $\mathbb{M}_3$.

Given the above-mentioned T_{ij}, we can consider the following operators:

$$\mathcal{T}_1 = T_{12}, \qquad \mathcal{T}_2 = \frac{T_{22} - T_{11}}{2},$$

so that we are able to define the following ladder operators:

$$\mathbb{T}_2^{(\pm)} := \mathcal{T}_1 \pm i\mathcal{T}_2 = -\frac{\partial}{\partial x}\frac{\partial}{\partial y} + xy \pm \frac{i}{2}\left(\frac{\partial^2}{\partial x^2} - \frac{\partial^2}{\partial y^2} + y^2 - x^2\right),$$

where $i = \sqrt{-1}$.

Theorem 8. *The ladder operators $\mathbb{T}_2^{(\pm)}$ satisfy the following commutation identity:*

$$[\mathbb{M}_3, \mathbb{T}_2^{(\pm)}] = \pm 2\mathbb{T}_2^{(\pm)}. \tag{17a}$$

Proof. If we expand the expression of the commutator in the left-hand side of (17a), we obtain:

$$[\mathbb{M}_3, \mathbb{T}_2^{(\pm)}] = i\left[y\frac{\partial}{\partial x} - x\frac{\partial}{\partial y}, -\frac{\partial}{\partial x}\frac{\partial}{\partial y} + xy \pm \frac{i}{2}\left(\frac{\partial^2}{\partial x^2} - \frac{\partial^2}{\partial y^2} + y^2 - x^2\right)\right]$$

$$= -i\left[y\frac{\partial}{\partial x}, \frac{\partial}{\partial x}\frac{\partial}{\partial y}\right] + i\left[y\frac{\partial}{\partial x}, xy\right] + i\left[x\frac{\partial}{\partial y}, \frac{\partial}{\partial x}\frac{\partial}{\partial y}\right] - i\left[x\frac{\partial}{\partial y}, xy\right]$$

$$\pm \frac{1}{2}\left\{\left[y\frac{\partial}{\partial x}, \frac{\partial}{\partial y}\frac{\partial}{\partial y}\right] + \left[y\frac{\partial}{\partial x}, x^2\right] + \left[x\frac{\partial}{\partial y}, \frac{\partial}{\partial x}\frac{\partial}{\partial x}\right] + \left[x\frac{\partial}{\partial y}, y^2\right]\right\}$$

$$= i\left(\frac{\partial^2}{\partial x^2} - \frac{\partial^2}{\partial y^2} + y^2 - x^2\right) \pm \left(-2\frac{\partial}{\partial x}\frac{\partial}{\partial y} + 2xy\right) = \pm 2\mathbb{T}_2^{(\pm)}.$$

□

Using Relations (12a), (12b), (14), and (17a), we can establish the following actions of the operators $\mathbb{T}_2^{(\pm)}$ on the eigenfunctions $\psi_{n,\ell,m}(\mathbf{r})$:

$$\mathbb{T}_2^{(+)}\psi_{n,\ell,m}(\mathbf{r}) = \sum_{k=0}^{(n-m-2)/2} c_k \psi_{n,n-2k,m+2}(\mathbf{r}), \quad \mathbb{T}_2^{(-)}\psi_{n,\ell,m}(\mathbf{r}) = \sum_{k=0}^{(n-m+2)/2} c_k \psi_{n,n-2k,m-2}(\mathbf{r}).$$

In order to prove that $\mathbb{T}_2^{(\pm)}$ are the ladder operators that give a clarification of accidental degeneracy, we have to determine the commutators $[A(\theta,\varphi),\mathbb{T}_2^{(+)}]$ and $[A(\theta,\varphi),\mathbb{T}_2^{(-)}]$. As in Theorem 8, we also obtain the commutators:

$$[\mathrm{M}_1,\mathbb{T}_2^{(+)}] = i\left[z\frac{\partial}{\partial y} - y\frac{\partial}{\partial z},\ -\frac{\partial}{\partial x}\frac{\partial}{\partial y} + xy + \frac{i}{2}\left(\frac{\partial^2}{\partial x^2} - \frac{\partial^2}{\partial y^2} + y^2 - x^2\right)\right]$$

$$= i\left[z\frac{\partial}{\partial y},\ xy\right] + i\left[y\frac{\partial}{\partial z},\ \frac{\partial}{\partial x}\frac{\partial}{\partial y}\right] - \frac{1}{2}\left[z\frac{\partial}{\partial y},\ y^2\right] - \frac{1}{2}\left[y\frac{\partial}{\partial z},\ \frac{\partial^2}{\partial y^2}\right]$$

$$= \frac{\partial}{\partial y}\frac{\partial}{\partial z} - yz + ixz - i\frac{\partial}{\partial x}\frac{\partial}{\partial z},$$

$$[\mathrm{M}_2,\mathbb{T}_2^{(+)}] = i\left[x\frac{\partial}{\partial z} - z\frac{\partial}{\partial x},\ -\frac{\partial}{\partial x}\frac{\partial}{\partial y} + xy + \frac{i}{2}\left(\frac{\partial^2}{\partial x^2} - \frac{\partial^2}{\partial y^2} + y^2 - x^2\right)\right]$$

$$= i\left[\frac{\partial}{\partial x}\frac{\partial}{\partial y},\ x\frac{\partial}{\partial z}\right] + i\left[xy,\ z\frac{\partial}{\partial x}\right] + \frac{1}{2}\left[\frac{\partial^2}{\partial x^2},\ x\frac{\partial}{\partial z}\right] + \frac{1}{2}\left[x^2,\ z\frac{\partial}{\partial x}\right]$$

$$= \frac{\partial}{\partial x}\frac{\partial}{\partial z} - xz - iyz + i\frac{\partial}{\partial y}\frac{\partial}{\partial z},$$

from which we can prove the following fundamental result.

Theorem 9 (Theorem of accidental degeneracy). *The commutator* $\left[A(\theta,\varphi),\mathbb{T}_2^{(+)}\right]$ *is the operator:*

$$\left[A(\theta,\varphi),\mathbb{T}_2^{(+)}\right] = 4\mathbb{T}_2^{(+)}\mathrm{M}_3 + 6\mathbb{T}_2^{(+)} + \left(-2i\frac{\partial}{\partial x}\frac{\partial}{\partial z} + 2\frac{\partial}{\partial y}\frac{\partial}{\partial z} + 2ixz - 2yz\right)\mathbb{T}_1^{(+)},$$

where $\mathbb{T}_1^{(+)}$ *is the raising operator of the natural degeneracy in* (13).

Proof. Using the relation $A(\theta,\varphi) \equiv \mathrm{M}_1^2 + \mathrm{M}_2^2 + \mathrm{M}_3^2$ and expanding the left-hand side, we have:

$$\left[A(\theta,\varphi),\mathbb{T}_2^{(+)}\right] = \left[\mathrm{M}_1^2 + \mathrm{M}_2^2 + \mathrm{M}_3^2,\ \mathbb{T}_2^{(+)}\right]$$

$$= \mathrm{M}_1\left[\mathrm{M}_1,\mathbb{T}_2^{(+)}\right] + \left[\mathrm{M}_1,\mathbb{T}_2^{(+)}\right]\mathrm{M}_1 + \mathrm{M}_2\left[\mathrm{M}_2,\mathbb{T}_2^{(+)}\right] + \left[\mathrm{M}_2,\mathbb{T}_2^{(+)}\right]\mathrm{M}_2$$

$$+ \mathrm{M}_3\left[\mathrm{M}_3,\mathbb{T}_2^{(+)}\right] + \left[\mathrm{M}_3,\mathbb{T}_2^{(+)}\right]\mathrm{M}_3$$

$$= i\left(z\frac{\partial}{\partial y} - y\frac{\partial}{\partial z}\right)\left(\frac{\partial}{\partial y}\frac{\partial}{\partial z} - yz + ixz - i\frac{\partial}{\partial x}\frac{\partial}{\partial z}\right)$$

$$+ i\left(\frac{\partial}{\partial y}\frac{\partial}{\partial z} - yz + ixz - i\frac{\partial}{\partial x}\frac{\partial}{\partial z}\right)\left(z\frac{\partial}{\partial y} - y\frac{\partial}{\partial z}\right)$$

$$+ i\left(x\frac{\partial}{\partial z} - z\frac{\partial}{\partial x}\right)\left(\frac{\partial}{\partial x}\frac{\partial}{\partial z} - xz - iyz + i\frac{\partial}{\partial y}\frac{\partial}{\partial z}\right)$$

$$+ i\left(\frac{\partial}{\partial x}\frac{\partial}{\partial z} - xz - iyz + i\frac{\partial}{\partial y}\frac{\partial}{\partial z}\right)\left(x\frac{\partial}{\partial z} - z\frac{\partial}{\partial x}\right)$$

$$+ 2i\left(y\frac{\partial}{\partial x} - x\frac{\partial}{\partial y}\right)\left[-\frac{\partial}{\partial x}\frac{\partial}{\partial y} + xy + \frac{i}{2}\left(\frac{\partial^2}{\partial x^2} - \frac{\partial^2}{\partial y^2} + y^2 - x^2\right)\right]$$

$$+ 2i\left[-\frac{\partial}{\partial x}\frac{\partial}{\partial y} + xy + \frac{i}{2}\left(\frac{\partial^2}{\partial x^2} - \frac{\partial^2}{\partial y^2} + y^2 - x^2\right)\right]\left(y\frac{\partial}{\partial x} - x\frac{\partial}{\partial y}\right).$$

Expanding the right-hand side yields:

$$4\mathbb{T}_2^{(+)}\mathbb{M}_3 + 6\mathbb{T}_2^{(+)} + \left(-2i\frac{\partial}{\partial x}\frac{\partial}{\partial z} + 2\frac{\partial}{\partial y}\frac{\partial}{\partial z} + 2ixz - 2yz\right)\mathbb{T}_1^{(+)}$$

$$= 4i\left(-\frac{\partial}{\partial x}\frac{\partial}{\partial y} + xy + \frac{i}{2}\frac{\partial^2}{\partial x^2} - \frac{i}{2}\frac{\partial^2}{\partial y^2} + \frac{iy^2}{2} - \frac{ix^2}{2}\right)\left(y\frac{\partial}{\partial x} - x\frac{\partial}{\partial y}\right)$$

$$+ 6\left(-\frac{\partial}{\partial x}\frac{\partial}{\partial y} + xy + \frac{i}{2}\frac{\partial^2}{\partial x^2} - \frac{i}{2}\frac{\partial^2}{\partial y^2} + \frac{iy^2}{2} - \frac{ix^2}{2}\right)$$

$$+ \left(-2i\frac{\partial}{\partial x}\frac{\partial}{\partial z} + 2\frac{\partial}{\partial y}\frac{\partial}{\partial z} + 2ixz - 2yz\right)\left(iz\frac{\partial}{\partial y} - iy\frac{\partial}{\partial z} - x\frac{\partial}{\partial z} + z\frac{\partial}{\partial z}\right).$$

With the help of some algebra, we can recognize that the two expansions are equal; hence, the proof is complete. □

Theorem 9 and the identity $\mathbb{T}_1^{(+)}\psi_{n\ell\ell} = 0$ lead to establishing the action of the commutator $[A(\theta,\varphi), \mathbb{T}_2^{(+)}]$ on the eigenfunction $\psi_{n,\ell,\ell}$, obtained when positing $m = \ell$.

$$\left[A(\theta,\varphi), \mathbb{T}_2^{(+)}\right]\psi_{n,\ell,\ell}$$

$$= \left[4\mathbb{T}_2^{(+)}\mathbb{M}_3 + 6\mathbb{T}_2^{(+)} + \left(-2i\frac{\partial}{\partial x}\frac{\partial}{\partial z} + 2\frac{\partial}{\partial y}\frac{\partial}{\partial z} + 2ixz - 2yz\right)\mathbb{T}_1^{(+)}\right]\psi_{n,\ell,\ell}$$

$$= \left[4\mathbb{T}_2^{(+)}\mathbb{M}_3 + 6\mathbb{T}_2^{(+)}\right]\psi_{n,\ell,\ell} + \left(-2i\frac{\partial}{\partial x}\frac{\partial}{\partial z} + 2\frac{\partial}{\partial y}\frac{\partial}{\partial z} + 2ixz - 2yz\right)\left[\mathbb{T}_1^{(+)}\psi_{n,\ell,\ell}\right]$$

$$= (4\ell + 6)\left[\mathbb{T}_2^{(+)}\psi_{n,\ell,\ell}\right],$$

that is we have found the fundamental commutator:

$$\left[A(\theta,\varphi), \mathbb{T}_2^{(+)}\right]\psi_{n,\ell,\ell} = (4\ell + 6)\left[\mathbb{T}_2^{(+)}\psi_{n,\ell,\ell}\right]. \tag{17b}$$

The function $\mathbb{T}_2^{(+)}\psi_{n,\ell,\ell}$ is either the null function or a simultaneous eigenfunction of the operator $\mathcal{L}$, with respect to the same eigenvalue λ_n as $\psi_{n,\ell,\ell}$, and of the operators $A(\theta,\varphi)$, $\mathbb{M}_3$, with respect to the eigenvalues $\ell(\ell+1) + 4\ell + 6 \equiv (\ell+2)(\ell+3)$ and $\ell+2$, respectively, that is:

$$\mathbb{T}_2^{(+)}\psi_{n,\ell,\ell} = C_{\ell+2}\,\psi_{n,\ell+2,\ell+2}.$$

Furthermore, the raising operator $\mathbb{T}_2^{(+)}$ provides a clarification of the accidental degeneracy of the spectrum of the operator $\mathcal{L}$ because its iterated action on the eigenfunction $\psi_{n,0,0}$, where n is even, gives:

$$\mathbb{T}_2^{(+)}\psi_{n,0,0} = C_2\,\psi_{n,2,2}, \quad \mathbb{T}_2^{(+)}\psi_{n,2,2} = C_4\,\psi_{n,4,4}, \quad \ldots, \quad \mathbb{T}_2^{(+)}\psi_{n,n-2,n-2} = C_n\,\psi_{n,n,n}$$

and analogously with n odd:

$$\mathbb{T}_2^{(+)}\psi_{n,1,1} = C_3\,\psi_{n,3,3}, \quad \mathbb{T}_2^{(+)}\psi_{n,3,3} = C_5\,\psi_{n,5,5}, \quad \ldots, \quad \mathbb{T}_2^{(+)}\psi_{n,n-2,n-2} = C_n\,\psi_{n,n,n},$$

where the coefficients C_i are coefficients of normalization, that is the action of the raising operator $\mathbb{T}_2^{(+)}$ on the eigenfunctions $\psi_{n,\ell,\ell}$ leaves the parameters n unchanged and modifies the parameters ℓ, m, only.

Regarding the operator $\mathbb{T}_2^{(-)}$, we have the relation (it can be proven by means of the same strategy as in Theorem 9):

$$\left[A(\theta, \varphi), \mathbb{T}_2^{(-)} \right] = -4\mathbb{T}_2^{(-)} \mathbb{M}_3 + 6\mathbb{T}_2^{(-)} + \left(-2i \frac{\partial}{\partial x}\frac{\partial}{\partial z} - 2\frac{\partial}{\partial y}\frac{\partial}{\partial z} + 2ixz + 2yz \right) \mathbb{T}_1^{(-)},$$

where $\mathbb{T}_1^{(-)}$ is the lowering operator of the natural degeneracy in (13), from which we obtain the action:

$$\left[A(\theta, \varphi), \mathbb{T}_2^{(-)} \right] \psi_{n,\ell,-\ell} = (4\ell + 6) \left[\mathbb{T}_2^{(-)} \psi_{n,\ell,-\ell} \right]. \tag{18}$$

Again, for the above reasons, the function $\mathbb{T}_2^{(-)} \psi_{n,\ell,-\ell}$ is either the null function or a simultaneous eigenfunction of the operator $\mathcal{L}$, with respect to the same eigenvalue λ_n as $\psi_{n,\ell,-\ell}$, and of the operators $A(\theta, \varphi)$, $\mathbb{M}_3$, with respect to the eigenvalues $\ell(\ell+1) + 4\ell + 6 \equiv (\ell+2)(\ell+3)$ and $-\ell-2$, respectively, that is:

$$\mathbb{T}_2^{(-)} \psi_{n,\ell,-\ell} = \widetilde{C}_{\ell+2} \psi_{n,\ell+2,-\ell-2}.$$

Since the action of the operator $\mathbb{T}_2^{(-)}$ on the eigenfunctions $\psi_{n,\ell,-\ell}$ raises the parameter ℓ by two units, as the operator $\mathbb{T}_2^{(+)}$, we can conclude that there is no lowering operator for the parameter ℓ, but this is not surprising because, by virtue of (17a), the operator $\mathbb{T}_2^{(-)}$ lowers the parameter m of the eigenfunctions $\psi_{n,\ell,-\ell}$ from $-\ell$ to $-\ell-2$. This means that the parameter ℓ cannot change from ℓ to $\ell-2$ because otherwise, we would have that:

$$|m| = |-\ell-2| > \ell-2,$$

which is absurd, due to the constraint $|m| \leqslant \ell$.

Furthermore, the operator $\mathbb{T}_2^{(-)}$ provides a clarification of the accidental degeneracy of the spectrum of the operator $\widetilde{\mathcal{L}}$ because its iterated action on the eigenfunction $\psi_{n,0,0}$, where n is even, gives:

$$\mathbb{T}_2^{(-)} \psi_{n,0,0} = \widetilde{C}_2 \psi_{n,2,-2}, \quad \mathbb{T}_2^{(-)} \psi_{n,2,-2} = \widetilde{C}_4 \psi_{n,4,-4}, \quad \ldots, \quad \mathbb{T}_2^{(-)} \psi_{n,n-2,-n+2} = \widetilde{C}_n \psi_{n,n,-n},$$

and also, if n is odd:

$$\mathbb{T}_2^{(-)} \psi_{n,1,-1} = \widetilde{C}_3 \psi_{n,3,-3}, \quad \mathbb{T}_2^{(-)} \psi_{n,3,-3} = \widetilde{C}_5 \psi_{n,5,-5}, \quad \ldots, \quad \mathbb{T}_2^{(-)} \psi_{n,n-2,-n+2} = \widetilde{C}_n \psi_{n,n,-n},$$

where the coefficients $\widetilde{C}_i$ are coefficients of normalization, i.e., the action of the operator $\mathbb{T}_2^{(-)}$ on the eigenfunctions $\psi_{n,\ell,-\ell}$ leaves the parameters n unchanged and modifies the parameters ℓ, m, only.

5. Discussion

In this paper, we focused on the accidental degeneracy of a second-order, Schrödinger-type differential operator, acting on a Hilbert space. Typically, in the theory of PDEs, the concept of degeneracy is connected to the number of parameters on which the eigenvalues depend. Natural degeneracy and accidental degeneracy were reformulated and characterized by using the ladder operators. Such a useful tool can be further employed to provide a new way to describe degeneracy in eigenvalue problems with elliptic operators.

Author Contributions: Methodology, S.P.; Writing—original draft, A.P.; Writing—review—editing, R.D.M. All the authors equally contributed to the present work. All authors have read and agreed to the published version of the manuscript.

Funding: This research received no external funding.

Institutional Review Board Statement: Not applicable.

Informed Consent Statement: Not applicable.

Data Availability Statement: Not applicable.

Conflicts of Interest: The authors declare no conflict of interest. The funders had no role in the design of the study, nor in the writing of the manuscript.

References

1. Gilbarg, D.; Trudinger, N.S. *Elliptic Partial Differential Equations of Second Order*, 3rd ed.; Springer: Berlin/Heiselberg, Germany; New York, NY, USA, 2015; Volume 224.
2. Gilmore, R. *Lie Groups, Physics, and Geometry: An Introduction for Physicists, Engineers and Chemists*; Cambridge University Press: Cambridge, UK, 2008.
3. Burkhardt, C.; Leventhal, J.J. Lenz vector operations on spherical hydrogen atom eigenfunctions. *Am. J. Phys.* **2004**, *72*, 1013–1016. [CrossRef]
4. Deshmukh, P.C.; Ganesan, A.; Banerjee, S.; Mandal, A. Accidental Degeneracy of the Hydrogen Atom and its Non-accidental Solution in Parabolic Coordinates. *Can. J. Phys.* **2021**, *99*, 853–860. [CrossRef]
5. Deshmukh, P.C.; Ganesan, A.; Shanthi, N.; Jones, B.; Nicholson, J.; Soddu, A. The "accidental" degeneracy of the hydrogen atom is no accident. *Can. J. Phys.* **2015**, *93*, 312–317. [CrossRef]
6. Hou, J.M.; Chen, W. Hidden antiunitary symmetry behind "accidental" degeneracy and its protection of degeneracy. *Front. Phys.* **2018**, *13*, 1–4. [CrossRef]

Article

A Mathematical Model of the Production Inventory Problem for Mixing Liquid Considering Preservation Facility

Md Sadikur Rahman [1], Subhajit Das [1], Amalesh Kumar Manna [1], Ali Akbar Shaikh [1], Asoke Kumar Bhunia [1], Leopoldo Eduardo Cárdenas-Barrón [2,*], Gerardo Treviño-Garza [2] and Armando Céspedes-Mota [2]

[1] Department of Mathematics, The University of Burdwan, Burdwan 713104, India; mdsadikur.95@gmail.com (M.S.R.); mathsubhajitdas@gmail.com (S.D.); akmanna1987@gmail.com (A.K.M.); aliashaikh@math.buruniv.ac.in (A.A.S.); akbhunia@math.buruniv.ac.in (A.K.B.)
[2] Tecnologico de Monterrey, School of Engineering and Sciences, Ave. Eugenio Garza Sada 2501, Monterrey 64849, Mexico; trevino@tec.mx (G.T.-G.); acespede@tec.mx (A.C.-M.)
* Correspondence: lecarden@tec.mx

Citation: Rahman, M.S.; Das, S.; Manna, A.K.; Shaikh, A.A.; Bhunia, A.K.; Cárdenas-Barrón, L.E.; Treviño-Garza, G.; Céspedes-Mota, A. A Mathematical Model of the Production Inventory Problem for Mixing Liquid Considering Preservation Facility. *Mathematics* **2021**, *9*, 3166. https://doi.org/10.3390/math9243166

Academic Editor: Arsen Palestini

Received: 28 September 2021
Accepted: 8 November 2021
Published: 9 December 2021

Publisher's Note: MDPI stays neutral with regard to jurisdictional claims in published maps and institutional affiliations.

Copyright: © 2021 by the authors. Licensee MDPI, Basel, Switzerland. This article is an open access article distributed under the terms and conditions of the Creative Commons Attribution (CC BY) license (https:// creativecommons.org/licenses/by/ 4.0/).

Abstract: The mixing process of liquid products is a crucial activity in the industry of essential commodities like, medicine, pesticide, detergent, and so on. So, the mathematical study of the mixing problem is very much important to formulate a production inventory model of such type of items. In this work, the concept of the mixing problem is studied in the branch of production inventory. Here, a production model of mixed liquids with price-dependent demand and a stock-dependent production rate is formulated under preservation technology. In the formulation, first of all, the mixing process is presented mathematically with the help of simultaneous differential equations. Then, the mixed liquid produced in the mixing process is taken as a raw material of a manufacturing system. Then, all the cost components and average profit of the system are calculated. Now, the objective is to maximize the corresponding profit maximization problem along with the highly nonlinear objective function. Because of this, the mentioned maximization problem is solved numerically using MATHEMATICA software. In order to justify the validity of the model, two numerical examples are worked out. Finally, to show the impact of inventory parameters on the optimal policy, sensitivity analyses are performed and the obtained results are presented graphically.

Keywords: mixing process; simultaneous differential equations; variable production rate; simulated annealing; differential evolution

1. Introduction

The mixing problem has a great impact on different sectors of business management, viz. the medicine industry (Gautam et al. [1], Essi [2], Ploypetchara et al. [3]), cosmetics industry (Bernardo and Saraiva [4], Kim et al. [5], Zhang et al. [6]), chemical industry (Funt [7], Wu et al. [8], Jasikova et al. [9]), and so on, to produce essential commodities in our daily life. Thus, in the area of inventory control, investigation of the production inventory problem of a mixed product along with the mixing process is an intersecting research area. In this connection, Nienow et al. [10], Cheng et al. [11], Fitschen et al. [12], and many others have had a valuable influence in this area. As various inventory parameters like production rate, demand rate, deterioration rate, and preservation technology play a significant role to control a production inventory, researchers should take more care of those inventory parameters in the studying of the production inventory problem with the mixing process.

In production inventory, the production rate of the product is the key parameter that may be constant or dependent on customers' demand/stock level of the product, among others. On the other hand, owing to the failure of machines, sometimes imperfect production occurs during the production process. Thus, imperfect production is also an important factor for production firm/manufacturing firm. Several researchers developed different production models by taking various production rates and imperfect production processes. De [13] analyzed a production problem with a variable rate of production. Su and Lin [14,15] investigated two production inventory models with a demand- as well as inventory-level-dependent production rate. After that, Giri et al. [16] analyzed an unreliable production system with variable production. Roy et al. [17] studied a production inventory model for defective products with rework policy. Considering an imperfect production process, Sana [18] formulated a production inventory model. A few years later, Sharmila and Uthayakumar [19] established the optimal policy of a production problem with three different production rates. Then, Patra and Maity [20] developed a production problem for defective items with a variable production rate. Dey [21] investigated an imperfect production model under an integrated system in an imprecise environment. Succeeding them, Mishra et al. [22] studied the sustainability of a production system under controllable carbon emission. Lu et al. [23] applied the Stackelberg gaming approach to determine the optimal policy of an imperfect production inventory model with collaborative investment policy for reducing emission. Recently, Öztürk et al. [24] studied an imperfect production process with random breakdowns, rework, and inspection costs and Khara et al. [25] formulated an imperfect production model considering advanced payment and trade credit facilities. Beside these, the works of Malik et al. [26], Lin et al. [27], and Rizky et al. [28] are valuable in this area.

Demand of customers is also an important factor in inventory control. It depends on several factors, such as selling price of the product, inventory level, frequency of the advertisements, time, and so on. In reality it is seen that, if the price of a commodity increases, the demand for that commodity must decrease, i.e., the selling-price-dependent demand rate is a decreasing function. On the other side, more customers are attracted because of the large number of items in stock, i.e., the stock-dependent demand rate is an increasing function of the stock level of the items. Sometimes, the customers' demand for a new product increases drastically owing to the advertisement of the product. Thus, advertisement frequency has a great impact on the demand rate. Resh et al. [29] first introduced the variable demand rate (selling-price-dependent) in the area of inventory control and modified Harris's EOQ model. Urban [30] analyzed an inventory model with stock-linked demand. Chang [31] studied a model for optimal lot sizing with a nonlinear stock-linked demand rate. Mukhopadhyay et al. [32] and You [33] studied different types of EOQ models with price-dependent demand. After a few years, Khanra et al. [34] constructed an inventory model with a time-dependent demand rate under trade credit policy. Further, Bhunia and Shaikh [35] studied a deterministic inventory model with price-dependent demand and a three-parameter Weibull distributed deterioration rate. Prasad and Mukherjee [36] proposed an inventory model where the demand rate is connected to stock and time, along with shortages. Manna et al. [37] investigated a production inventory model with imperfect production and advertisement-dependent demand. Jain et al. [38] investigated a fuzzy inventory model where the demand for an item is dependent on time. Recently, the contributions of Alfares and Ghaithan [39], Shaikh et al. [40], Rahman et al. [41], Cardenas-Barron et al. [42], Das et al. [43], Halim et al. [44], Rahman et al. [45], and others on this topic are worth mentioning.

Deterioration is also important in the control of inventory. Most of the commodities in our daily life deteriorate with the passing of time owing to the several factors. Thus, to study an inventory problem for deteriorating items, we cannot avoid the effect of deterioration. Naturally, the deterioration rate of an item cannot be predicted accurately. However, it was taken as constant or time-dependent or probabilistic by several researchers. In their work, for the first time, Ghare and Schrader [46] proposed the concept of deterioration (constant). Then, Emmons [47] proposed the concept of stochastic deterioration with two-parameter Weibull distribution. Since then, a number of research works have been reported in the existing literature. Among those, the works of Datta and Pal [48], Wee [49], Ouyang et al. [50], Min et al. [51], Dash et al. [52], Dutta and Kumar [53], Shah [54], Tiwari et al. [55],

Shaw et al. [56], Mashud et al. [57], Khakzad and Gholamian et al. [58], Mishra et al. [59], Khanna and Jaggi [60], and Naik and Shah [61] are worth mentioning.

On the other side, the economy of an industry is badly affected by reckless deterioration. Thus, in the case of more deterioration, the control of deterioration is highly required. Usually, to prevent more deterioration, some policies/techniques are adopted, named preservation policies/technologies. For the first time, Hsu et al. [62] investigated the concept of preservation technology in the area of inventory control. After that, Dye [63] discussed the preservation investment effect on deterioration rate. Zhang et al. [64] solved an inventory problem for perishable goods by considering stock-dependent demand and investment in preservation technology. Yang et al. [65] proposed an inventory model under preservation technology and trade-credit policy. Tayal et al. [66] studied an inventory problem for a perishable product with a permissible delay in payment along with investment in preservation technology. Dhandapanin and Uthayakumar [67] analyzed the optimal policy of a multi-item inventory model under preservation technology. Recently, Shaikh et al. [68], Das et al. [69], Saha et al. [70], Mashud et al. [71], Sepehri et al. [72], and others contributed through their works on preservation technology.

The organization of the paper is according to Figure 1. In this work, a production problem for mixed liquid and price-dependent demand is formulated. In this formulation, at first, the mixing process is presented mathematically by the simultaneous differential equations under some restrictions. Then, the corresponding optimization problem related to this model is obtained as the profit maximization problem. Because of the high non-linearity of the objective function (average profit), the mentioned maximization problem is solved by differential evolution and simulated annealing in Mathematica software. Then, to investigate the validation of the model, two numerical examples are solved. Finally, sensitivity analyses are performed graphically and this work is concluded with some future scopes. A summary of some of the literature is presented in Table 1.

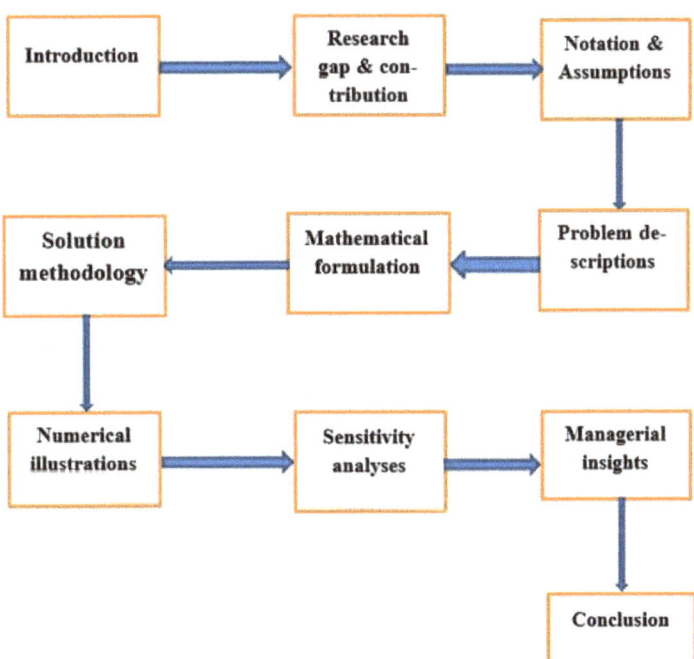

Figure 1. Organization of the paper.

Table 1. Summary of the related literature.

Literature	Simultaneous Differential Equation	Production Rate	Demand	Deterioration
Su and Lin [14]	No	Variable	Variable	———
Kapuscinki and Tayur [73]	No	Constant	Periodic	———
Sana et al. [74]	No	Constant	Time varying	Constant
Lo et al. [75]	No	Constant	Constant	Weibull distributed
Roy et al. [17]	No	Imprecise	Imprecise	Imprecise
Sarkar [76]	No	Constant	Constant	Probabilistic
Samanta [77]	No	Constant	Constant	Probabilistic
Bhunia et al. [78]	No	Constant	Variable	———
Rastogi and Singh [79]	No	Demand-dependent	Selling-price-dependent	Time-dependent
Ullah et al. [80]	No	Constant	Constant	Constant
Salas-Navarro et al. [81]	No	Constant	Probabilistic	———
Das and Islam [82]	No	Time-dependent	Time-dependent and imprecise	———
Saren et al. [83]	No	Constant	Selling-price- and time-dependent	Constant
Khanna and Jaggi [60]	No	———	Price- and stock-dependent	Preservation-technology-dependent
Sepehri et al. [72]	No	Constant	Selling-price-dependent	Constant
This Work	Yes	Variable	Selling-price-dependent	Preservation-technology-dependent

2. Research Gap and Contributions

After a brief survey of the literature, it is conjectured that many works have been accomplished on production inventory (Table 1) for different types of products, such as food, electrical goods, garments, medicine, and so on, with various assumptions regarding the production rate, demand rate, deterioration rate, and so forth. On the other hand, the concepts of the mixing problem are essential in the production manufacturing of liquid products (like, medicine, juice, cosmetics, and so on). To the best of our knowledge, few works on the mixing process (viz. Essi [2], Ploypetchara et al. [3], Kim et al. [5], Jasikova et al. [9], and Fitschen et al. [12], among others) are available in the literature. However, very few researchers ([84,85]) considered the combination of the mixing process as well as manufacturing process in his/her work. Though Su et al. [84] accomplished their work on production inventory for mixed products, they did not consider the mathematical formulation of the mixing process.

To fill this gap, a production inventory model for mixed liquid was formulated by defining the mixing process mathematically. Here, the mixing process of liquids is considered as a part of the production process. The mixing process is presented mathematically by simultaneous differential equations. Then, in the manufacturing part of this modelling, the variable production rate (dependent on the stock level of mixed liquid) and preservation technology are considered. The mentionable contributions of this study are as follows:

(i). Application of simultaneous linear differential equations (to the present mixing process) in the production inventory system.

(ii). Linkage between the mixing process and manufacturing process.

(iii). Consideration of the variable production rate in the manufacturing process dependent upon the stock level of mixed liquid.

All of the above represent the novelty of this work.

3. Notation and Assumptions

The following notations and assumptions are used thought the manuscript.

3.1. Notation

The notations used in this paper are as follows:

$x(t)$	Concentration of liquid at time t in container-I (%)
$y(t)$	Concentration of liquid at time t in container-II (%)
$q(t)$	Stock level of mixed liquid (L)
A	Capacity of container-I (L)
B	Capacity of container-II (L)
α	Incoming rate of liquid with concentration k in container-I (L/unit time)
β	Outgoing rate of liquid from container-I to container-II (L/unit time)
γ	Incoming rate of liquid from container-II to container-I (L/unit time)
δ	Outgoing rate of liquid 2 from container-II (L/unit time)
η	Initial concentration of liquid in container-II (%)
k	Concentration of liquid supplied from outside (%)
a, b	Demand parameters
$D(p)$	Demand of the customers
P	Production rate (L/time unit)
θ_1	Wastage rate during production without preservation
m	Preservation controlling parameter
ξ	Preservation investment ($)
c_p	Processing cost ($/L)
p	Selling price per unit ($/L)
C_o	Set up cost ($/order)
h	Carrying cost per unit per unit time ($/L/time unit)
t_1	Duration of production (time unit)
T	Cycle length (time unit)
$TP(t_1, p, \xi)$	Average profit ($/time unit)

3.2. Assumptions

(i). This work deals with a mixture of three different concentrations of a liquid.
(ii). The capacity of container-I filled with liquid with an initial concentration of zero (container) is less than the capacity of container-II filled with liquid with an initial concentration of k.
(iii). At first, the liquid with concentration η is sent to container-I at the rate α. Then, the mixture of liquid is sent to container-II at the rate β, and the liquid is sent back to container-I from container-II at the rate γ; this process continues to obtain the best desirable mixture. After reaching the desired mixture, the mixed liquid from container-II at the rate δ is used in the production process.
(iv). The production rate of the mixed product $P(t)$ is proportional to the level of mixed liquids ($y(t)$). The mathematical form of $P(t)$ is $P(t) = \frac{\delta}{B}y(t)$.
(v). The wastage/deterioration rate θ during production is dependent on preservation technology. The mathematical form of the deterioration rate is $\theta = \theta_1 e^{-m\xi}$, where ξ is the preservation investment, m is the preservation controlling parameter, and θ_1 is the original deterioration rate.
(vi). The demand of an item is dependent on selling price and its mathematical form is $D(p) = a - bp$, $a, b, p > 0$, such that $p < \frac{a}{b}$.
(vii). Shortages are not allowed.
(viii). Time horizon is infinite and lead time is constant.

4. Problem Description

The problem of the proposed model has two parts: (i) the mixing problem and (ii) the production inventory problem. In the mixing problem, the process of mixing takes place on an instrument made by two containers (Figure 2). In this instrument, container-I is connected to container-II by a pipe line so that the liquid can pass from container-I to container-II, and vice versa. Initially, liquids of two different concentrations (η and k) are taken to make the initial mixture. During mixing, the liquid with a concentration η is passed through container-I at the rate α and then from container-I to container-II with the rate β. Again, the mixed liquid is returned back from container-II to container-I with the rate γ, and this process is continued to obtain the desired mixed liquid. Finally, the desired mixed liquid exits from container-II at the rate δ. The entire process of mixing is presented in Figure 2. Then, in the part of production process, the desired mixture is taken as a raw material and a single product is produced at the production rate $P(t)$ $\left(P(t) = \frac{\delta}{B}y(t)\right)$. During the production period, owing to the customers' demand, the produced product is stored with the rate $(P - D)$ per unit time and the level of inventory reaches its pick level at time $t = t_1$. After that, the level of stock gradually decreases because of fulfilling the demand of the customer and the stock level reaches zero at time $t = T$. The variation in the level of inventory at any time t is shown in Figure 3.

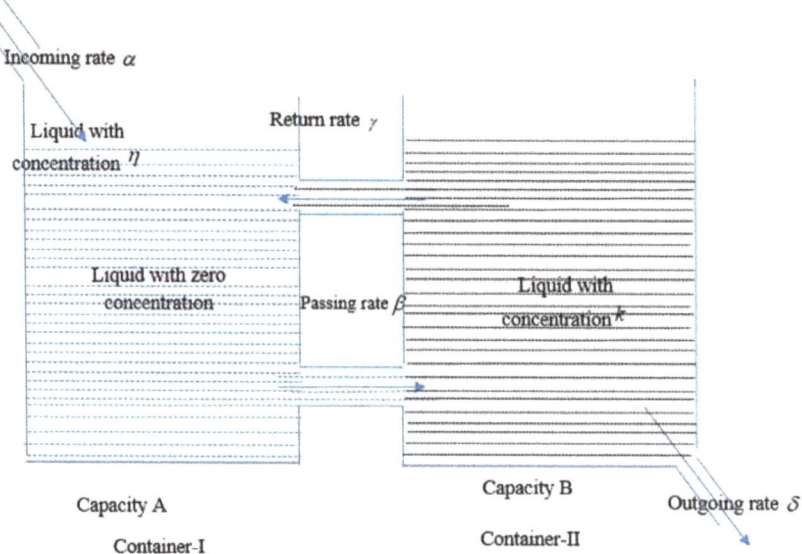

Figure 2. Representation of the mixing procedure in the production process.

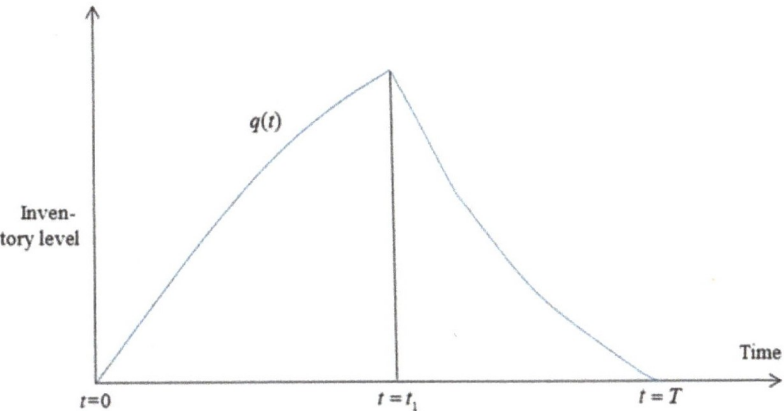

Figure 3. Changes in inventory level with respect to time.

5. Mathematical Formulation

Here, we have discussed the mathematical formulation of mixing and the production inventory system.

5.1. Mathematical Formulation of Mixing Problem

The mixing process described in the previous section is presented mathematically by the following simultaneous differential equations:

$$\begin{aligned} \dot{x} &= \eta\alpha - \tfrac{\beta}{A}x + \tfrac{\gamma}{B}y \\ \dot{y} &= \tfrac{\beta}{A}x - \tfrac{\gamma+\delta}{B}y \end{aligned} \quad (1)$$

Subject to the initial conditions $x(0) = 0, y(0) = kB$, where $\delta < \gamma < \beta$ and $0 < k < 1$. Moreover, from the principle of flow, we get

$$\beta = \alpha + \gamma = \gamma + \delta \quad (2)$$

Solving the system (1), one can obtain the concentrations of the liquids in container-I and container-II as follows:

$$x(t) = \exp\left(-\tfrac{k_1}{2}t\right)\{c_1\exp(k_4 t) + c_2\exp(-k_4 t)\} + \tfrac{k_3}{k_2} \quad (3)$$

$$y(t) = \tfrac{B}{\gamma}\left[c_1\left(k_4 - \tfrac{k_1}{2} + \tfrac{\beta}{A}\right)\exp\left\{\left(k_4 - \tfrac{k_1}{2}\right)t\right\} + c_2\left(-k_4 - \tfrac{k_1}{2} + \tfrac{\beta}{A}\right)\exp\left\{\left(-k_4 - \tfrac{k_1}{2}\right)t\right\}\right] - \tfrac{\eta}{\gamma}\alpha B + \tfrac{\beta B k_3}{\gamma A k_2} \quad (4)$$

where

$$k_1 = \tfrac{\beta}{A} + \tfrac{\gamma+\delta}{B},$$
$$k_2 = \tfrac{\beta\delta}{AB}$$
$$k_3 = \eta\tfrac{\alpha(\gamma+\delta)}{B}$$
$$k_4 = \tfrac{\sqrt{k_1^2 - 4k_2}}{2}$$
$$c_1 = -\tfrac{k_3}{2k_2} + \tfrac{1}{2k_4}\left[k\gamma + \eta\alpha + \tfrac{k_3}{k_2}\left(\tfrac{\beta}{A} - \tfrac{k_1}{2}\right) - \tfrac{\beta k_3}{Ak_2}\right]$$

and

$$c_2 = -\tfrac{k_3}{2k_2} - \tfrac{1}{2k_4}\left[k\gamma + \eta\alpha + \tfrac{k_3}{k_2}\left(\tfrac{\beta}{A} - \tfrac{k_1}{2}\right) - \tfrac{\beta k_3}{Ak_2}\right].$$

5.2. Mathematical Formulation of the Production Problem

The inventory level of the problem at any time t satisfies the governing differential equations

$$\frac{dq(t)}{dt} + \theta q(t) = P(t) - D \text{ for } 0 \leq t \leq t_1 \tag{5}$$

$$\frac{dq(t)}{dt} + \theta q(t) = -D \text{ for } t_1 < t \leq T \tag{6}$$

with the conditions $q(0) = 0$, $q(t_1) = Q$ and $q(T) = 0$.
The solutions of Equations (5) and (6) are given by

$$\begin{aligned}q(t) &= \left(\frac{\beta \delta k_3}{\gamma \theta k_2 A} - \frac{D}{\theta} - \frac{\eta \alpha \delta}{\gamma \theta}\right)\{1 - \exp(-\theta t)\} \\ &+ \frac{c_1}{\left(k_4 - \frac{k_1}{2} + \theta\right)}\left\{\left(k_4 - \frac{k_1}{2}\right)\frac{\delta}{\gamma} + \frac{\beta \delta}{\gamma A}\right\}\left[\exp\left\{\left(k_4 - \frac{k_1}{2}\right)t\right\} - \exp(-\theta t)\right] \\ &+ \frac{c_2}{\left(k_4 + \frac{k_1}{2} - \theta\right)}\left\{\left(k_4 + \frac{k_1}{2}\right)\frac{\delta}{\gamma} - \frac{\beta \delta}{\gamma A}\right\}\left[\exp\left\{-\left(k_4 + \frac{k_1}{2}\right)t\right\} - \exp(-\theta t)\right] \text{ for } 0 < t \leq t_1\end{aligned} \tag{7}$$

and

$$q(t) = \frac{D}{\theta}\{\exp(\theta(T - t)) - 1\} \text{ for } t_1 < t \leq T \tag{8}$$

Again, using the continuity of $q(t)$ at $t = t_1$, we have

$$\begin{aligned}T &= \frac{1}{\theta}\log\left[\frac{\theta}{D}\left[\left(\frac{\beta \delta k_3}{\gamma \theta k_2 A} - \frac{D}{\theta} - \frac{\eta \alpha \delta}{\gamma \theta}\right)\{1 - \exp(-\theta t_1)\}\right.\right. \\ &+ \frac{c_1}{\left(k_4 - \frac{k_1}{2} + \theta\right)}\left\{\left(k_4 - \frac{k_1}{2}\right)\frac{\delta}{\gamma} + \frac{\beta \delta}{\gamma A}\right\}\left[\exp\left\{\left(k_4 - \frac{k_1}{2}\right)t_1\right\} - \exp(-\theta t_1)\right] \\ &\left.\left.+ \frac{c_2}{\left(k_4 + \frac{k_1}{2} - \theta\right)}\left\{\left(k_4 + \frac{k_1}{2}\right)\frac{\delta}{\gamma} - \frac{\beta \delta}{\gamma A}\right\}\left[\exp\left\{-\left(k_4 + \frac{k_1}{2}\right)t_1\right\} - \exp(-\theta t_1)\right]\right] + 1\right] + t_1\end{aligned} \tag{9}$$

5.3. Various Components of the System

The various components of the system are calculated as follows:

(i). Sales revenue (SR):

$$SR = p \int_0^T D \, dt = pDT$$

(ii). Ordering cost (C_o):

(iii). Holding cost (HC):

$$\begin{aligned}HC &= h\int_0^{t_1} q(t)\,dt + h\int_{t_1}^T q(t)\,dt \\ &= h\left(\frac{\beta \delta k_3}{\gamma \theta k_2 A} - \frac{D}{\theta} - \frac{\eta \alpha \delta}{\gamma \theta}\right)\left\{t_1 - \frac{1}{\theta}(1 - \exp(-\theta t_1))\right\} \\ &+ \frac{hc_1}{\left(k_4 - \frac{k_1}{2} + \theta\right)}\left\{\left(k_4 - \frac{k_1}{2}\right)\frac{\delta}{\gamma} + \frac{\beta \delta}{\gamma A}\right\}\left[\frac{\exp\left\{\left(k_4 - \frac{k_1}{2}\right)t_1\right\} - 1}{\left(k_4 - \frac{k_1}{2}\right)} - \frac{1}{\theta}(1 - \exp(-\theta t_1))\right] \\ &+ \frac{hc_2}{\left(k_4 + \frac{k_1}{2} - \theta\right)}\left\{\left(k_4 + \frac{k_1}{2}\right)\frac{\delta}{\gamma} - \frac{\beta \delta}{\gamma A}\right\}\left[\frac{1 - \exp\left\{-\left(k_4 + \frac{k_1}{2}\right)t_1\right\}}{\left(k_4 + \frac{k_1}{2}\right)} - \frac{1}{\theta}(1 - \exp(-\theta t_1))\right] \\ &+ \frac{hD}{\theta^2}[\exp\{\theta(T - t_1)\} - 1] - \frac{hD}{\theta}(T - t_1)\end{aligned}$$

(iv). Production cost (PC):

$$\begin{aligned}
PC &= c_p \int_0^{t_1} P(t)\, dt \\
&= c_p \frac{\delta}{B} \int_0^{t_1} y(t)\, dt \\
&= c_p \frac{\delta}{\gamma} \left[\frac{c_1 \left(k_4 - \frac{k_1}{2} + \frac{\beta}{A}\right)}{\left(k_4 - \frac{k_1}{2}\right)} \left(\exp\left\{\left(k_4 - \frac{k_1}{2}\right) t_1\right\} - 1 \right) + \frac{c_2 \left(-k_4 - \frac{k_1}{2} + \frac{\beta}{A}\right)}{\left(k_4 + \frac{k_1}{2}\right)} \left(1 - \exp\left\{\left(-k_4 - \frac{k_1}{2}\right) t_1\right\}\right) \right] \\
&\quad + c_p \frac{\delta}{\gamma} \left(\frac{\beta k_3}{A k_2} - \eta \alpha \right) t_1
\end{aligned}$$

(v). Preservation cost: $CP = \xi T$.

Therefore, the profit per unit time of the system is given by

$$TP(t_1, p, \xi) = \frac{1}{T}[SR - PC - HC - C_o - CP]$$

Now, the corresponding maximization problem of the system is given by

$$\begin{aligned} &\text{Maximize } TP(t_1, p, \xi) \\ &\text{subject to } t_1 > 0,\ 0 < p < \frac{a}{b} \end{aligned} \qquad (10)$$

6. Solution Methodology

The corresponding optimization problem (10) of the proposed production system is clearly highly non-linear in nature with respect to the decision variables t_1, p, ξ. It is difficult to solve (10) by any analytical method, such as the gradient-based technique, Lagrange's multiplier method, Newton's method, saddle point optimization techniques, and so on. Thus, in order to solve the mentioned optimization problem (10), the following algorithms built in MATHEMATICA software are used:

(i) Differential evolution (Price, 1996);
(ii) Simulated annealing (Marchesi, 1988).

The discussions of the above-mentioned algorithms are done based on the following generalized optimization problem:

$$\begin{aligned} &\text{Maximize } f(u) \\ &\text{subject to } t \in S \subseteq \mathbb{R}^n \\ &\text{where } f : S \to \mathbb{R} \end{aligned}$$

(i) Differential Evolution (DE)

Differential evolution is one of the popular search techniques in the area of optimization. The algorithm of this optimizer has the following attributes:

- The initial positions of the population of size m are $\{u_1, u_2, \ldots, u_m\}$, $m \gg n$
- In the evaluation process for each iteration, the algorithm generates a new population with m points. Using the three points u_u, u_v and u_m, the algorithm generated the jth new point randomly from the previous population.
- The mathematical form is $u_s = u_w + s(u_u - u_v)$, where s is a scaling parameter.
- The new point u_{new} is created from u_j and u_s with the help of the ith coordinate from u_s along with probability ρ, otherwise it will take the coordinate from u_j.
- If $f(u_{new}) > f(u_j)$, then u_{new} replaces u_j in the new population.
- The probability ρ is controlled by the "cross probability" option.

Generally, this process is converged if deviation in between the best functional values in the new position and old population as well as the deviation between the new best point and the old best point are less than the tolerances.

The values of parameters used in the Differential Evolution are given in Table 2.

Table 2. The values of parameters used in the Differential Evolution.

Operator Name	Default Value	Descriptions
"Cross Probability"	0.5	Probability of a gene taken from t_i
"Random Seed"	0	It is a starting value of random number generator
"Scaling Factor"	0.6	Scale applied to the deviation vector in creating a mate
"Tolerance"	0.001	It is accepting constraint violations

(ii) Simulated Annealing (SA)

Simulated annealing is another random search-based meta-heuristic maximizer. The algorithm of this maximizer is inspired by physical activity of annealing, in which a metallic object is warmed up to an extreme temperature and allowed to cool gently. In this process, the atomic structure of metal reaches the lower energy level from the upper, and thus becomes a tougher metal. Exploring this concept in optimization, the algorithm of simulated annealing allows to move away from a local minimizer, and to traverse and settle on a better position and, ultimately, on the global maximizer.

During the iterative process, a new point u_{new} is created in the neighboring point u. Thus, the radius of the neighborhood is decreased from iteration to iteration. The best-found point u_{best} obtained so far is tracked as follows:

If $f(u_{new}) > f(u_{best})$, u_{new} replaces u_{best} and u.

Otherwise, u_{new} replaces u with a probability $e^{b(i,\Delta f, f_0)}$, where b is the Boltzmann exponent, I is the current iteration, Δf is the change in the objective value, and f_0 is the last iteration objective function value.

The default function for b is taken as $\frac{-\Delta f \log(i+1)}{10}$.

Simulated annealing is used for multi-initial points and obtains an optimizer among them. In general, the default number of initial points is taken as $\min\{2n, 50\}$.

The starting points is repeated until achieving of the maximum number of iterations and this method converges to a point.

The values of the parameters of the Simulated annealing are given in Table 3.

Table 3. The values of parameters used in the Simulated annealing.

Option Name	Default Value	Descriptions
"Level Iterations"	50	Maximum number of iterations to stay at a given point
"Perturbation Scale"	1.0	Scale for the random jump
"Random Seed"	0	It is a starting value of random number generator
"Tolerance"	0.001	Tolerance for accepting constraint violations

Solution Procedure

To solve the optimization Problem (10), the following steps are followed:

Step 1: Set the initial values of all input inventory parameters.
Step 2: Define the objective Function (10) in MATHEMATICA.
Step 3: Use the following comments:
"NMaximize [objective, decision variables, Method → "SimulatedAnnealing"]
"NMaximize [objective, decision variables, Method → "DifferentialEvaluation"]
Step 4: Compile and execute.
Step 5: Check the result.
Step 6: If the program is convergent and the results are feasible, go to **Step 8**, otherwise go to **Step 7**.
Step 7: Repeat **Steps 1** to **6**.
Step 8: Print the optimal results.
Step 9: Stop.

7. Numerical Illustrations

Here, we have discussed validation of the proposed work. During the validation process, two numerical examples of a hypothetical system are considered as follows:

Example 1: In this numerical example, the hypothetical data of input parameters are taken in the following way:

$A = 690, B = 700, \alpha = 325, \beta = 690, \gamma = 365, \delta = 325, \theta_1 = 0.22, \eta = 0.9, k = 0.2, a = 150, b = 0.5, C_o = 450, c_p = 50, h = 0.5.$

Example 2: Here, the values of preservation parameters are taken as $m = 0.7$ and the other input parameters are taken to be the same as Example 1.

Example 1 and Example 2 are solved by DE and SA, which are codded in Mathematica software, and the obtained results are displayed in Tables 4 and 5, respectively. Moreover, to show the concavity of the objective function, the pictorial representations of the average profit function versus independent variables taken two at a time w.r.t. Example 2 are depicted in Figures 4–6.

Table 4. Best-found solution of Example 1.

Unknown Parameters	Best-Found Result Obtained by DE	Best-Found Result Obtained by SA
Production time (t_1) (month)	1.9851	1.9851
Cycle length (T) (month)	2.2615	2.2615
Selling price (p) ($/L)	170.746	170.746
Average profit (TP) ($/month)	7591.65	7591.65

Table 5. Best-found solution of Example 2.

Unknown Parameters	Best-Found Result Obtained by DE	Best-Found Result Obtained by SA
Production time (t_1) (month)	3.92474	3.92474
Cycle length (T) (month)	7.005	7.005
Selling price (p) ($/L)	174.89	174.89
Preservation investment (ξ) ($)	8.97837	8.97836
Average profit (TP) ($/month)	7703.15	7703.15

Discussion

From the solution of Examples 1 and 2 (cf. Tables 2 and 3), the following findings are observed.

(i) The average profit of Example 2 (model with preservation technology) is higher than that of the Example 1 (model without preservation technology). From this finding, it may be concluded that the model with preservation technology is more economical than the model without preservation technology.

(ii) The best-found results of both Examples 1 and 2 obtained by DE and SA are same up to a certain degree of accuracy. Thus, from here, it can also be concluded that both of the algorithms are equally efficient to solve the corresponding optimization problem of the proposed model.

(iii) Figures 4–6 indicate pictorial evidence for the near optimality of the obtained results for Examples 1 and 2.

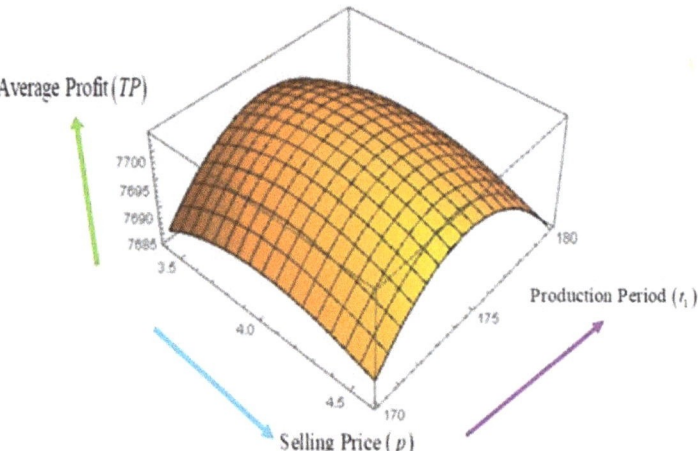

Figure 4. Profit function with respect to t_1 and p.

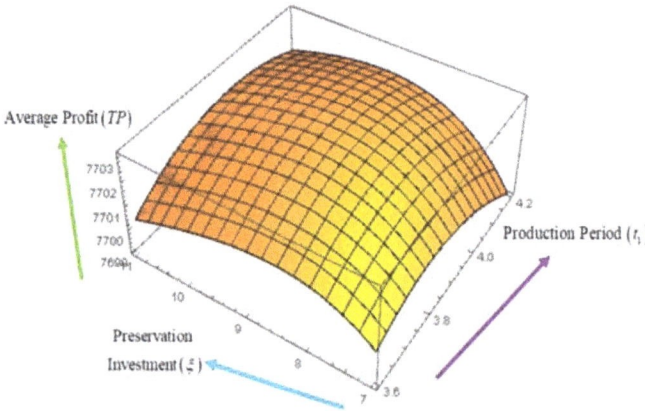

Figure 5. Profit function with respect to t_1 and ξ.

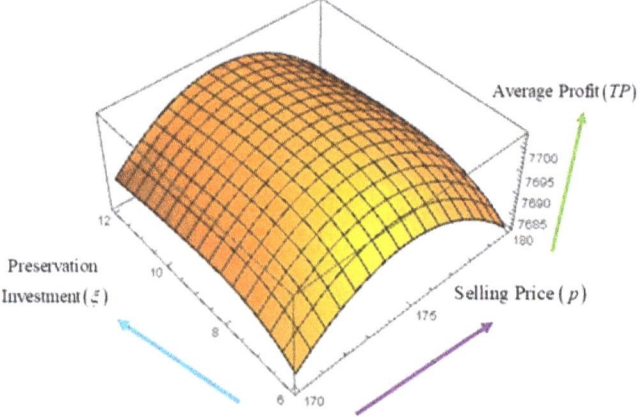

Figure 6. Profit function with respect to ξ and p.

8. Sensitivity Analyses

To show the impact of various known inventory parameters on the average profit (TP), production time (t_1), selling price (p), and cycle length (T), sensitivity analyses are performed with respect to Example 2 by changing the parameters from -20% to 20%. Then, the obtained results of these analyses are depicted graphically in Figures 7–12.

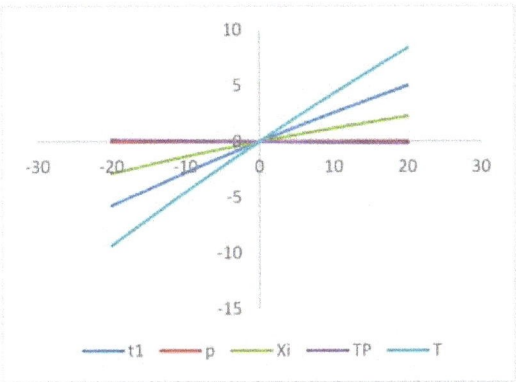

Figure 7. Impact of C_o on the optimal policy.

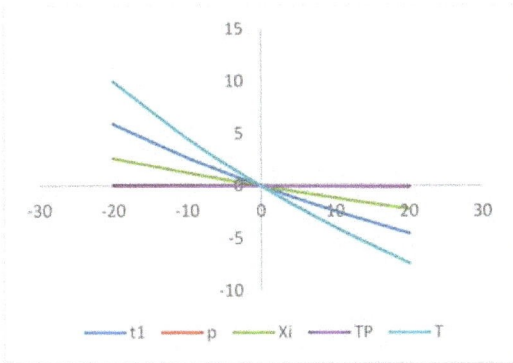

Figure 8. Impact of h on the optimal policy.

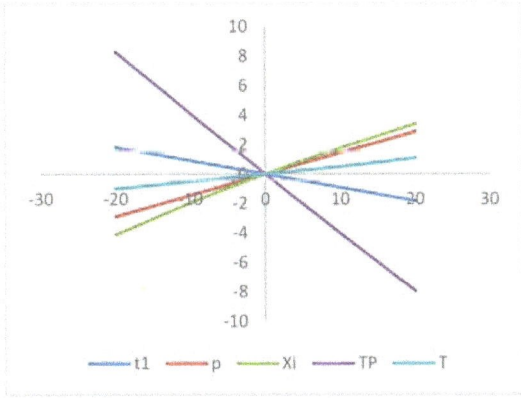

Figure 9. Impact of c_p on the optimal policy.

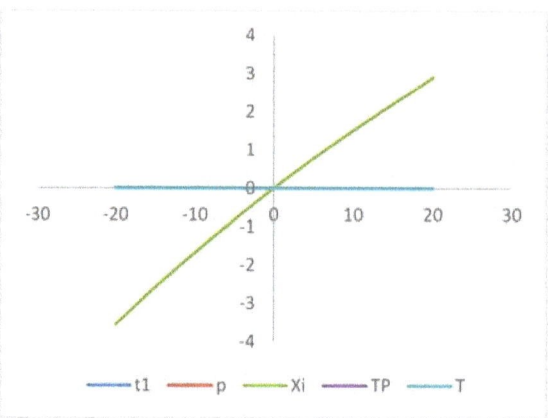

Figure 10. Impact of θ_1 on the optimal policy.

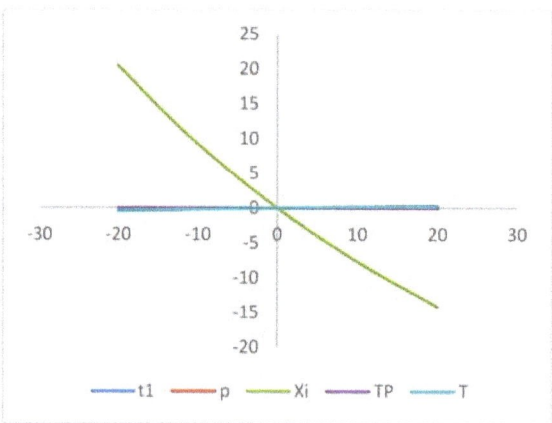

Figure 11. Impact of m on the optimal policy.

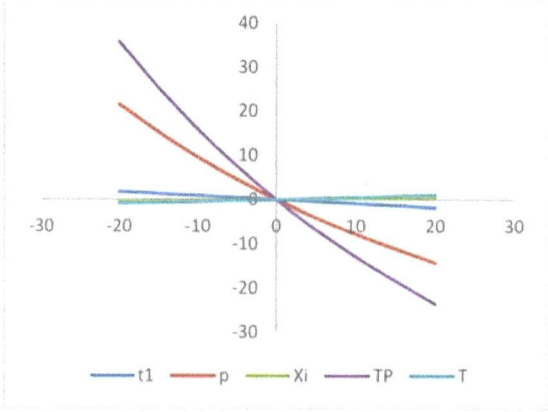

Figure 12. Impact of b on the optimal policy.

From Figures 7–12, the following observations can be made:

- The profit per unit (TP) is moderately sensitive with a reverse effect with respect to c_p, whereas it is insensitive with the change of θ_1, m, h and C_o, and highly sensitive with a reverse effect with respect to b.
- The production time (t_1) is less sensitive directly with respect to C_o, c_p, and slightly sensitive with a reverse effect with respect to h. On the other hand, it is insensitive with the changes in θ_1, m & b.
- The selling price (p) is slightly sensitive with respect to c_p, whereas it is insensitive with the changes in C_o, h, θ_1 & m, and fairly sensitive with a reverse effect with respect to b.
- The preservation investment (ξ) is slighter sensitive with respect to C_o, c_p, h & θ_1, whereas it is insensitive with the changes in b, and highly sensitive with a reverse effect with respect to m.
- The cycle length (T) is slightly sensitive with respect to c_p, and moderately sensitive with a reverse effect with respect to h. On the other hand, it is insensitive with the changes in b, θ_1 and m and fairly sensitive with respect to C_o.

9. Managerial Implications

From the numerical and sensitivity analyses, a few advisories or awareness may be given to the manager of the manufacturing system of mixed products, which are presented below:

(i). As the model with preservation technology is more economical than the model without preservation technology, it will be a good choice for the manager to consider the preservation facility during the manufacturing process of perishable products.

(ii). On the other hand, the manager should be careful about the preservation controlling factor (m), which has a high reverse effect on the preservation investment, the ignorance of which may be the cause of higher compensation on preservation technology.

(iii). The average profit is highly sensitive with respect to the demand controlling parameter b and inventory cost components in the reverse sense, thus a manager/model analyst should take more care about these parameters when making the optimal decision.

10. Conclusions

In this work, the concept of the mixing problem is implemented in the production inventory model for a liquid product with selling-price-dependent demand and a variable production rate under preservation technology. The mixing process is formulated mathematically by the system of differential equations. The non-linear average profit is maximized numerically by the meta-heuristic optimizers: differential evaluation and simulated annealing.

It may be concluded from the numerical result that, if the enterprise/organization applies the preservation facility, it will be more beneficial for them. From the sensitivity analyses, it can also be concluded that the demand parameters and different inventory costs have a significant negative impact on average profit.

As a practical implication, the concept of this proposed model can be applied in various industries, such as medicine, cosmetics, detergent, food industries, and so on. Although the concept of this model can be implemented in the various fields mentioned above, this work has some limitations. Firstly, there is no theoretical proof of the optimal policy of the proposed model. Secondly, under uncertainty, this model cannot be directly implemented in the such industrial sectors and, finally, the shortages case is not considered in this model.

Keeping the above limitations of the proposed model in mind, in the future, the concept of the mixing problem can be extended in other production inventory models, such as models with shortages, a production model with an imperfect production process, and a model with trade credit policy, among others. Finally, the concept of this work may be extended in an uncertain environment-fuzzy, stochastic, fuzzy-stochastic, and interval environment, among others.

Author Contributions: Conceptualization, M.S.R., S.D., A.K.M., A.A.S., A.K.B., L.E.C.-B., G.T.-G. and A.C.-M.; Data curation, M.S.R., S.D. and L.E.C.-B.; Formal analysis, M.S.R., S.D., A.K.M., A.A.S., A.K.B., L.E.C.-B., G.T.-G. and A.C.-M.; Investigation, M.S.R., S.D., A.K.M., A.A.S., A.K.B., L.E.C.-B., G.T.-G. and A.C.-M.; Methodology, M.S.R., S.D., A.K.M., A.A.S., A.K.B., L.E.C.-B., G.T.-G. and A.C.-M.; Supervision, L.E.C.-B.; Validation, M.S.R., S.D., A.K.M., A.A.S., A.K.B., L.E.C.-B., G.T.-G. and A.C.-M.; Visualization, M.S.R.; Writing—original draft, M.S.R., S.D. and A.K.M.; Writing—review and editing, A.A.S., A.K.B., L.E.C.-B., G.T.-G. and A.C.-M. All authors have read and agreed to the published version of the manuscript.

Funding: This research received no external funding.

Institutional Review Board Statement: Not applicable.

Informed Consent Statement: Not applicable.

Data Availability Statement: The data is in the paper.

Conflicts of Interest: The authors declare no conflict of interest.

References

1. Gautam, C.S.; Utreja, A.; Singal, G.L. Spurious and counterfeit drugs: A growing industry in the developing world. *Postgrad. Med. J.* **2009**, *85*, 251–256. [CrossRef] [PubMed]
2. Essi, D.F. Mixing Dinner and Drugs—Is It Ethically Contraindicated? *AMA J. Ethics* **2015**, *17*, 787–795. [PubMed]
3. Ploypetchara, N.; Suppakul, P.; Atong, D.; Pechyen, C. Blend of polypropylene/poly (lactic acid) for medical packaging application: Physicochemical, thermal, mechanical, and barrier properties. *Energy Procedia* **2014**, *56*, 201–210. [CrossRef]
4. Bernardo, F.P.; Saraiva, P.M. Integrated process and product design optimization: A cosmetic emulsion application. In *Computer Aided Chemical Engineering*; Elsevier: Amsterdam, The Netherlands, 2005; Volume 20, pp. 1507–1512.
5. Kim, K.-M.; Oh, H.M.; Lee, J.H. Controlling the emulsion stability of cosmetics through shear mixing process. *Korea-Aust. Rheol. J.* **2020**, *32*, 243–249. [CrossRef]
6. Zhang, X.; Zhou, T.; Ng, K.M. Optimization-based cosmetic formulation: Integration of mechanistic model, surrogate model, and heuristics. *AIChE J.* **2021**, *67*, 17064. [CrossRef]
7. Funt, J.M. Mixing of Rubber. 2009. Available online: https://ccsuniversity.ac.in/ccsu/syllabus_camp/379syl.pdf (accessed on 13 August 2021).
8. Wu, J.; Graham, L.; Nguyen, B. Mixing intensification for the mineral industry. *Can. J. Chem. Eng.* **2010**, *88*, 447–454. [CrossRef]
9. Jasikova, D.; Kotek, M.; Kysela, B.; Sulc, R.; Kopecky, V. Compiled visualization with IPI method for analysing of liquid liquid mixing process. In Proceedings of the EPJ Web of Conferences, Mikulov, Czech Republic, 21–24 November 2018; Volume 180, p. 02039.
10. Nienow, A.W.; Edwards, M.F.; Harnby, N. Mixing in the Process Industries. 1997. Available online: https://books.google.com.hk/books?hl=zh-CN&lr=&id=LxdFnHQcXhgC&oi=fnd&pg=PP1&dq=10.%09Nienow,+A.W.%3B+Edwards,+M.F.%3B+Harnby,+N.+Mixing+in+the+process+industries.+In+Butterworth-Heinemann%3B+1997.&ots=IbEy8GkBXx&sig=FqlgYuB327J9lHv5lBqZSs9ERy4&redir_esc=y&hl=zh-CN&sourceid=cndr#v=onepage&q=10.%09Nienow%2C%20A.W.%3B%20Edwards%2C%20M.F.%3B%20Harnby%2C%20N.%20Mixing%20in%20the%20process%20industries.%20In%20Butterworth-Heinemann%3B%201997.&f=false (accessed on 13 August 2021).
11. Cheng, D.; Feng, X.; Cheng, J.; Yang, C. Numerical simulation of macro-mixing in liquid–liquid stirred tanks. *Chem. Eng. Sci.* **2013**, *101*, 272–282. [CrossRef]
12. Fitschen, J.; Hofmann, S.; Wutz, J.; Kameke, A.; Hoffmann, M.; Wucherpfennig, T.; Schlüter, M. Novel evaluation method to determine the local mixing time distribution in stirred tank reactors. *Chem. Eng. Sci. X* **2021**, *10*, 100098. [CrossRef]
13. De Kok, A.G. Approximations for operating characteristics in a production-inventory model with variable production rate. *Eur. J. Oper. Res.* **1987**, *29*, 286–297. [CrossRef]
14. Su, C.T.; Lin, C.W. A production inventory model for variable demand and production. *Yugosl. J. Oper. Res.* **1999**, *9*, 197–206.
15. Su, C.T.; Lin, C.W. A production inventory model which considers the dependence of production rate on demand and inventory level. *Prod. Plan. Control* **2001**, *12*, 69–75. [CrossRef]
16. Giri, B.C.; Yun, W.; Dohi, T. Optimal design of unreliable production–inventory systems with variable production rate. *Eur. J. Oper. Res.* **2005**, *162*, 372–386. [CrossRef]
17. Roy, A.; Maity, K.; Kar, S.; Maiti, M. A production–inventory model with remanufacturing for defective and usable items in fuzzy-environment. *Comput. Ind. Eng.* **2009**, *56*, 87–96. [CrossRef]
18. Sana, S.S. A production-inventory model of imperfect quality products in a three-layer supply chain. *Decis. Support Syst.* **2011**, *50*, 539–547. [CrossRef]

19. Sharmila, D.; Uthayakumar, R. An inventory model with three rates of production rate under stock and time dependent demand for time varying deterioration rate with shortages. *Int. J. Adv. Eng. Manag. Sci.* **2016**, *9*, 2.
20. Patra, K.; Maity, R. A Single Item Inventory Model with Variable Production Rate and Defective Items. *Int. J. Appl. Comput. Math.* **2017**, *3*, 19–29. [CrossRef]
21. Dey, O. A fuzzy random integrated inventory model with imperfect production under optimal vendor investment. *Oper. Res.* **2019**, *19*, 101–115. [CrossRef]
22. Mishra, U.; Wu, J.-Z.; Sarkar, B. A sustainable production-inventory model for a controllable carbon emissions rate under shortages. *J. Clean. Prod.* **2020**, *256*, 120268. [CrossRef]
23. Lu, C.-J.; Yang, C.-T.; Yen, H.-F. Stackelberg game approach for sustainable production-inventory model with collaborative investment in technology for reducing carbon emissions. *J. Clean. Prod.* **2020**, *270*, 121963. [CrossRef]
24. Öztürk, H. Optimal production run time for an imperfect production inventory system with rework, random breakdowns and inspection costs. *Oper. Res.* **2021**, *21*, 167–204. [CrossRef]
25. Khara, B.; Mondal, S.K.; Dey, J.K. An imperfect production inventory model with advance payment and credit period in a two-echelon supply chain management. *RAIRO-Oper. Res.* **2021**, *55*, 189–211. [CrossRef]
26. Malik, A.I.; Sarkar, B. Disruption management in a constrained multi-product imperfect production system. *J. Manuf. Syst.* **2020**, *56*, 227–240. [CrossRef] [PubMed]
27. Lin, H.J. An economic production quantity model with backlogging and imperfect rework process for uncertain demand. *Int. J. Prod. Res.* **2021**, *59*, 467–482. [CrossRef]
28. Rizky, N.; Wangsa, I.D.; Jauhari, W.A.; Wee, H.M. Managing a sustainable integrated inventory model for imperfect production process with type one and type two errors. *Clen Technol. Environ. Policy* **2021**, *23*, 2697–2712. [CrossRef]
29. Resh, M.; Friedman, M.; Barbosa, L.C. On a General Solution of the Deterministic Lot Size Problem with Time-Proportional Demand. *Oper. Res.* **1976**, *24*, 718–725. [CrossRef]
30. Urban, T.L. Inventory models with the demand rate dependent on stock and shortage levels. *Int. J. Prod. Econ.* **1995**, *40*, 21–28. [CrossRef]
31. Chang, C.-T. Inventory models with stock-dependent demand and nonlinear holding costs for deteriorating items. *Asia-Pac. J. Oper. Res.* **2004**, *21*, 435–446. [CrossRef]
32. Mukhopadhyay, S.; Mukherjee, R.N.; Chaudhuri, K.S. An EOQ model with two-parameter Weibull distribution deterioration and price-dependent demand. *Int. J. Math. Educ. Sci. Technol.* **2005**, *36*, 25–33. [CrossRef]
33. You, P.-S. Ordering and pricing of service products in an advance sales system with price-dependent demand. *Eur. J. Oper. Res.* **2006**, *170*, 57–71. [CrossRef]
34. Khanra, S.; Mandal, B.; Sarkar, B. An inventory model with time dependent demand and shortages under trade credit policy. *Econ. Model.* **2013**, *35*, 349–355. [CrossRef]
35. Bhunia, A.K.; Shaikh, A.A. A deterministic inventory model for deteriorating items with selling price dependent demand and three-parameter Weibull distributed deterioration. *Int. J. Ind. Eng. Comput.* **2014**, *5*, 495–510. [CrossRef]
36. Prasad, K.; Mukherjee, B. Optimal inventory model under stock and time dependent demand for time varying deterioration rate with shortages. *Ann. Oper. Res.* **2014**, *243*, 323–334. [CrossRef]
37. Manna, A.K.; Dey, J.K.; Mondal, S.K. Imperfect production inventory model with production rate dependent defective rate and advertisement dependent demand. *Comput. Ind. Eng.* **2017**, *104*, 9–22. [CrossRef]
38. Jain, S.; Tiwari, S.; Cárdenas-Barrón, L.E.; Shaikh, A.A.; Singh, S.R. A fuzzy imperfect production and repair inventory model with time dependent demand, production and repair rates under inflationary conditions. *RAIRO-Oper. Res.* **2018**, *52*, 217–239. [CrossRef]
39. Alfares, H.K.; Ghaithan, A.M. Inventory and pricing model with price-dependent demand, time-varying holding cost, and quantity discounts. *Comput. Ind. Eng.* **2016**, *94*, 170–177. [CrossRef]
40. Shaikh, A.A.; Cárdenas-Barrón, L.E.; Tiwari, S. A two-warehouse inventory model for non-instantaneous deteriorating items with interval-valued inventory costs and stock-dependent demand under inflationary conditions. *Neural Comput. Appl.* **2017**, *31*, 1931–1948. [CrossRef]
41. Rahman, S.; Duary, A.; Shaikh, A.A.; Bhunia, A.K. An application of parametric approach for interval differential equation in inventory model for deteriorating items with selling-price-dependent demand. *Neural Comput. Appl.* **2020**, *32*, 14069–14085. [CrossRef]
42. Cárdenas-Barrón, L.E.; Shaikh, A.A.; Tiwari, S.; Treviño-Garza, G. An EOQ inventory model with nonlinear stock dependent holding cost, nonlinear stock dependent demand and trade credit. *Comput. Ind. Eng.* **2020**, *139*, 105557. [CrossRef]
43. Das, S.; Manna, A.K.; Mahmoud, E.E.; Abualnaja, K.M.; Abdel-Aty, A.-H.; Shaikh, A.A. Product Replacement Policy in a Production Inventory Model with Replacement Period-, Stock-, and Price-Dependent Demand. *J. Math.* **2020**, *2020*, 6697279. [CrossRef]
44. Halim, M.A.; Paul, A.; Mahmoud, M.; Alshahrani, B.; Alazzawi, A.Y.; Ismail, G.M. An overtime production inventory model for deteriorating items with nonlinear price and stock dependent demand. *Alex. Eng. J.* **2021**, *60*, 2779–2786. [CrossRef]
45. Rahman, S.; Duary, A.; Khan, A.-A.; Shaikh, A.A.; Bhunia, A.K. Interval valued demand related inventory model under all units discount facility and deterioration via parametric approach. *Artif. Intell. Rev.* **2021**, 1–40. Available online: https://link.springer.com/article/10.1007%2Fs10462-021-10069-1 (accessed on 13 August 2021). [CrossRef]

46. Ghare, P.M.; Schrader, G.F. An inventory model for exponentially deteriorating items. *J. Ind. Eng.* **1963**, *14*, 238–243.
47. Emmons, H. A Replenishment Model for Radioactive Nuclide Generators. *Manag. Sci.* **1968**, *14*, 263–274. [CrossRef]
48. Datta, T.A.; Pal, A.K. Order level inventory system with power demand pattern for items with variable rate of deterioration. *Indian J. Pure Appl. Math.* **1988**, *19*, 1043–1053.
49. Wee, H.-M. A replenishment policy for items with a price-dependent demand and a varying rate of deterioration. *Prod. Plan. Control.* **1997**, *8*, 494–499. [CrossRef]
50. Ouyang, L.Y.; Wu, K.S.; Yang, C.T. A study on an inventory model for non-instantaneous deteriorating items with permissible delay in payments. *Comput. Ind. Eng.* **2006**, *51*, 637–651. [CrossRef]
51. Min, J.; Zhou, Y.-W.; Zhao, J. An inventory model for deteriorating items under stock-dependent demand and two-level trade credit. *Appl. Math. Model.* **2010**, *34*, 3273–3285. [CrossRef]
52. Dash, B.P.; Singh, T.; Pattnayak, H. An Inventory Model for Deteriorating Items with Exponential Declining Demand and Time-Varying Holding Cost. *Am. J. Oper. Res.* **2014**, *4*, 1–7. [CrossRef]
53. Dutta, D.; Kumar, P. A partial backlogging inventory model for deteriorating items with time-varying demand and holding cost. *Int. J. Math. Oper. Res.* **2015**, *7*, 281–296. [CrossRef]
54. Shah, N.H. Three-layered integrated inventory model for deteriorating items with quadratic demand and two-level trade credit financing. *Int. J. Syst. Sci. Oper. Logist.* **2015**, *4*, 1–7. [CrossRef]
55. Tiwari, S.; Cárdenas-Barrón, L.E.; Goh, M.; Shaikh, A.A. Joint pricing and inventory model for deteriorating items with expiration dates and partial backlogging under two-level partial trade credits in supply chain. *Int. J. Prod. Econ.* **2018**, *200*, 16–36. [CrossRef]
56. Shaw, B.K.; Sangal, I.; Sarkar, B. Joint Effects of Carbon Emission, Deterioration, and Multi-stage Inspection Policy in an Integrated Inventory Model. In *Optimization and Inventory Management*; Springer: Singapore, 2020; pp. 195–208.
57. Mashud, A.H.M.; Roy, D.; Daryanto, Y.; Ali, M.H. A Sustainable Inventory Model with Imperfect Products, Deterioration, and Controllable Emissions. *Mathematics* **2020**, *8*, 2049. [CrossRef]
58. Khakzad, A.; Gholamian, M.R. The effect of inspection on deterioration rate: An inventory model for deteriorating items with advanced payment. *J. Clean. Prod.* **2020**, *254*, 120117. [CrossRef]
59. Mishra, U.; Mashud, A.; Tseng, M.-L.; Wu, J.-Z. Optimizing a Sustainable Supply Chain Inventory Model for Controllable Deterioration and Emission Rates in a Greenhouse Farm. *Mathematics* **2021**, *9*, 495. [CrossRef]
60. Khanna, A.; Jaggi, C.K. An inventory model under price and stock dependent demand for controllable deterioration rate with shortages and preservation technology investment: Revisited. *OPSEARCH* **2021**, *58*, 181–202.
61. Naik, M.K.; Shah, N.H. A coordinated single-vendor single-buyer inventory system with deterioration and freight discounts. In *Soft Computing in Inventory Management*; Springer: Singapore, 2021; pp. 205–224.
62. Hsu, P.; Wee, H.; Teng, H. Preservation technology investment for deteriorating inventory. *Int. J. Prod. Econ.* **2010**, *124*, 388–394. [CrossRef]
63. Dye, C.-Y. The effect of preservation technology investment on a non-instantaneous deteriorating inventory model. *Omega* **2013**, *41*, 872–880. [CrossRef]
64. Zhang, J.; Bai, Z.; Tang, W. Optimal pricing policy for deteriorating items with preservation technology investment. *J. Ind. Manag. Optim.* **2014**, *10*, 1261–1277. [CrossRef]
65. Yang, C.-T.; Dye, C.-Y.; Ding, J.-F. Optimal dynamic trade credit and preservation technology allocation for a deteriorating inventory model. *Comput. Ind. Eng.* **2015**, *87*, 356–369. [CrossRef]
66. Tayal, S.; Singh, S.R.; Sharma, R. An integrated production inventory model for perishable products with trade credit period and investment in preservation technology. *Int. J. Math. Oper. Res.* **2016**, *8*, 137. [CrossRef]
67. Dhandapani, J.; Uthayakumar, R. Multi-item EOQ model for fresh fruits with preservation technology investment, time-varying holding cost, variable deterioration and shortages. *J. Control. Decis.* **2016**, *4*, 1–11. [CrossRef]
68. Shaikh, A.A.; Panda, G.C.; Sahu, S.; Das, A.K. Economic order quantity model for deteriorating item with preservation technology in time dependent demand with partial backlogging and trade credit. *Int. J. Logist. Syst. Manag.* **2019**, *32*, 1–24.
69. Das, S.C.; Zidan, A.; Manna, A.K.; Shaikh, A.A.; Bhunia, A.K. An application of preservation technology in inventory control system with price dependent demand and partial backlogging. *Alex. Eng. J.* **2020**, *59*, 1359–1369.
70. Saha, S.; Chatterjee, D.; Sarkar, B. The ramification of dynamic investment on the promotion and preservation technology for inventory management through a modified flower pollination algorithm. *J. Retail. Consum. Serv.* **2021**, *58*, 102326. [CrossRef]
71. Mashud, A.H.M.; Wee, H.-M.; Huang, C.-V. Preservation technology investment, trade credit and partial backordering model for a non-instantaneous deteriorating inventory. *RAIRO Oper. Res.* **2021**, *55*, S51–S77. [CrossRef]
72. Sepehri, A.; Mishra, U.; Sarkar, B. A sustainable production-inventory model with imperfect quality under preservation technology and quality improvement investment. *J. Clean. Prod.* **2021**, *310*, 127332. [CrossRef]
73. Kapuscinski, R.; Tayur, S. A Capacitated Production-Inventory Model with Periodic Demand. *Oper. Res.* **1998**, *46*, 899–911. [CrossRef]
74. Sana, S.; Goyal, S.; Chaudhuri, K. A production–inventory model for a deteriorating item with trended demand and shortages. *Eur. J. Oper. Res.* **2004**, *157*, 357–371. [CrossRef]
75. Lo, S.T.; Wee, H.M.; Huang, W.C. An integrated production-inventory model with imperfect production processes and Weibull distribution deterioration under inflation. *Int. J. Prod. Econ.* **2007**, *106*, 248–260. [CrossRef]

76. Sarkar, B. A production-inventory model with probabilistic deterioration in two-echelon supply chain management. *Appl. Math. Model.* **2013**, *37*, 3138–3151. [CrossRef]
77. Samanta, G.; Roy, A. A production inventory model with deteriorating items and shortages. *Yugosl. J. Oper. Res.* **2004**, *14*, 219–230. [CrossRef]
78. Bhunia, A.K.; Shaikh, A.A.; Cárdenas-Barrón, L.E. A partially integrated production-inventory model with interval valued inventory costs, variable demand and flexible reliability. *Appl. Soft Comput.* **2017**, *55*, 491–502. [CrossRef]
79. Rastogi, M.; Singh, S.R. A production inventory model for deteriorating products with selling price dependent consumption rate and shortages under inflationary environment. *Int. J. Procure. Manag.* **2018**, *11*, 36–52. [CrossRef]
80. Ullah, M.; Sarkar, B.; Asghar, I. Effects of Preservation Technology Investment on Waste Generation in a Two-Echelon Supply Chain Model. *Mathematics* **2019**, *7*, 189. [CrossRef]
81. Salas-Navarro, K.; Acevedo-Chedid, J.; Árquez, G.M.; Florez, W.F.; Ospina-Mateus, H.; Sana, S.S.; Cárdenas-Barrón, L.E. An EPQ inventory model considering an imperfect production system with probabilistic demand and collaborative approach. *J. Adv. Manag. Res.* **2019**, *17*, 282–304. [CrossRef]
82. Das, S.K.; Islam, S. Multi-item a supply chain production inventory model of time dependent production rate and demand rate under space constraint in fuzzy environment. *Indep. J. Manag. Prod.* **2020**, *11*, 304–323. [CrossRef]
83. Saren, S.; Sarkar, B.; Bachar, R.K. Application of Various Price-Discount Policy for Deteriorated Products and Delay-In-Payments in an Advanced Inventory Model. *Inventions* **2020**, *5*, 50. [CrossRef]
84. Su, R.-H.; Weng, M.-W.; Yang, C.-T.; Li, H.-T. An Imperfect Production–Inventory Model with Mixed Materials Containing Scrap Returns Based on a Circular Economy. *Processes* **2021**, *9*, 1275. [CrossRef]
85. Chen, T.-L.; Lin, J.T.; Wu, C.-H. Coordinated capacity planning in two-stage thin-film-transistor liquid-crystal-display (TFT-LCD) production networks. *Omega* **2014**, *42*, 141–156. [CrossRef]

 *mathematics*

Article

A Dynamical Model for Financial Market: Among Common Market Strategies Who and How Moves the Price to Fluctuate, Inflate, and Burst?

Annalisa Fabretti

Department of Economics and Finance, University of Rome Tor Vergata, 00133 Rome, Italy; annalisa.fabretti@uniroma2.it

Abstract: A piecewise linear dynamical model is proposed for a stock price. The model considers the price is driven by three rather standard demand components: chartist, fundamental and market makers. The chartist demand component is related to the study of differences between moving averages. This generates a high order system characterized by a piecewise linear map not trivial to study. The model has been studied analytically in its fixed points and dynamics and then numerically. Results are in line with the related literature: the fundamental demand component helps the stability of the system and keeps prices bounded; market makers satisfy their role of restoring stability, while the chartist demand component produces irregularity and chaos. However, in some cases, the chartist demand component assumes the role to compensate the fundamental demand component, felt in an autogenerated loop, and pushes the dynamics to equilibrium. This fact suggests that the instability must not be searched into the nature of the different investment styles rather in the relative proportion of the contribution of market actors.

Keywords: dynamical systems; financial markets; investment style; border collision bifurcation; fundamental analysis; technical analysis; market maker

MSC: 39A60; 91-10; 91B69

Citation: Fabretti, A. A Dynamical Model for Financial Market: Among Common Market Strategies Who and How Moves the Price to Fluctuate, Inflate, and Burst? *Mathematics* **2022**, *10*, 679. https://doi.org/10.3390/math10050679

Academic Editor: Arsen Palestini

Received: 10 January 2022
Accepted: 17 February 2022
Published: 22 February 2022

Publisher's Note: MDPI stays neutral with regard to jurisdictional claims in published maps and institutional affiliations.

Copyright: © 2022 by the author. Licensee MDPI, Basel, Switzerland. This article is an open access article distributed under the terms and conditions of the Creative Commons Attribution (CC BY) license (https://creativecommons.org/licenses/by/4.0/).

1. Introduction

Financial markets are complex systems whose functioning has been studied and discussed largely in literature. Conventionally, markets are seen as populated by rational investors that arbitrage away any possible predictable gain, thus what is left is just perturbation with null returns. However psychological forces unquestionably play a role in financial crashes, for example, it happened in 1929, on the Black Monday of October 1987, or in the dot.com bubble of 2001. Bubbles and crashes cannot be explained by an efficient market, where prices are supposed to reflect all the available information. Starting from empirical facts that cannot be explained by the efficient market hypothesis and observable features that can be seen as the outcome of speculative activities, a large stream of literature developed models in which prices are driven by the demand of heterogeneous market participants. The addressed issues consisted in understanding how irregular patterns, alternating periods of bull and bear markets, can be derivable from the way actors participate in the market. One of the first behavioral model in this direction was proposed in [1] with linear trading rules that were successively extended to non-linear versions in [2,3]. At the same time, imitative behavior and switching between investment styles have been also largely addressed to explain the emergence of fads, herding behavior, and financial bubbles [3–5]. Such a field intersects also with some empirical literature that looks at financial data searches for chaotic traces instead of randomness [6–9].

In the mentioned literature two rather standard approaches in terms of investment styles are considered: fundamental analysis and technical analysis. The fundamental analysis supports the trading through a deep analysis of the real economy behind the asset and evaluating the future earnings; in this respect, a fundamental value will summarize the outcome of such analysis and will drive the trader's order submission. The technical analysis, based on graphs and indices, return trends and the market sentiment, provides concise tools to understand where the market is going. Professional traders rely both on technical and fundamental analysis to determine whether and how to participate in the market. Hence the model considers the price driven by a composite demand in which fundamentals and indices contribute together to move the price. Moreover, the third typology of component is considered, hereafter referred to as market makers' demand: market makers are specific entrepreneurs who accomplish the task to absorb excess demand if any. The fundamental and chartist demand components are assumed piecewise linear, indeed it is quite common that an investor does not participate continuously in the market rather she enters (buy) or exits (sell) the market if something gives her a signal of unfair prices or trend inversion; in other words, an investor submits an order, whatever it is, when something happens to suggest the presence of earning opportunities. Thus the model belongs to that part of literature that sees markets as financial dynamical systems and applies continuous and discontinuous piecewise smooth maps in economics and finance, as [10–12]; in the specific financial markets, see [13] for a review. In the present model, the chartist demand component is given by a common chartist investment strategy that uses the difference of moving averages to catch trend inversions. From the mathematical point of view, this leads to a large first-order difference equation system whose study is not so straightforward. The equilibrium points and their stability can be studied only partially; the bifurcations that occur belong to the class of border collision bifurcations for which analytical results are still limited to low order systems [14–16].

The analytical and numerical analysis confirm that demand based on fundamental analysis keeps prices around the fundamental value even when chaos appears. Demand based on technical analysis can in large amount contribute to enhancing the chaos of the system and the price oscillations, while market makers assume the role to stabilize the market. The presence in the market of investors, those who try to speculate without caring about fundamentals, generates dynamics that remove the price from its fundamental value because their action drives the market in the same direction the market goes, giving strength to the trend. A clear example of such a phenomenon is represented by the financial bubble (see [17,18]): increasing prices lead investors to buy, which feeds the price increase far away from its fundamental. On the other hand, when the price is so pumped, it starts a period of instability, then a crash can occur, or a smooth deflation will bring back the price near its fundamental. In the model each demand component is weighted by a specific parameter, the ratios between these parameters give the balance between the investment styles relative dominance. Results are anything but surprising, and in line with the related literature, however, the emergence of a situation in which the fundamental demand component alone generates periodic prices and small amounts of chartist demand push prices to converge. How can chartist demand push to equilibrium a periodic dynamic triggered by the fundamentals? In an attempt to answer this question: while the fundamental demand component generates a loop that feeds a periodic up and down of prices, the chartist demand component that moves in an opposite direction operates as softening the fundamental force resulting in a convergent price. One could argue that the interaction of different investments styles in the market generates disequilibrium in prices when their contribution is out of proportion, otherwise, the market moves chaotic without spikes or anomalies, apparently in line with the efficient market hypothesis. In other words, one can conclude that the observed instability does not derive from the presence of some specific investment style in itself, rather from a disproportion of their reciprocal contributions to form the total demand.

The novelty of the model stays in introducing: (a) a common chartist investment strategy that sees applied the moving averages; in particular, the difference between two moving averages, as used by technical analysis, involves the use of past prices in the long and short term, leading to a high order system whose study is anything but trivial to face; (b) the market makers demand so far has not experienced enough attention in the related literature. Future investigations will move in the direction of studying deeply the border collisions bifurcation in high order system as it occurs here; adding sophistication to the market makers demand via a piecewise map, which would be more reasonable from the economic point of view; developing a stochastic version of the model to replicate more realistically the market and allowing for calibration on real data.

The rest of the paper is organized as follows: Section 2 presents the model with all its components in details; Section 3 presents the analytical study of the system in each component, in the limit of their tractability; Section 4 presents numerical examples with relative observations and results; in Section 5 a general discussion on the model is provided; finally Section 6 concludes.

2. A Financial Market Model

The proposed model considers the price as moved by the market demand, driven by three rather standard components: a fundamental component, set according to a "fair" price deriving from fundamental analysis; a chartist component, that follows the market trend by using technical analysis, and a market makers component, that helps liquidity and price fluidity absorbing demand in excess.

Let x_t and y_t be the stock price and the demand at time t, respectively. They can be put in relation by a difference equation system of the type

$$\begin{aligned} x_t &= ax_{t-1} + by_{t-1} \\ y_t &= y_t^f + y_t^c + y_t^{mm} \end{aligned} \quad (1)$$

where y_t^f, y_t^c and y_t^{mm} are the fundamental, chartist and market makers demands, respectively. The price is driven by past prices, just one step before, and the demand y_{t-1}. The price dependence with respect to the past and the demand could be modeled in many different maps, for the sake of tractability the linear map remains one of the most adopted choices.

Under the action of the three market forces, prices will move up and down, showing stable, periodic, or chaotic behavior. Each market component can dominate more than others pushing the market to an equilibrium price or an erratic movement, that even in a stylized fashion can remind real market reproducing known stylized facts. Each component will be studied analytically and numerically, varying the specific parameters that balance the weight of each component. In the following, each component will be described in detail.

2.1. Fundamental Demand

The fundamental strategy is built around the fundamental price that each agent evaluates according to her perception and belief, selecting the relevant economic and financial factors which contribute to producing the supposed security's intrinsic value. For the sake of simplicity, we consider a demand driven by a unique fundamental price as all the investors agree on it. A heterogenous specification of the fundamental value could be adopted to incorporate heterogenous agents' beliefs; for example, we could select a fundamental value following a random walk which can incorporate also the effect of news arrival, as in [5,19], however, it would add more complexity to the model.

Given v the fundamental price, the stock results overvalued if $x_t > v$, the stock is correctly valued if $x_t = v$, and the stock is undervalued if $x_t < v$; then an investor sells, holds her position, or buys, respectively, because she expects prices decreasing or increasing accordingly. In literature this has been often modeled by a linear function $y_t^f \sim (v - x)$, which can generate an unlimited demand; however limited money availability could suggest that a bounded function could fit better the bounded reality, for example, the following

$$y^f = c \arctan(V - x). \quad (2)$$

The Equation (2) owns the quality to be continuous and smooth, however its analytical tractability could be hard. Then a piecewise linearized version around v could be more suitable:

$$y^f = \begin{cases} d & \text{if} \quad x < v - \delta \\ c(v-x) & \text{if} \quad v - \delta \leq x \leq v + \delta \\ -d & \text{if} \quad x > v + \delta \end{cases}. \quad (3)$$

Note that the map is continuous if $d = c\delta$, discontinuous otherwise. This map can be written also as

$$y^f = c(v-x)\chi_{[v-\delta,v+\delta]} - d\chi_{(v+\delta,\infty)} + d\chi_{(\infty,v-\delta)}.$$

where χ_A is the indicator function of set A.

The dynamics of these maps will be analyzed in Section 3.1.

2.2. Chartist Demand

The technical analysis attempts to interpret the evolution of the market by looking at charts, for this reason, the investors using such analysis are called often chartists. According to the technical analysis, the price charts present recurrent figures (head and shoulders, Elliot's wave, triangular forms, just for citing some examples); such figures can indicate evolution, persistence, or inversion of trend. If the market is in a down-trend (bearish) the technical analysis suggests selling, and if it is in an up-trend (bullish) to buy; price dynamics are often summarized by indicators as moving averages, those are built such that they can generate a signal of market changes.

Investment decisions in technical analysis are the result of complex evaluations based on market observation by means of charts, signals, oscillators involving prices, volumes, and any variable of interest. Among the most commonly used indicators, there are moving averages, that smooth the price dynamics, clearing it from temporary oscillations. The difference between two moving averages, a long and a short one is a common indicator sensible to a trend inversion. The moving average (ma) at time t on K days is defined by

$$ma_K(t) = \frac{1}{K} \sum_{i=t-K+1}^{t} x_i; \quad (4)$$

it is a smooth line of prices that shows the development of the price following it without anticipating. It is a popular practice to use and compare two moving averages, one on the long term, one on the short term; the former catches the main trend while the latter is more sensitive to short time fluctuations; their difference, called a difference of averages (*doa*), is such that it generates a signal as they cross each other; indeed, in the short term, ma is lower than the long-term ma and their position inverts, the short ma is catching an increasing trend inversion; while when the short term is greater than the long one and their position inverts, their intersection signals a decreasing trend beginning. Formally, let doa_t be

$$doa_t = ma_S(t) - ma_L(t), \quad (5)$$

where $S < L$, i.e., $ma_S(t)$ is the short term moving average and $ma_L(t)$ is the long term moving average, briefly we have:

$$\begin{array}{ll} \text{if} \quad doa_{t-1} < 0 < doa_t & \text{then buy,} \\ \text{if} \quad doa_{t-1} > 0 > doa_t & \text{then sell.} \end{array} \quad (6)$$

In a few words, the signal is generated when the *doa*-line crosses zero, if it does from below, the signal is to buy, if it does from above is to sell. Introducing such an indicator in the chartist demand, we get

$$y^c = e \cdot (doa_t - doa_{t-1}) \cdot \chi(doa_t \cdot doa_{t-1} < 0) \quad (7)$$

where e is the specific chartist parameter and χ is the indicator function. Given (4), we have

$$doa_t - doa_{t-1} = \frac{1}{S}(x_t - x_{t-S}) - \frac{1}{L}(x_t - x_{t-L}), \tag{8}$$

it results

$$y_t^c = e \cdot \left(\frac{1}{S}(x_t - x_{t-S}) - \frac{1}{L}(x_t - x_{t-L})\right)\chi(D), \tag{9}$$

where $D = \{x_i, \ i = t - L, \ldots, t \mid doa_t \cdot doa_{t-1} < 0\}$.

2.3. Market Makers Demand

Market makers clean the market by excess demand, so they buy or sell in opposition to the market behavior. For this reason, the easiest expression is

$$y_t^{mm} = -d_m y_{t-1},$$

where d_m is the reaction parameter that balances the market makers' presence in the market.

3. The Analytical Study

Fundamental and chartist components are piecewise linear maps of first and $L+1$ order. In the present section, fundamental and chartist demand components are first considered singularly and analytically studied to the limit of their tractability, then they will be studied together. The market makers' demand will not be considered alone because this lacks economic sense.

3.1. The Model with Fundamental Demand

Let us start with the map

$$\begin{cases} x_t = ax_{t-1} + by_{t-1} \\ y_t = c \arctan(v - x_{t-1}). \end{cases} \tag{10}$$

The system can be re-written in one equation

$$x_t = ax_{t-1} + bc \arctan(v - x_{t-2}), \tag{11}$$

which is a one-dimensional map but a second-order difference equation. This map admits a positive fixed point lower than v for $\frac{1-a}{bc} > 0$, a negative fixed point for $\frac{1-a}{bc} < m^*$ and one negative and two positive fixed points greater than v for $m^* < \frac{1-a}{bc} < 0$, where m^* is given by

$$m^* = \frac{1}{1 + (v - x_s^*)^2}, \tag{12}$$

given x_s^* to be the solution of the equation

$$\frac{x_s^*}{1 + (v - x_s^*)^2} + \arctan(v - x_s^*) = 0.$$

The local/global stability of such points can be studied numerically; the trajectories appear in some cases non trivial, but a full analytical study is hindered by the presence of the arctang. The map in (10) can be approximated by a two-dimensional piecewise smooth map, which shows interesting behavior, and it is more analytically tractable. Note that parameters in the piecewise smooth map can be set to have a continuous map that approximates (10), the calculation is straightforward. For the sake of simplicity, we use the same notations even if they might differ.

Let us consider now the piecewise linear map

$$\begin{cases} x_t = ax_{t-1} + by_{t-1} \\ y_t = c(v - x_{t-1})\chi(x_{t-1})_{[v-\delta,v+\delta]} - d\chi(x_{t-1})_{(v+\delta,\infty)} + d\chi(x_{t-1})_{(\infty,v-\delta)} \end{cases} \tag{13}$$

which can be written in a normal form

$$z_t = \begin{cases} A_1 z_{t-1} + d\overrightarrow{1} & x_n < v - \delta \\ A_2 z_{t-1} + c\overrightarrow{v} & v - \delta \leq x_n \leq v + \delta \\ A_1 z_{t-1} - d\overrightarrow{1} & x_n > v + \delta \end{cases}, \quad (14)$$

where $z_t = (x_t, y_t)$, $\overrightarrow{v} = (v, 0)'$, $\overrightarrow{1} = (0, 1)'$ and

$$A_1 = \begin{pmatrix} a & b \\ 0 & 0 \end{pmatrix}, \quad A_2 = \begin{pmatrix} a & b \\ -c & 0 \end{pmatrix}.$$

The phase space of this map is divided by the borderlines $x = v - \delta$, $x = v + \delta$ into 3 regions $\mathcal{L}_1 := \{(x, y) \in \mathbb{R}^2 : x < v - \delta\}$, $\mathcal{L}_2 := \{(x, y) \in \mathbb{R}^2 : v - \delta \leq x \leq v + \delta\}$ and $\mathcal{L}_3 := \{(x, y) \in \mathbb{R}^2 : x > v + \delta\}$; in each region the dynamics follows a linear map continuous in its relative region. The map is invertible if $bc \neq 0$. By a straightforward calculation we find that the map owns three fixed points $O_i \in \mathcal{L}_i$ with $i = 1, 2, 3$,

$$\begin{array}{lll} O_1 = \left(\frac{bd}{1-a}, d\right) & if & \frac{bd}{1-a} < v - \delta \\ O_2 = \left(\frac{bcv}{1-a+bc}, cv\frac{1-a}{1-a+bc}\right) & if & v - \delta \leq \frac{bcv}{1-a+bc} \leq v + \delta \\ O_3 = \left(-\frac{bd}{1-a}, -d\right) & if & -\frac{bd}{1-a} > v + \delta \end{array} \quad (15)$$

Each of these three points exists in an own existence region according to parameters value (a, b, c, d, δ, v). In order to determine the stability, we need to calculate the eigenvalues of matrices A_1 and A_2, where the characteristic polynomials are

$$p_1(\lambda) = \lambda(a - \lambda), \quad p_2(\lambda) = \lambda^2 - a\lambda + bc.$$

Since $p_1(\lambda)$ admits $\lambda = 0$ and $\lambda = a$ as roots, O_1 and O_3 are stable if $a < 1$. The polynomial $p_2(\lambda)$ has discriminant $\Delta = a^2 - 4bc$ that depicts different stability regions according to a, b, c values. The curve $\Delta = 0$ partitions the space $\mathbb{R}^3$ into two regions where the eigenvalues are

- real and distinct if $\Delta > 0$,
- real and equal if $\Delta = 0$,
- complex if $\Delta < 0$.

The bifurcation conditions are given by

$$\begin{array}{ll} Period \ doubling(flip): & 1 + a + bc = 0 \\ Saddle - node(foldbif.): & 1 - a + bc = 0 \\ Neimark \ Sacker: & bc = 1. \end{array} \quad (16)$$

In Figure 1 (**left**) the stability regions and the bifurcation curves are represented in the (a, b) plane with $c = 1$, while in (**middle**) the stability regions and the bifurcation curves are represented in the (b, c) plane with $a = 1$. In Figure 2 (**left:right**) the bifurcation surfaces are shown in the (a, b, c) space. The conditions for the asymptotic stability are

$$\begin{array}{rcl} 1 - Tr(A_2) + Det(A_2) & = & 1 + a + bc > 0 \\ 1 + Tr(A_2) + Det(A_2) & = & 1 - a + bc > 0 \\ Det(A_2) & = & bc < 1. \end{array}$$

In Figure 1 the asymptotic stability region is highlighted by the striped area. Simulations and relative discussion of this case are reported in Section 4.

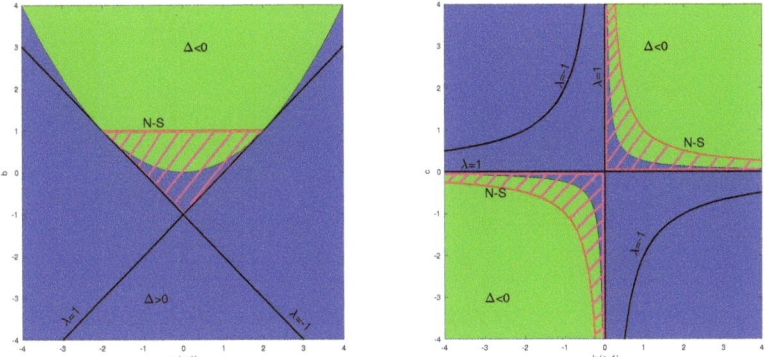

Figure 1. In (**a**) on the left hand side the bifurcation conditions together with the asymptotic stability region of the map in Equation (14) are represented in the plane (a,b) with c = 1; In (**b**) on the right-hand side the bifurcation conditions together with the asymptotic stability region are represented in the plane (b,c) with a = 1. The green area corresponds to complex eigenvalues, the blue one to real eigenvalues; the black lines denote the flip and fold bifurcation, the red line marks the Neimarck Sacker bifurcation and the striped area characterizes the asymptotic stability region.

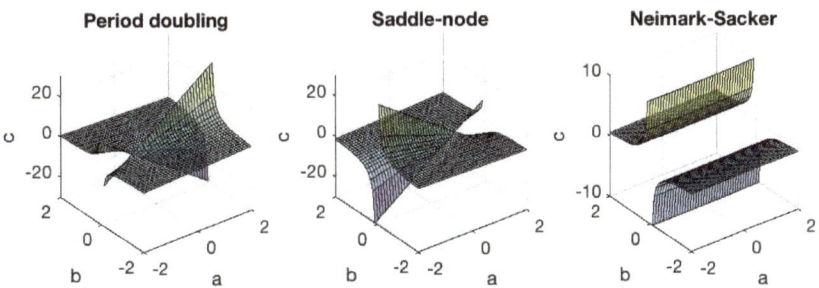

Figure 2. (**left**), (**middle**), (**right**) show the three bifurcation conditions in Equation (16) represented in the space (a,b,c).

3.2. The Model with Fundamental and Market Makers Demands

In the following section, we consider fundamental demand together with market makers. Considering market makers alone have a poor economical meaning, for this reason, it is more of interest to the presented case. We have the following system

$$\begin{cases} x_t = ax_{t-1} + by_{t-1} \\ y_t = c(v - x_{t-1})\chi(x_{t-1})_{[v-\delta,v+\delta]} - d\chi(x_{t-1})_{(v+\delta,\infty)} + d\chi(x_{t-1})_{(\infty,v-\delta)} - d_m y_{t-1} \end{cases}, \quad (17)$$

which corresponds to a normal form as in (14) where

$$A_1 = \begin{pmatrix} a & b \\ 0 & -d_m \end{pmatrix}, \quad A_2 = \begin{pmatrix} a & b \\ -c & -d_m \end{pmatrix}.$$

Matrices A_1 and A_2 are invertible if $ad_m \neq 0$ and $-ad_m + bc \neq 0$, respectively. As in (13) the phase space is divided in 3 regions $\mathcal{L}_i$, with $i = 1, 2, 3$ and a straightforward calculation brings to the following fixed points

$$O_1 = \left(\frac{bd}{(1-a)(1+d_m)}, \frac{d}{1+d_m}\right) \quad if \quad \frac{bd}{(1-a)(1+d_m)} < v - \delta$$
$$O_2 = \left(\frac{bcv}{(1-a)(1+d_m)+bc}, cv\frac{1-a}{(1-a)(1+d_m)+bc}\right) \quad if \quad v - \delta \leq \frac{bcv}{(1-a)(1+d_m)+bc} \leq v + \delta \quad . \quad (18)$$
$$O_3 = \left(-\frac{bd}{(1-a)(1+d_m)}, -\frac{d}{1+d_m}\right) \quad if \quad -\frac{bd}{(1-a)(1+d_m)} > v + \delta$$

Now the parameters set includes the new parameter d_m. The characteristics of polynomials are

$$p_1(\lambda) = (-d_m - \lambda)(a - \lambda), \quad p_2(\lambda) = \lambda^2 + (d_m - a)\lambda - ad_m + bc.$$

In $\mathcal{L}_1$ and $\mathcal{L}_3$ eigenvalues are always real and fixed points are stable if $a < 1$ and $d_m < 1$. Flip bifurcation occurs at $a = 1$ and $d_m = 1$, fold bifurcation occurs at $a = 1$ and $d_m = -1$, while Neimarck Sacker bifurcation occurs when $a = -\frac{1}{d_m}$. The stability region in $\mathcal{L}_2$ is given by the conditions

$$\begin{aligned} (1-a)(1+d_m) + bc &> 0 \\ (1+a)(1-d_m) + bc &> 0 \\ bc - ad_m &< 1 \end{aligned} \quad (19)$$

and bifurcation conditions are

$$\begin{aligned} Period\ doubling(flip): & \quad (1+a)(1-d_m) + bc = 0 \\ Saddle-node(foldbif.): & \quad (1-a)(1+d_m) + bc = 0 \\ Neimark\ Sacker: & \quad bc - ad_m = 1 \end{aligned}.$$

Assuming that $d_m \in [0,1]$ which is economically reasonable, in Figure 3 stability regions and bifurcation curves are plotted with $c = 1$ (lhs) and $a = 1$ (rhs). The triangular region moves accordingly the effect of d_m, while the hyperboles on the right-hand side moves up and down accordingly.

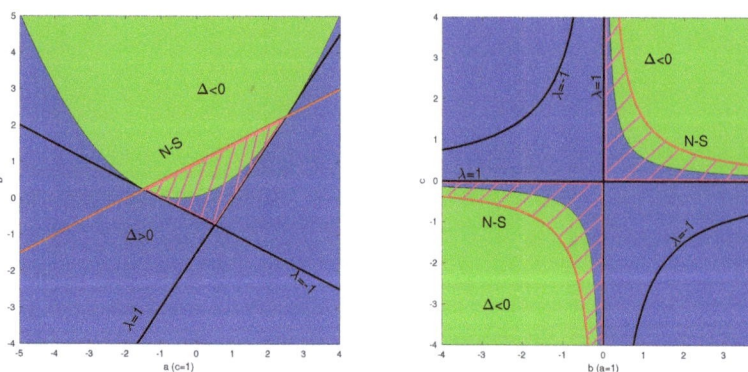

Figure 3. In (**a**) on the left hand side the bifurcation conditions together with the asymptotic stability region of the map in Equation (17) are represented in the plane (*a*, *b*) with *c* = 1; In (**b**) on the right-hand side the bifurcation conditions together with the asymptotic stability region are represented in the plane (*b*,*c*) with *a* = 1. In green the area in which eigenvalues are complex, in blue where eigenvalues are real, the black lines denote the flip and fold bifurcations, the red line marks the Neimarck Sacker bifurcation, and the striped area characterizes the asymptotic stability region. The Figure can be compared with Figure 1 to see that the presence of market makers enlarge the stability region.

3.3. The Model with Chartist Demand

Considering only the chartist component, the model takes the form

$$\begin{cases} x_t = ax_{t-1} + by_{t-1} \\ y_t = e \cdot \left(\frac{1}{S}(x_{t-1} - x_{t-1-S}) - \frac{1}{L}(x_{t-1} - x_{t-1-L}) \right) \chi(D), \end{cases} \quad (20)$$

where $D = \{x_i \text{ with } i = t - L - 1, \ldots, t - 1 \mid doa_{t-1} \cdot doa_{t-2} < 0\}$. It is a system of order $L + 1$, that can be transformed into a $L + 2$ system of first order as following

$$\begin{cases} x_{t+1}^{(1)} = ax_t^{(1)} + bx_t^{(2)}(t) \\ x_{t+1}^{(2)} = e \cdot \left(\frac{1}{S}(x_t^{(1)} - x_t^{(S+2)}) - \frac{1}{L}(x_t^{(1)} - x_t^{(L+2)}) \right) \chi(D) \\ x_{t+1}^{(3)} = x_t^{(1)} \\ x_{t+1}^{(4)} = x_t^{(3)} \\ \vdots \\ x_{t+1}^{(S)} = x_t^{(S-1)} \\ \vdots \\ x_{t+1}^{(L+2)} = x_t^{(L+1)}. \end{cases} \quad (21)$$

Let be $\mathbf{z}_t = (x_t^{(1)}, x_t^{(2)}, \ldots, x_t^{(L+2)})$, the system takes the normal form $\mathbf{z}_t = A\mathbf{z}_{t-1}$ in D, where

$$A = \begin{pmatrix} a & b & 0 & \cdots & & \cdots & 0 \\ \frac{e}{S} - \frac{e}{L} & 0 & 0 & \cdots & 0 & -\frac{e}{S} & \cdots & \frac{e}{L} \\ 1 & 0 & 0 & & 0 & & \cdots & 0 \\ 0 & 0 & 1 & 0 & & \cdots & 0 \\ \vdots & 0 & 0 & 1 & 0 & \cdots & 0 \\ \vdots & & 0 & \vdots & 0 & \ddots & \cdots & 0 \\ \vdots & & 0 & & 0 & \ddots & 1 & 0 \\ 0 & \cdots & & 0 & & \cdots & 0 & 1 \end{pmatrix}. \quad (22)$$

Outside D the system collapses in $x_t = ax_{t-1}$, which has the trivial solution $x_t = a^t x_0$. The characteristic polynomial is given by

$$p(\lambda) = a_1 \lambda^{L+2} + a_2 \lambda^{L+1} + a_3 \lambda^L + a_4 \lambda^{L-S-1} + a_5$$

where $a_1 = (-1)^L$, $a_2 = (-1)^{L+1}a$, $a_3 = (-1)^{L+1}b\left(\frac{e}{S} - \frac{e}{L}\right)$, $a_4 = (-1)^L \frac{eb}{S}$, and $a_5 = (-1)^{L+1} \frac{eb}{L}$. In this case the study of the stability region is not trivial.

3.4. The Complete Model

When all the components are considered the model takes a normal form $\mathbf{z}_t = A\mathbf{z}_{t-1}$ in $D \cup [v - \delta, v + \delta]$ where

$$A = \begin{pmatrix} a & b & 0 & \cdots & & \cdots & 0 \\ -c + \frac{e}{S} - \frac{e}{L} & dm & 0 & \cdots & 0 & -\frac{e}{S} & \cdots & \frac{e}{L} \\ 1 & 0 & 0 & & 0 & & \cdots & 0 \\ 0 & 0 & 1 & 0 & & \cdots & 0 \\ \vdots & 0 & 0 & 1 & 0 & \cdots & 0 \\ \vdots & & 0 & \vdots & 0 & \ddots & \cdots & 0 \\ \vdots & & 0 & & 0 & \ddots & 1 & 0 \\ 0 & \cdots & & 0 & & \cdots & 0 & 1 \end{pmatrix}. \quad (23)$$

Also, in this case, we can write the characteristic polynomial, however, the stability region study is not trivial, and it can be performed only partially. For this reason, in the following, we settle for numerical simulation to discuss the dynamics scenario and the economic implications.

4. Numerical Simulation

In the following, we study numerically all the presented cases. In detail, we start with the fundamental map; then we consider fundamental and market makers' demand together; as a third step we consider chartist demand firstly alone then jointly with fundamental demand and, finally, we combine all the demands. The market makers' demand is studied only associated with fundamental and chartist demands, indeed, as already mentioned, being thought to absorb excess demand, alone it loses reasonability from the economic point of view. In all the simulations it holds $v = 5$, $\delta = \frac{v}{2}$ and $d = 2$. The main discussion is about parameters a, b, c, d_m, e which give the impact of each demand and past prices on the dynamics.

4.1. Fundamental Demand

We investigate the dynamics starting from the analytical results. In the asymptotic stability region, prices go to one of the fixed points with speed according to the parameters. Closer the parameters to the border of the stability region slower the convergence, as it can be seen in Figure 4, comparing the scenario in the top with parameters $a = 1$, $b = 1.9$ and $c = 0.4$ to that in the bottom with $a = 1$, $b = 0.7$ and $c = 1.4$, where the value of c at the border would be $\frac{1}{b} = 1.4286$. Each figure in the following shows price dynamics on the left-hand side and the phase space (x, y) on the right-hand side. Outside the stability region, the dynamic scenarios include periodic orbits and chaotic motion. Some examples of periodic orbits are reported in Figure 5, where on the top there is an orbit of period 6 to be read clockwise; note that in terms of price and demand the orbit is 3-period but they are combined giving 6 couples of price and demand. On the bottom a periodic elliptic orbit appears, this dynamics holds for any value of $a \in (0,1)$ when b and c are equal 1. In this case, the effect of the demand is fixed, while the price drift matters: the higher a the closer the ellipse center to the fixed point $(v, 0)$ and the closer the amplitude to the range $(v - \delta, v + \delta)$. Examples of chaotic motion are reported in Figures 6 and 7. In Figure 6 the plot on the top panel shows prices almost regularly oscillating in the range $(v - \delta, v + \delta)$, since parameters are closed to the stability region border; while on the bottom panel parameters are far from the border and prices oscillate widely. In Figure 7, c is negative; being c the fundamental demand parameter, negative values mimic a trend follower demand, indeed the dynamics show bear and bull period (on the top), a wide range of prices (in the center) and price overvaluation (on the bottom). In Figure 8 bifurcation diagrams with respect c show the map behavior varying c.

4.2. Fundamental and Market Makers

As already discussed, stability regions, see again Figure 3, the presence of market makers tends to regularize prices enlarging the stability region. Outside of this region dynamics scenarios appear very similar to those in the already studied case with only the fundamental demand component. We focus on $d_m \in [0, 1]$ because values outside this interval own low interest from an economic perspective, indeed such a case complies with a reverse effect of market maker that rather absorbing amplifies the excess demand effect. Even if such dynamics could be interesting from the mathematical point of view, its absence of interest from the economical point of view suggests skipping this study. The simulation outcomes do not add any insight to those already discussed in the fundamental demand map, thus no figures about this case are reported.

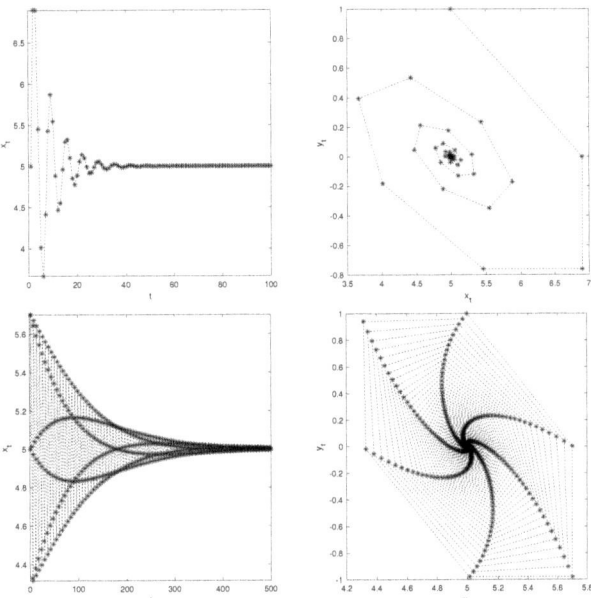

Figure 4. The (**top-left**) shows the price evolution and (**top-right**) the phase space of fundamental map dynamics with $a = 1$, $b = 1.9$ and $c = 0.4$, while (**bottom-left**) and (**bottom-right**) show the price evolution and the phase space of fundamental map dynamics with $a = 1$, $b = 0.7$ and $c = 1.4$ note that the value of c at the border would be $\frac{1}{b} = 1.4286$.

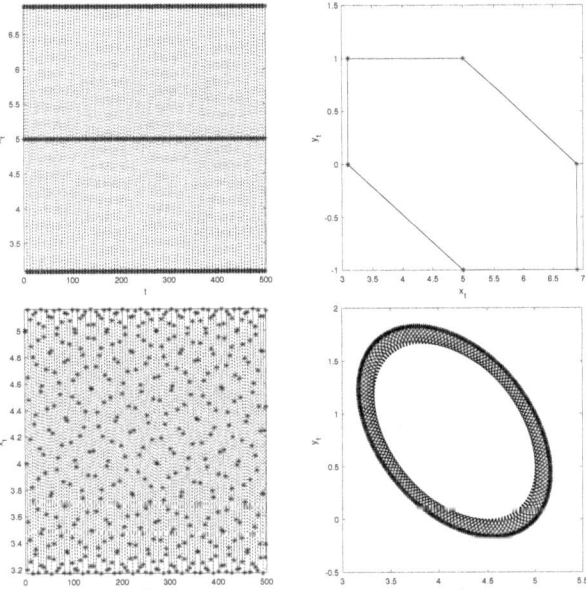

Figure 5. The (**top-left**) shows the price evolution and (**top-right**) the phase space of the fundamental map dynamics with $a = 1$, $b = 1.9$ and $c = \frac{1}{b}$; while (**bottom-left**) and (**bottom-right**) show the price evolution and the phase space of fundamental map dynamics with $a = 0.8$, $b = 1$ and $c = 1$.

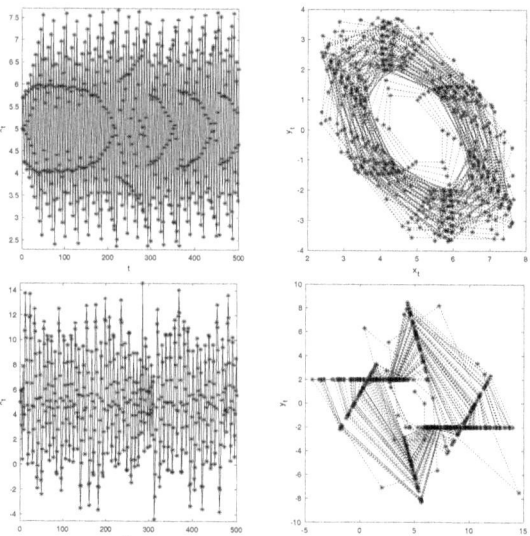

Figure 6. The (**top-left**) shows the price evolution and (**top-right**) the phase space of the fundamental map dynamics with $a = 1$, $b = 0.7$ and $c = 1.5$, note that $\frac{1}{b} = 1.4286$; while (**bottom-left**) and (**bottom-right**) show the price evolution and the phase space of fundamental map dynamics with $a = 1$, $b = 0.9$ and $c = 3.4$.

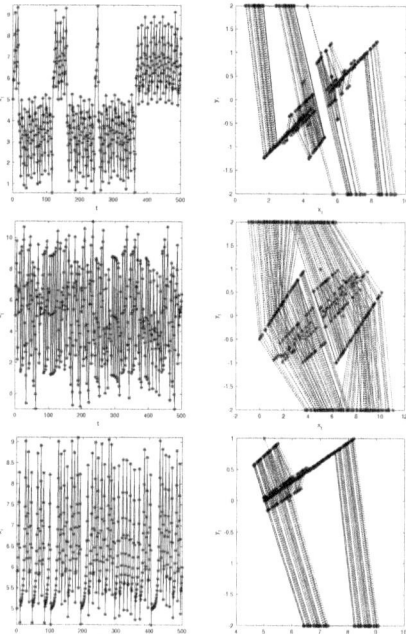

Figure 7. The (**top-left**) shows the price evolution and (**top-right**) the phase space of the fundamental map dynamics with $a = 1$, $b = 0.9$ and $c = -0.5$; while (**middle-left**) and (**middle-right**) show the price evolution and the phase space of fundamental map dynamics with $a = 1$, $b = 1.9$ and $c = -0.4$, while in the (**bottom**) it holds $a = 1$, $b = 0.9$ and $c = -0.4$.

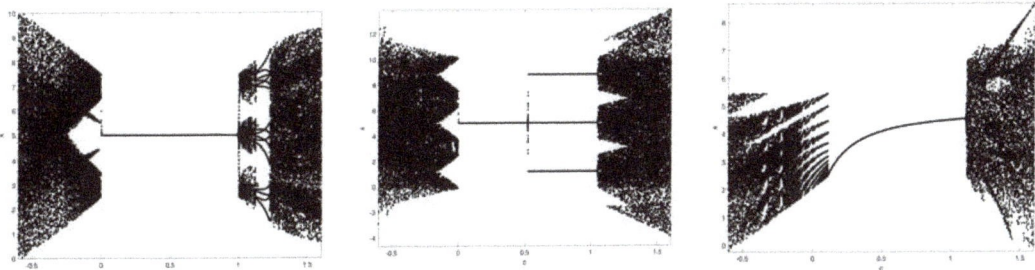

Figure 8. Bifurcation diagrams with respect c of the fundamental map. (**left**) shows the diagram with $a = 1$, $b = 1.9$ and $c \in [-0.6, 1.6]$. (**middle**) shows the diagram with $a = 1$, $b = 1$ and $c \in [-0.6, 1.6]$. (**right**) shows the diagram with $a = 0.9$, $b = 0.9$ and $c \in [-0.6, 1.6]$. Note that having a and b lower than 1 enlarge the area in which a lower/negative c generates chaos.

4.3. Chartist Demand

It is of interest to see how the system behaves when only chartist demand is active. When $a = 1$ and $b = 1$, no matter the chartist contribution, the system converges to a fixed point determined by the initial conditions. When $a < 1$ and $b = 1$ the system shows a rough periodicity for small value of e, i.e., for small contribution of the chartist investment style, and a chaotic behavior for high values of e, see bifurcation diagrams in Figure 9. Lower the b later the chaos appears, since a low b reduces the amplitude of the chartist demand and hence its impact on prices, see Figure 9 in the center. Finally, if a is greater than 1, but still in that range in which prices do not explode, the contribution of the chartist leads directly to chaos, see Figure 9 (rhs).

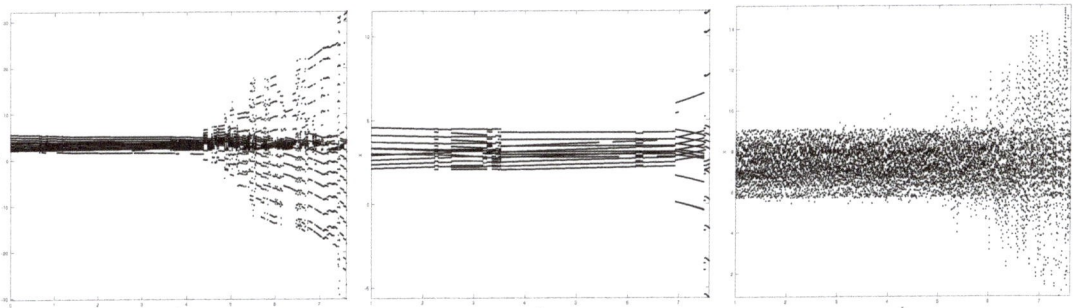

Figure 9. Bifurcation diagrams for the chartist map with respect to the parameter e. (**left**) shows the diagram with $a = 0.9$, $b = 1$ and $e \in [0, 7.6]$. (**middle**) shows the diagram with $a = 0.9$, $b = 0.8$ and $e \in [0, 7.6]$. (**right**) shows the diagram with $a = 1.1$, $b = 0.8$ and $e \in [0, 7.6]$. Note that having the lower the b the later the chaos appears.

4.4. Fundamental and Chartist Demand

Let us now consider the dynamics with the fundamental and chartist demands. In Figure 10 (lhs), a, b, c are the same as those in the bottom of Figure 5, while $e \in [0, 7.6]$. The bifurcation diagrams show that low values of e do not change the dynamics, then the presence of chartist investors stabilizes the price pushing it to converge to a slightly overvalued price. Increasing e the dynamics becomes chaotic with small intervals in which the contribution of chartist demand pushes prices to converge or to oscillate around the equilibrium, not far from the fundamental value. How and why chartist demand can do this is not straightforward to understand and appears counterintuitive. Note that when $a = 1.1$, $b = 0.8$ and $c < \frac{1}{b}$ the fundamental map converges and chartist investors do not affect the convergence, even a large amount of chartists do not change the dynamics. Similarly when $a = 1$ and $b = 1.9$ and $c = \frac{1}{b}$ chartist demand has no effect on the periodic dynamics of fundamental map. Differently, when $a < 1$, $b < 1$ and $c < \frac{1}{b}$, such that the fundamental map dynamics is asymptotically stable, a small presence of chartist has no effect, while high values of e move the dynamics into chaos. Note that in Figure 10 (rhs) there is a range of e in which the price oscillates chaotic into the range $(v - \delta, v + \delta)$, while for e approaching values near 7 prices move chaotic in a very large range. This fact suggests the following picture: prices oscillate in a reasonable range under the action of fundamental and chartist forces, for some reason, chartist investors increase in number till to surpass a certain threshold, after that, prices start to oscillate widely as it happens in case of market turbulence, with prices going up and down crazily. This confirms the belief that chartist investors participate in instability and bubble inflation. However, it appears that the responsibility of instability stays more in the unequal proportion of force pressures on the market than the specific action of an investment style itself. In other words, it is not the adoption of the technical analysis in itself the problem but their dominance in proportion.

Figures 11 and 12 propose three dynamics with comparable parameters. On the left-hand side, only fundamental demand is considered, while in the center fundamental demand is coupled with chartist demand and on the right-hand side, all the components are effective. The dynamics changes according to the demand: with only fundamental demand, the price stays in a narrow neighborhood of $\mathcal{O}_2$, when chartist demand intervenes, the regular dynamics moves into a chaotic elliptic attractor (see the plot in the center), while the intervention of market maker regularizes and pushes the price to converge fast (see rhs). In this case, chartist demand moves prices to chaos, and market makers restore the convergence. Differently in Figure 12, fundamental parameters are set to generate a periodic elliptic attractor (lhs), chartist demand has the effect to shrink the price to the fixed point $\mathcal{O}_2$ (see in the center) and again the market makers accelerate the convergence (rhs). In this example, chartist demand has the effect to push prices to equilibrium.

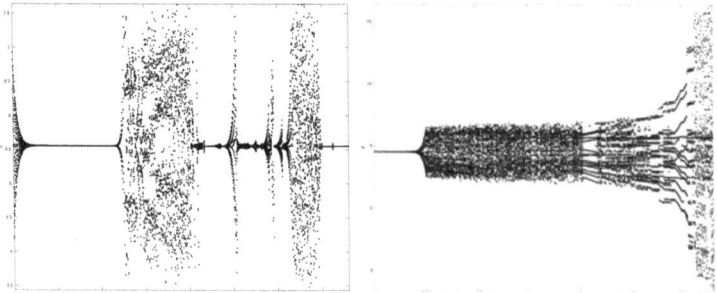

Figure 10. Bifurcation diagrams for the map that considers together fundamentalist, and chartist demands. The diagrams are presented with respect to e. (**left**) shows the diagram with $a = 1.1$, $b = 0.8$, $c = \frac{1}{b}$ and $e \in [0, 7.6]$. (**right**) shows the diagram with $a = 0.9$, $b = 0.8$, $c = \frac{1}{b}$ and $e \in [0, 7.6]$.

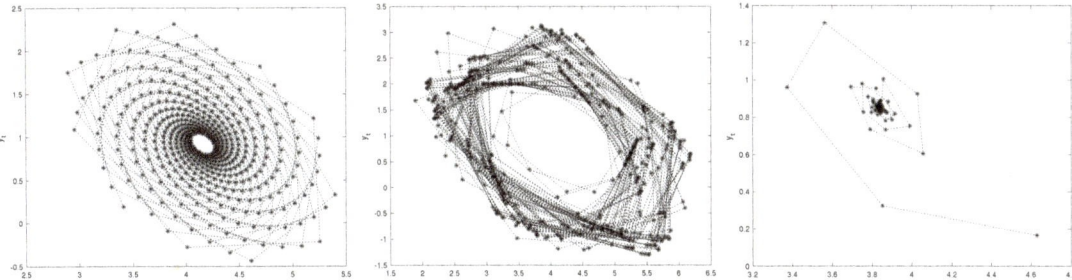

Figure 11. (**left**) shows the phase space of the fundamental map with $a = 0.8$, $b = 0.9$ and $c = 1.1$, (**middle**) shows the phase space of fundamental and chartist map with $a = 0.8$, $b = 0.9$ and $c = 1.1$ and $e = 2.0$, and (**right**) shows the phase space of the complete map with the same values of previous plot and $d_m = 0.5$.

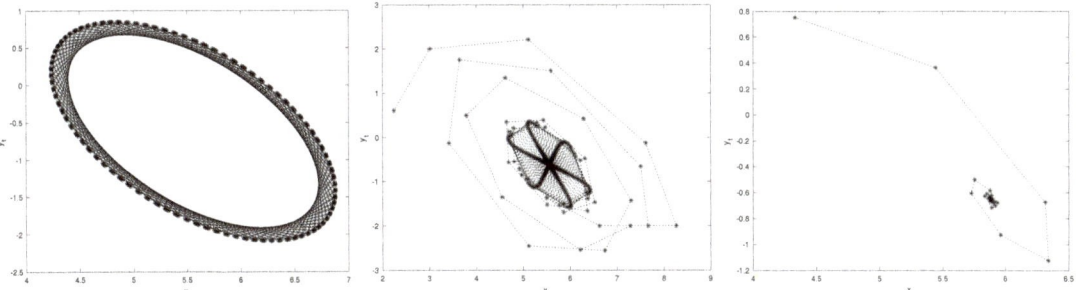

Figure 12. (**left**) shows the phase space of the fundamental map with $a = 1.1$, $b = 0.9$ and $c = \frac{1}{b}$ (periodic dynamics), (**middle**) shows the phase space of fundamental and chartist map with $a = 1.1$, $b = 0.9$ and $c = \frac{1}{b}$ and $e = 2.0$, (**right**) shows the phase space of the complete map with the same values of previous plot and $d_m = 0.5$.

5. Further Discussions

The present section addresses a general discussion about the model, its limits, and some possible future evolutions. The presented model is deterministic and pointed toward considering how market participants, their styles, and their attitudes have an impact on prices and market instability. The model considers three rather standard strategies and provides stylized explanations of empirical market features. Thanks to its simplicity the model is flexible with respect to many future variations. One could include the possibility to have fundamental value varying over time, following for example a random walk as in [4]. This can be done substituting in Equation (10) v by

$$v_t = v_{t-1} + \epsilon,$$

where $\epsilon \sim N(0, \sigma^2)$.

Another variation could consider the switching between investment styles; this can be done by allowing the reaction parameters c, d, e, and d_m also including the tolerance δ to change in time as in [19]. Indeed, in the full demand, we can see the contribution of investment styles accounted by traders simultaneously in the proportion given by the reaction parameters. Traders can consider differently the misalignment by fundamentals or the trend, thus reaction parameters can vary according to the strength of the investors' belief in each specific investment style. In other words, there could be phases in the market in which investors believe and adopt more fundamental analysis than technical one or vice versa. For doing so a mechanism of imitation and profitability evaluation must be implemented. Alternatively, although more simplistic it could be done by considering parameters varying randomly in time. A stochastic version of the model can also be considered, including a random perturbation of prices to incorporate the effect of traders moved by liquidity needs or the effect of exogenous news arrival on the market. The stochastic version has the advantage to replicate more realistically the market features. Indeed, a deterministic model has mainly the aim to offer a stylized explanation of market features and not the presumption to be completely realistic as it is needed to be used for forecasting purposes for example. The stochastic version could be also subjected to a calibration procedure following the simulated method of moments as in [20,21]. Although the undeniable value of work pointed towards the reproduction of real market dynamics in its entirety, such an issue is outside the aims of the present paper and left for future investigations.

6. Conclusions

In the present model, a simple financial market model is considered with three rather standard market forces contributing simultaneously to the total demand: fundamental, chartist, and market makers. The model is given by a discrete difference equation system with a piecewise linear map of a high order. Each component has been studied separately to understand and highlight its contribution to the dynamics. Results are not surprising and in line with the related literature [1,4,12,13]: fundamental demand helps the stability of the system and keeps prices bounded; market makers satisfy their role of restoring stability, while the chartist demand component adds instability and chaotic movement to prices. However, we see that in some cases chartist demand can compensate for fundamental demand, felt in the loop, and pushes the dynamics to equilibrium. The lesson we can take from this fact is that the instability does not stay intrinsically in the nature of the demands but their combination and proportion. Indeed, markets are places where a mix of different beliefs and attitude meets. The market dynamics cannot be anything else than the outcome of such a variety of agents. In the market, the heterogeneity of actors finds an equilibrium that can show regular dynamics and smooth oscillations coherent with the efficient market hypothesis. Nevertheless, if any kind of disequilibrium occurs in the market forces, prices can oscillate widely, bear and bull periods can arrive, and bubbles can inflate and explode.

The contribution of the paper goes in three directions: (1) it considers a common, rather so far unstudied, chartist demand implying moving averages difference; (2) the model includes market maker participation, so far that it has not received so much attention; (3) the model uses a high order piecewise linear map that provides interesting bifurcation diagrams belonging to the class of border collision bifurcations but those deserve much attention for the future, also for their economic implications.

Future investigations can move in the following directions: (1) the study of border collisions bifurcations in high order systems as the one proposed here; (2) the sophistication of the market maker demand via a piecewise map; (3) the implementation of a stochastic version of the model with a mechanism of changing the weight of each investment style; (4) the calibration of a stochastic version of the model to reproduce real markets dynamics.

Funding: A.F. acknowledges financial support from the project HiDEA (Advanced Econometric methods for High-frequency Data) financed by the Italian Ministry of Education, University and Research (MIUR) under the program "PRIN: PROGETTI DI RICERCA DI RILEVANTE INTERESSE NAZIONALE—Bando 2017" Prot. 2017RSMPZZ.

Institutional Review Board Statement: Not applicable.

Informed Consent Statement: Not applicable.

Data Availability Statement: Data were generated during the study. The paper presents any information needed to replicate the study.

Conflicts of Interest: The author declares no conflict of interest.

References

1. Beja, A.; Goldman, M.B. On the dynamic behavior of prices in disequilibrium. *J. Financ.* **1980**, *35*, 235–248. [CrossRef]
2. Day R.; Huang, W. Bulls, Bears, and Market Sheep. *J. Econ. Behav. Organ.* **1990**, *14*, 299–329. [CrossRef]
3. Chiarella, C. The dynamics of speculative behavior. *Ann. Oper. Res.* **1992**, *37*, 101–123. [CrossRef]
4. Lux, T. The socio-economic dynamics of speculative markets: Interacting agents, chaos, and the fat tails return distributions. *J. Econ. Behav. Organ.* **1998**, *33*, 143–165. [CrossRef]
5. Lux, T.; Marchesi, M. Scaling and criticality in a stochastic multi-agent model of a financial market. *Nature* **1999**, *397*, 498–500. [CrossRef]
6. Gilmore, C.G. A new approach to testing for chaos, with applications in finance and economics. *Int. J. Bifurc. Chaos* **1992**, *3*, 583–587. [CrossRef]
7. Gilmore, C.G. Detecting linear and non linear dependence in stock returns: New methods derived from chaos theory. *J. Bus. Financ. Account.* **1996**, *23*, 1357–1377. [CrossRef]
8. Holyst, J.A.; Zebrowska, M.; Urbanowicz, K. Observation of deterministic chaos in financial time series by Recurrence Plots, can one control chaotic economy? *Eur. Phys. J. B* **2001**, *20*, 531–535. [CrossRef]
9. McKenzie, M.D. Chaotic behavior in national stock market indices. *Glob. Financ. J.* **2001**, *12*, 35–53. [CrossRef]
10. Lorenz, H.W. *Non Linear Dynamical Equation and Chaotic Economy*; Springer: Berlin, Germany, 1993.
11. Hommes, C.H.; Nusse, H. Period three to period two bifurcations for piecewise linear models. *J. Econ.* **1991**, *54*, 157–169. [CrossRef]
12. Tramontana, F.; Westerhoff, F.; Gardini, L. On the complicated price dynamics of a simple one-dimensional discontinuous financial market model with heterogeneous interacting traders. *J. Econ. Behav. Organ.* **2010**, *74*, 187–205. [CrossRef]
13. Tramontana, F.; Westerhoff, F. Piecewise-Linear Maps and Their Application to Financial Markets. *Front. Appl. Math. Stat.* **2016**, *2*, 10. [CrossRef]
14. Banerjee, S.; Grebogi, C. Border collision bifurcations in two-dimensional piece wise smooth maps. *Phys. Rev. E* **1999**, *59*, 4052–4061. [CrossRef]
15. Nusse, H.E.; Yorke, J.A. Border collision bifurcations for piecewise smooth one-dimensional maps. *Int. J. Bifurc. Chaos* **1995**, *5*, 189–207. [CrossRef]
16. De, S.; Sharathi Dutta, P.; Banerjee, S.; Ranjan, A. Local and global bifurcations in three dimensional continuous piecewise smooth maps. *Int. J. Bifurc. Chaos* **2011**, *21*, 1617–1636. [CrossRef]
17. Sornette, D.; Johansen, A.; Bouchaud, J.P. Stock Market Crashes, Precursors and Replicas. *J. Phys. I Franc.* **1996**, *6*, 167–175. [CrossRef]
18. Sornette, D. *Why Stock Markets Crash: Critical Events in Complex Financial Systems*; Princeton University Press: Princeton, NJ, USA, 2004; p. 448.
19. Westerhoff, F.; Reitz, S. Nonlinearities and Cyclical Behavior: The Role of Chartists and Fundamentalists. *Stud. Nonlinear Dyn. Econom.* **2007**, *7*, 4. [CrossRef]
20. Franke, R.; Westerhoff, F. Structural stochastic volatility in asset pricing dynamics: Estimation and model contest. *J. Econ. Dyn. Control.* **2012**, *36*, 1193–1211. [CrossRef]
21. Fabretti, A. Markov chain analysis in agent-based model calibration by classical and simulated minimum distance. *Knowl. Inf. Syst.* **2019**, *61*, 259–276. [CrossRef]

Article

Stability of Solutions to Systems of Nonlinear Differential Equations with Discontinuous Right-Hand Sides: Applications to Hopfield Artificial Neural Networks

Ilya Boykov [1,*], Vladimir Roudnev [2] and Alla Boykova [1]

[1] Department of Higher and Applied Mathematics, Penza State University, 40, Krasnaya Str., 440026 Penza, Russia; aiboikova@pnzgu.ru
[2] Department of Computational Physics, Saint Petersburg State University, 1 Ulyanovskaya Str., 198504 Saint Petersburg, Russia; v.rudnev@spbu.ru
* Correspondence: boikov@pnzgu.ru

Citation: Boykov, I.; Roudnev, V.; Boykova, A. Stability of Solutions to Systems of Nonlinear Differential Equations with Discontinuous Right-Hand Sides: Applications to Hopfield Artificial Neural Networks. *Mathematics* 2022, *10*, 1524. https://doi.org/10.3390/math10091524

Academic Editor: Maria C. Mariani

Received: 31 March 2022
Accepted: 29 April 2022
Published: 2 May 2022

Publisher's Note: MDPI stays neutral with regard to jurisdictional claims in published maps and institutional affiliations.

Copyright: © 2022 by the authors. Licensee MDPI, Basel, Switzerland. This article is an open access article distributed under the terms and conditions of the Creative Commons Attribution (CC BY) license (https://creativecommons.org/licenses/by/4.0/).

Abstract: In this paper, we study the stability of solutions to systems of differential equations with discontinuous right-hand sides. We have investigated nonlinear and linear equations. Stability sufficient conditions for linear equations are expressed as a logarithmic norm for coefficients of systems of equations. Stability sufficient conditions for nonlinear equations are expressed as the logarithmic norm of the Jacobian of the right-hand side of the system of equations. Sufficient conditions for the stability of solutions of systems of differential equations expressed in terms of logarithmic norms of the right-hand sides of equations (for systems of linear equations) and the Jacobian of right-hand sides (for nonlinear equations) have the following advantages: (1) in investigating stability in different metrics from the same standpoints, we have obtained a set of sufficient conditions; (2) sufficient conditions are easily expressed; (3) robustness areas of systems are easily determined with respect to the variation of their parameters; (4) in case of impulse action, information on moments of impact distribution is not required; (5) a method to obtain sufficient conditions of stability is extended to other definitions of stability (in particular, to p-moment stability). The obtained sufficient conditions are used to study Hopfield neural networks with discontinuous synapses and discontinuous activation functions.

Keywords: differential equations with discontinuous right-hand sides; Hopfield artificial neural networks; stability

MSC: 34D20; 34A36

1. Introduction

Hopfield, Cohen–Grossberg and similar neural networks have been actively studied recently due to their applications in physics and engineering [1–4]. Hopfield neural networks (HNNs) have found many applications in associative memory, repetitive learning, classification of patterns, optimization problems and many others.

Today, two basic mathematical models are employed for neural network research: either local field neural network models or static neural models. The basic model of local field neural network is described as

$$\frac{dx_i(t)}{dt} = -x_i(t) + \sum_{j=1}^{n} w_{ij} g_j(x_j(t)) + I_i, i = 1, 2, \ldots, n, \qquad (1)$$

where g_i is a function of the ith neuron activation, x_i is the state of the ith neuron, I_i is the external input imposed on the ith neuron, w_{ij} stands for the synaptic connectivity value between the jth neuron and the ith neuron, and n is the number of neurons in the network.

A static neural network is defined by the system of equations

$$\frac{dx_i(t)}{dt} = -x_i(t) + g_i\left(\sum_{j=1}^n w_{ij}x_j(t) + I_i\right), i = 1,2,\ldots,n, \qquad (2)$$

where we used the same notation as above.

The local fields neural network (1) was introduced by Hopfield and it is the Hopfield neural network that is usually referred to in the literature. The neural network (1) models bidirectional associative memory networks [5] and cellular neural networks [6].

Static neural networks (2) are often referred to as Cohen–Grossberg networks. They are widely used in optimization problems and in modeling brain processes, so-called brain-state-in-a-box neural networks [7]. The research on stability for models such as (2) was opened with the classical work [8].

The stability results for the basic model (2) as well as the results for a more general model,

$$\frac{dx_i(t)}{dt} = a_i(x_i)[b_i(x_i) - \sum_{i=1}^n c_{ij}\varphi_j(x_j)]$$

were obtained in [8,9].

Below, we present a brief review of the papers devoted to the stability of solutions for systems of ordinary differential equations with discontinuous right-hand sides. Here, we examined the stability of dynamic neural networks and obtained sufficient conditions for their absolute and local asymptotic stability. The fixed points of the neural network are associated with local minima of the network energy function. Interest in seeking for local minima is due to the study of the memory problem for neural networks. Clearly, the more local minima a neural network has, the greater potential memory it holds.

When solving computational mathematics problems on neural networks, asymptotically stable networks appear to be more preferable in general.

The derivation of sufficient conditions for stable neural networks in general is a rather complicated problem. Its solution is known only in a few special cases.

In [10], sufficient conditions for stability for neural networks (1) have been obtained based on Gershgorin circles. In [11], sufficient conditions for the global stability of solutions of systems of Equation (1) have been obtained by a mapping method. In [12], the results of works [10,11] have been generalized and new Lyapunov functions have been constructed.

In [13], it was proven that the diagonal stability of the interconnection matrix implies the existence and uniqueness of an equilibrium and global stability of the equilibrium.

In [14], it was shown that the negative semidefiniteness of matrices ensures the stability of Hopfield neural networks described by the Equation (1). In [15], the number of sufficient conditions for the local exponential stability of HNNs was presented. In [16], the algorithm of matrix norms was applied to the study of nonlinear dynamical systems.

The stability of recurrent systems that model identification problems was investigated in [17].

Extensive literature is devoted to researching the stability of neural networks with various time delays [18–22].

Constructing a mathematical model, we have to abstract from many phenomena—for example, from the uncertainty. In [21], the stability of fuzzy cellular neural networks based on the union of cellular neural networks and fuzzy logic methods has been studied. The cellular neural networks are modeled by systems of differential equations with discontinuous right-hand sides.

Along with continuous activation functions, there are a great number of applications that are modeled by neural networks with discontinuous activation functions. Similar models have been studied in [23].

The theory of differential equations with discontinuous right-hand sides is given in [24].

Recall, following [24], the definitions of solutions for differential equations with discontinuous right-hand sides and their stability.

Consider an equation or a system of equations in vector form

$$\frac{dx}{dt} = f(t, x), \quad (3)$$

where $f(t, x)$ is a piece-wise continuous function or a vector function in domain $\Omega : \{x \in R_n, t \in [0, \infty)\}$; M is a measure zero set of the function $f(t, x)$ discontinuity points.

Each point (t, x) we associate with a set $F(t, x)$ in n dimensional space. This set is constructed as follows. If the function $f(t, x)$ is continuous at the point (t, x), the set $F(t, x)$ contains just one point which matches with $f(t, x)$. If f has a discontinuity point at (t, x), the set $F(t, x)$ is defined according to the related physical problem. One such method is described in Section 1.5 in [25].

Definition 1 ([24]). *A solution of the Equation (3) is called a solution of differential inclusion*

$$\frac{dx}{dt} \in F(t, x), \quad (4)$$

i.e., absolutely continuous vector function $x(t)$ defined in interval or segment I and for which the inclusion $\frac{dx}{dt} \in F(t, x)$ is satisfied almost everywhere in I.

Definition 2 ([24]). *The solution $x = \varphi(t), t_0 \leq t < \infty$ of differential inclusion (4) is called stable if, for any $\epsilon > 0$, there exists $\delta > 0$ so that, for every $\tilde{x}_0$, $|\tilde{x}_0(t_0) - \varphi(t_0)| < \delta$ each solution $\tilde{x}(t)$ with the initial condition $\tilde{x}(t_0) = \tilde{x}_0, t_0 \leq t < \infty$ exists and satisfies the inequality*

$$|\tilde{x}(t) - \varphi(t)| < \epsilon \quad \text{for} \quad t_0 \leq t < \infty.$$

Definition 3 ([24]). *The solution $x = \varphi(t), t_0 \leq t < \infty$ of differential inclusion (4) is called asymptotically stable if it is stable and, in addition, $\lim_{t \to \infty} |\tilde{x}(t) - \varphi(t)| = 0$.*

Definition 4 ([24]). *The solution $x = \varphi(t), t_0 \leq t < \infty$, of differential inclusion (4) is called stable in general if it is asymptotically stable for any initial $x_0 \in R_n$, where R_n is n-dimensional vector space.*

Intense research on the stability of systems of ordinary differential equations with discontinuous right-hand sides began in the middle of the last century in connection with increasing interest in automatic control problems. In addition to the issues of automatic control, automatic regulation [26] and the theory of relay systems, differential equations with discontinuous right-hand sides are widely used to model various problems in physics and engineering—in particular, the classical problem of dry friction [27]. Differential equations for automatic control with variable structures and discontinuous right-hand sides are obtained from differential equations with continuous right-hand sides when passing to the limit along a parameter [24].

Today, the stability of solutions of systems of ordinary differential equations with discontinuous right-hand sides is an active and growing field.

This is because there are numerous applications of systems of differential equations with discontinuous right-hand sides (Filippov systems) for various problems in physics, techniques, biology and medicine. A detailed bibliography is given in [28].

Recently, stability theory with discontinuous coefficients has been extended to numerical mathematics. There are widely used various methods to determine solutions for systems of linear and nonlinear algebraic equations.

In [29], the authors have developed a continuous method for solving nonlinear operator equations. Each nonlinear operator equation is assigned with the Cauchy problem. Convergence of the method is based on Lyapunov stability theory.

Collocation methods for solving initial and boundary problems for differential equations and the theory of B, D, G, P stability of their solutions has been developed and presented in [30–32]. The latter also contains an extensive bibliography.

In [33], the second Lyapunov's method was used to investigate semistability finite-time stability differential inclusions for systems of differential equations with discontinuity of the first kind on various manifolds. Semistability has a wider range of applications than the stability condition.

Research is performed in several directions: (1) systems of differential equations with one [34] and two [35] relays have been studied.

Stability of solutions of differential equations with one relay

$$\frac{dx_i(t)}{dt} = p_i \operatorname{sgn} x_i + \sum_{j=1}^{n} c_{ij} x_j, i = 1, 2, \ldots, n. \tag{5}$$

has been studied in [34].

In [35], the author investigates the stability of solutions of systems of differential equations

$$\begin{aligned}
\frac{dx_1(t)}{dt} &= a_1 \operatorname{sgn} x_1(t) + b_1 \operatorname{sgn} x_2(t) + \sum_{j=2}^{n} c_{1,j} x_j(t), \\
\frac{dx_2(t)}{dt} &= a_2 \operatorname{sgn} x_1(t) + b_2 \operatorname{sgn} x_2(t) + \sum_{j=2}^{n} c_{2,j} x_j(t), \\
\frac{dx_i(t)}{dt} &= \sum_{j=1}^{n} c_{i,j} x_j(t), i = 3, \ldots, n,
\end{aligned} \tag{6}$$

with constant coefficients.

Stability of solutions of systems of differential equations with relay [34,35] is based on the study of transfer functions. There have been obtained necessary and sufficient conditions for the stability of solutions for the systems (5), (6) expressed in terms of coefficients of equations.

Numerous works have been devoted to the stability of systems of nonlinear switching differential equations. For a bibliography, see [36].

Another class of problems is related to the study of sliding modes in automatic regulation and control systems [37]. It is interesting to note that sliding modes are present in ecology models [28].

When studying the stability of systems of nonlinear differential equations with discontinuous right-hand sides, Lyapunov's functions method [38–40] has been used.

Stability of neural networks described by the equations

$$\frac{dx_i}{dt} = -c_i x_i + \sum_{j=1}^{n} a_{ij} \varphi_j(x_j), \tag{7}$$

$i = 1, 2, \ldots, n$ and more general equations

$$\frac{dx_i}{dt} = -c_i x_i - \sum_{j=1}^{n} a_{ij} \sum_{k=1}^{n} a_{jk} g_k(x_k), \tag{8}$$

$i = 1, 2, \ldots, n$ by the second Lyapunov method has been investigated in [41] assuming that the functions $g_k(x), k = 1, 2, \ldots, n$ are continuous. The following conditions are imposed on the functions $\varphi_j(x_j)$

A1. Each function $\varphi_j(x_j)$ is defined everywhere for $-\infty < x_j < \infty$, continuous and one-valued;

A2. Each function $\varphi_j(x_j)$ lies in the first and the third quadrant; $x_j \neq 0$, moreover, the inequalities are fulfilled $x_j \varphi_j(x_j) > 0, j = 1, 2, \ldots, n$;

A3. $\lim_{|x_j| \to \infty} \int_0^{x_j} \varphi_j(\rho) d\rho = +\infty, j = 1, 2, \ldots, n$.

Stability of neural networks with discontinuous coefficients $g_i(x)$, $i = 1, 2, \ldots, n$ has been studied in [42,43].

It was assumed in [42] that

$$g_i(x) = g(x) = \begin{cases} 1, & x > 0, \\ 0, & x < 0, \end{cases}$$

$i = 1, 2, \ldots, n$. To ensure the stability of a neural network, the method based on the majorization of the nonlinear part of Equation (7) by a constant and further solving the differential has been proposed.

Stability of the solutions of Equation (7) with discontinuous nonlinear functions was investigated with the second Lyapunov method in [43]. The study of sliding mode stability is also reported in [43].

The detailed research of neural networks including Hopfield networks is given in [44]. The stability of neural networks with various activation functions in general has been studied, as well as the stability at separated stationary points. The basic technique of neural network stability in [44] appears to be the use of Lyapunov's and energy functions. In [44], one can find an extensive bibliography on the stability of neural networks described with differential and difference equations.

The exponential stability of a Hopfield neural network on the timeline has been investigated in [45]. Stability of the neural networks described by differential equations

$$\frac{dx_i(t)}{dt} = -e_i x_i + \sum_{j=1}^{n} g_{ij}(x_j), i = 1, 2, \ldots, n, \tag{9}$$

with functions $g_{ij}(x_j)$, $i, j = 1, 2, \ldots, n$ having discontinuities of the first kind at separate points has been studied in [25,46].

In this paper, we investigate the stability of solutions of systems of linear and nonlinear equations with discontinuous right-hand sides. We obtained sufficient conditions for the asymptotic stability for systems of differential equations used when studying HNNs' stability with discontinuous synapses and activation functions.

We study the stability of solutions for systems of differential equations regardless of how an inclusion equation is defined. With this approach, it is essential to use the first Lyapunov method.

It is possible to suggest that in applying the second Lyapunov method, one has to construct separate Lyapunov–Krasovski functionals for each area where the right-hand side of the differential equation system is continuous.

The paper is divided into the Introduction, three sections and the Conclusions. Section 2 introduces the definitions and the notation used throughout the paper. Section 3 examines the stability of solutions of differential equations with discontinuous right-hand sides. In Section 4, we analyze the stability of Hopfield neural networks. The obtained results are drawn in the final section.

2. Definitions and Notations

We now introduce a few definitions used in this paper.

Here, $D^k g(t, u_1, \ldots, u_n)$ stands for a partial derivative $D^k g(t, u_1, \ldots, u_n) = \partial g(t, u_1, \ldots, u_n)/\partial u_k$, $k = 1, 2, \ldots, n$.

Moreover, we employ the following notation: $B(a, r) = \{z \in B : \|z - a\| \leq r\}$, $S(a, r) = \{z \in B : \|z - a\| = r\}$, $Re(K) = \Re(K) = (K + K^*)/2$, $\Lambda(K) = \lim_{h \downarrow 0}(\|I + hK\| - 1)h^{-1}$. Here, B is a Banach space, $a \in B$, K is a linear and bounded operator on B, $\Lambda(K)$ is the logarithmic norm [47] of the operator K, K^* is the conjugate operator to K, and I stands for the identity operator.

The main properties of the logarithmic norm are given in [47].

If A is an $n \times n$ matrix, then $\Lambda(A)$ can readily be computed for the corresponding norms of linear vector spaces.

The logarithmic norm is known for operators in the most frequently used spaces.

Let $A = \{a_{ij}\}, i,j = 1, 2, \ldots, n$ be a real matrix.

In the n-dimensional space R_n of vectors $x = (x_1, \ldots, x_n)$, the following norms are often used:

- $\|x\|_1 = \sum_{i=1}^{n} |x_i|$;
- $\|x\|_2 = \max_{1 \leq i \leq n} |x_i|$;
- $\|x\|_3 = (\sum_{i=1}^{n} x_i^2)^{1/2}$.

Below are some expressions of the logarithmic norm of a matrix $A = (a_{ij})$ corresponding to the norms of the vectors given above:

$$\Lambda_1(A) = \max_{1 \leq j \leq n} \left(a_{jj} + \sum_{i \neq j} |a_{ij}| \right);$$

$$\Lambda_2(A) = \max_{1 \leq i \leq n} \left(a_{ii} + \sum_{j \neq i} |a_{ij}| \right);$$

$$\Lambda_3(A) = \lambda_{\max}\left(\frac{A + A^*}{2} \right),$$

where A^* is the conjugate matrix for A.

3. Stability of Solutions to Equations Systems with Discontinuous Right-Hand Sides

3.1. Stability of Solutions to Linear Equations Systems with Discontinuous Coefficients

Consider the Cauchy problem

$$\frac{dx_i(t)}{dt} = \sum_{j=1}^{n} a_{ij}(t) x_j(t), t \geq 0, \tag{10}$$

$$x_i(0) = x_i, i = 1, 2, \ldots, n, \tag{11}$$

with discontinuous coefficients $a_{ij}(t), i,j = 1, 2, \ldots, n$.

We assume that the functions $a_{ij}(t)$ are continuous everywhere except a countable set of points $\zeta_1, \zeta_2, \ldots$, where the functions have discontinuities.

The following statement is valid.

Theorem 1. *Let the following conditions be satisfied:*

(1) Functions $a_{ij}(t)$ are continuous everywhere except a countable set of points $\zeta_1, \zeta_2, \ldots$, where the functions have discontinuities. There is at most a finite number of discontinuities on each $[0, A], 0 < A < \infty$. The coefficients $\{a_{ij}(t)\}$ at $\zeta_1, \zeta_2, \ldots$, have discontinuities of the first kind or discontinuities of the second kind integrable in L-metric:

$$\int_{\zeta_l^1}^{\zeta_{l+1}^1} |a_{ij}(t)| dt \leq c_{lij} < \infty, i,j = 1, 2, \ldots, n, l = 1, 2, \ldots$$

Here, ζ_l^1 are the points that satisfy $\zeta_i < \zeta_i^1 < \zeta_{i+1}, i = 0, 1, \ldots, \zeta_0 = 0$;

(2) The Cauchy problem (10)–(11) has a solution for $t \geq 0$ and any initial conditions;

(3) The inequality $\Lambda(A(t)) \leq -\kappa, \kappa > 0$ is valid everywhere except a set of points $\zeta_1, \zeta_2, \ldots$ Here, $A(t) = \{a_{ij}(t)\}_{i,j=1}^{n}$.

Then, zero solution of the system (10) is asymptotically stable in general.

Set $\Lambda(A(t))$ equal to zero at discontinuity points ζ_i. By the theorem, we have a finite number of discontinuities in each time interval. Thus, it does not change the value $\int_0^t \Lambda(A(\tau))d\tau$.

Proof of Theorem 1. Consider a time interval $[0, \zeta_1)$. The Wintner estimate is valid [47] within this interval

$$\|x(t)\| \leq \|x(0)\| \exp\left\{\int_0^t \Lambda(A(\tau))d\tau\right\}, t \in [0, \zeta_1). \tag{12}$$

The function $\|x(t)\|$ is continuous for $t \geq 0$, and then the Inequality (12) is correct for $t \in [0, \zeta_1]$. Therefore,

$$\|x(\zeta_1)\| \leq \|x(0)\| \exp\left\{\int_0^{\zeta_1} \Lambda(A(\tau))d\tau\right\}.$$

Consider an interval $[\zeta_1, \zeta_2]$. First, assume that functions $a_{ij}(t)$ have discontinuities of the first kind at ζ_2. Let $A^+(t) = \{a_{ij}^+(t)\}, i,j = 1,2,\ldots,n$ be a matrix with elements defined by

$$a_{ij}^+(t) = \begin{cases} a_{ij}(t), t \neq \zeta_2, \\ \lim_{t \to \zeta_2+0} a_{ij}(t), t = \zeta_2. \end{cases}$$

We take $x_i(\zeta_1), i = 1,2,\ldots,n$, as initial values. Repeat the arguments above, for $t \in [\zeta_1, \zeta_2]$, and we have

$$\|x(t)\| \leq \|x(\zeta_1)\| \exp\left\{\int_{\zeta_1}^t \Lambda(A^+(\tau))d\tau\right\} =$$
$$= \|x(\zeta_1)\| \exp\left\{\int_{\zeta_1}^t \Lambda(A(\tau))d\tau\right\} \leq \|x(0)\| \exp\left\{\int_0^t \Lambda(A(\tau))d\tau\right\}.$$

Next, we consider the case where functions $a_{ij}(t)$ have discontinuities of the second kind and integrals $\int_0^\infty |a_{ij}(t)|dt$ exist. Obviously, for $t \in [0, \zeta_1)$, the Inequality (12) is valid. Since the function $x(t)$ is continuous, the inequality is valid on the interval $[0, \zeta_1]$. From the continuity of $\|x(t)\|$, it follows that a point $\zeta_1^1(\zeta_1 < \zeta_1^1 < \zeta_2)$ such that

$$\|x(t)\| \leq \|x_0\| + \|x_0\| \frac{\exp\left\{\int_0^t \Lambda(A(\tau))d\tau\right\} - 1}{2}$$

exists for $t \in [\zeta_1, \zeta_1^1]$.

By taking $x_i(\zeta_1^1), i = 1,2,\ldots,n$ as initial conditions and repeating the arguments above, we verify immediately the validity of the inequality

$$\|x(t)\| \leq \|x_0\| \exp\left\{\int_0^t \Lambda(A(\tau))d\tau\right\},$$

for $0 \leq t \leq \zeta_2$. Repeating the process in each interval $[\zeta_l, \zeta_{l+1}]$, we can observe that the inequality is correct for $0 \leq t \leq \infty$. □

Let us consider the case when coefficients $a_{ij}(t)$ have a countable number of discontinuity points.

Let the function $a_{11}(t)$ have a countable number of discontinuity points located in interval $[b_1, b_2]$ with measure $\Delta = |b_2 - b_1|, b_1 > 0$.

The following assertion is true.

Theorem 2. *Let the following conditions be satisfied:*

(1) The functions a_{ij} are continuous everywhere except a countable number of points located in the interval $[b_1, b_2], b_1 > 0, \Delta = |b_2 - b_1|$.

(2) The Cauchy problem (10), (11) has a solution for all $t \geq 0$ and for any initial conditions.

(3) The inequality $\Lambda(A(t)) \leq -\kappa, \kappa > 0$ holds everywhere except the interval $[b_1, b_2]$. Here, $A(t) = \{a_{ij}(t)\}, i, j = 1, 2, ..., n;$

(4) The inequality is valid

$$\int_0^{b_1} \Lambda(A(\tau))d\tau + A\Delta < 0,$$

where $A = \sup_{\tau \in [b_1, b_2]} \|A(\tau)\|$.

Then, a trivial solution of the system of Equation (10) is asymptotically stable.

Proof of Theorem 2. Consider $[0, b_1]$. From Wintner inequality [47], it follows that for $t \in [0, b_1]$

$$\|x(t)\| \leq \|x(0)\| \exp\left\{\int_0^t \Lambda(A(\tau))d\tau\right\}.$$

Take $[b_1, b_2]$. Here, we have

$$x(t) = x(b_1) + \int_{b_1}^t A(\tau)x(\tau)d\tau,$$

and the integral is understood in the sense of Lebesgue.

Thus,

$$\|x(t)\| \leq \|x(b_1)\| + \int_{b_1}^t \|A(\tau)\|\|x(\tau)\|d\tau \leq \|x(b_1)\| + A\int_{b_1}^t \|x(\tau)\|d\tau.$$

where $A = \max_{b_1 \leq t \leq b_2} \|A(t)\|$.

From Gronwall–Bellman inequality, it follows that

$$\|x(t)\| \leq \|x(b_1)\| \exp\{A(t - b_1)\}.$$

Thus, for $t \in [b_1, b_2]$,

$$\begin{aligned}\|x(t)\| &\leq \|x(0)\| \exp\left\{\int_0^{b_1} \Lambda(A(\tau))d\tau + A(t - b_1)\right\} \\ &\leq \exp\left\{\int_0^{b_1} \Lambda(A(\tau))d\tau + A(b_2 - b_1)\right\}\|x(0)\|.\end{aligned} \quad (13)$$

Therefore, if $\int_0^{b_1} \Lambda(A(\tau))d\tau + A\Delta < 0$, then $\|x(b_2)\| \leq \|x(0)\|$ and a trivial solution of the system of Equation (10) is stable. □

It is easy to see that the obtained results can be extended to systems of switching differential equations. At the same time, the stability condition is extended to systems of differential equations with an arbitrary number of relays. Moreover, the suggested method allows one to obtain sufficient conditions for the stability of solutions of systems of nonlinear equations with relay. Similarly, based on the results presented in Sections 2 and 3, one can formulate sufficient conditions for the stability of switching systems.

Example. We consider a system of differential equations with relay

$$\frac{dx_k(t)}{dt} = \sum_{l=1}^m a_{kl}(t) \operatorname{sgn} x_l(t) + \sum_{l=1}^n b_{kl}(t)x_l(t), \quad k = 1, 2, \ldots, n.$$

Theorem 1 implies that for the asymptotic stability of the trivial solution of this system, it is sufficient to fulfill the following conditions: for each $t \in [0, \infty)$

$$b_{kk}(t) + \sum_{l=1}^{m} |a_{kl}(t)| + \sum_{l=1, l \neq k}^{n} |b_{kl}(t)| \leq -\xi, \xi > 0.$$

3.2. Stability of Solutions for Systems of Nonlinear Non-Autonomous Differential Equations with Discontinuous Right-Hand Sides

First, let us recall the sufficient stability conditions for systems of nonlinear differential equations with continuous right-hand sides that we gave previously [48], and which we extensively use below.

Consider the system of equations

$$\frac{dx_i(t)}{dt} = a_i(t, x_1(t), \ldots, x_n(t)), \, i = 1, 2, \ldots, n, \tag{14}$$

with the initial conditions

$$x_i(0) = x_i, \, i = 1, 2, \ldots, n. \tag{15}$$

Let $x^*(t) = (x_1^*(t), \ldots, x_n^*(t))$ be a steady-state solution of the Cauchy problems (14) and (15).

Let the functions $a_i(t, u_1, \ldots, u_n)$ be continuous with respect to the first variable and have partial derivatives with respect to other variables satisfying the Lipschitz condition with a coefficient A:

$$|D^j a_i(t, x_1^*, \ldots, x_n^*) - D^j a_i(t, y_1^*, \ldots, y_n^*)| \leq A(|x_1^* - y_1^*| + \ldots + |x_n^* - y_n^*|), \, i, j = 1, \ldots, n. \tag{16}$$

Let $\chi = \text{const} > 0$. Let, for $t \in [0, \infty)$, the following conditions be satisfied

$$D^i a_i(t, x_1^*(t), \ldots, x_n^*(t)) + \sum_{j=1, j \neq i}^{n} \left| D^j a_i(t, x_1^*(t), \ldots, x_n^*(t)) \right| < -\chi < 0, \, i = 1, \ldots, n. \tag{17}$$

Theorem 3 ([48]). *Let the system (14) have a steady-state solution $x^*(t) = (x_1^*(t), \ldots, x_n^*(t))$. Let the functions $a_i(t, x_1, \ldots, x_n), i = 1, 2, \ldots, n$ be continuous with respect to the first variable, continuously differentiate to other variables and partial derivatives satisfy the Lipschitz condition (16). Let, for all $t \geq 0$, the conditions (17) be satisfied. Then, the steady-state solution $x^*(t)$ of the system of Equation (14) is asymptotically stable in the R_n^3 space metric of n-dimensional vectors $v = (v_1, \ldots, v_n)$ with norm $\|v\| = \max_{1 \leq j \leq n} |v_j|$.*

Consider a system of nonlinear equations

$$\frac{du_i(t)}{dt} = a_i(t, u_1(t), \ldots, u_n(t)), \, i = 1, 2, \ldots, n, \, t \geq 0, \tag{18}$$

with initial conditions

$$u_i(0) = u_i, \, i = 1, 2, \ldots, n. \tag{19}$$

Their right-hand sides are continuous everywhere except a countable set of values $(\zeta_i, u_1^i, \ldots, u_n^i), i = 1, 2, \ldots,$ in which they have discontinuities.

For the sake of simplicity, we consider two cases here:
(1) there are discontinuities with respect to variable t;
(2) there are discontinuities with respect to variable u_1.

Consider the first case. Assume that the functions $a_j(t; u_1, \ldots, u_n), j = 1, 2, \ldots, n$ have discontinuities with respect to t at points $\zeta_i, i = 1, 2, \ldots; 0 < \zeta_1 < \zeta_2 < \ldots$. For convenience, let $j = 1$. The functions $a_i(t; u_1, \ldots, u_n), i = 2, 3, \ldots, n$ are assumed to be continuous.

We impose the following constraints on $a_i(t, u_1, \ldots, u_n), i = 1, 2, \ldots, n$:

(1) functions $a_i(t, u_1, \ldots, u_n)$, $i = 2, \ldots, n$ are continuous with respect to $t(t \in [0, \infty))$ and have partial derivatives that satisfy the Lipschitz condition with coefficient q with respect to other variables

$$|D^k a_i(t, u_1, \ldots, u_n) - D^k a_i(t, v_1, \ldots, v_n)| \leq q \sum_{i=1}^{n} |u_i - v_i|, k = 1, 2, \ldots, n, \ t \in [0, \infty); \quad (20)$$

(2) the function $a_1(t, u_1, \ldots, u_n)$ is continuous for $t \in [0, \zeta_1) \cup_{i=1}^{\infty} (\zeta_i, \zeta_{i+1})$. For t, it has partial derivatives with respect to other variables satisfying the Lipschitz condition with coefficient q

$$|D^j a_1(t, u_1, \ldots, u_n) - D^j a_1(t, v_1, \ldots, v_n)| \leq q \sum_{i=1}^{n} |u_i - v_i|, \, , j = 1, 2, \ldots, n; \quad (21)$$

(3) for $t \in [0, \infty)$

$$D^i a_i(t, x_1^*(t), \ldots, x_n^*(t)) + \sum_{j=1, j \neq i}^{n} \left| D^j a_i(t, x_1^*(t), \ldots, x_n^*(t)) \right| < -\chi < 0, \ i = 2, 3, \ldots, n; \quad (22)$$

(4) for $t \in [0, \zeta_1) \cup_{i=1}^{\infty} (\zeta_i, \zeta_{i+1})$

$$D^1 a_1(t, x_1^*(t), \ldots, x_n^*(t)) + \sum_{j=2}^{n} \left| D^j a_1(t, x_1^*(t), \ldots, x_n^*(t)) \right| < -\chi < 0, \quad (23)$$

where $\chi = \text{const} > 0$.

Now, consider the time interval $t \in [0, \zeta_1]$.

Let $\|u(0)\| \leq \delta$, where $\delta \leq \chi/(4qn^2)$. In [48], it was shown that in order to fulfill the conditions (20)–(23) in time interval $t \in [0, \zeta_1]$, the trajectory of the solution of the Cauchy problems (18) and (19) does not leave a ball $B(0, \delta)$. It was also shown that for $t \in [0, \zeta_1]$, it holds that

$$\|u(t)\| \leq e^{-\chi t/4} \|u(0)\| \leq e^{-\chi t/4} \delta. \quad (24)$$

Since the function $\|u(t)\|$ is continuous for $t \in [0, \infty)$, we can find ζ_1', $\zeta_1 < \zeta_1' < \zeta_2$ such that $|\zeta_1' - \zeta_1| < |\zeta_2 - \zeta_1|/10$ and $\|u(t)\| \leq e^{-\chi \zeta_1/8} \|u(0)\|$ for $t \in [\zeta_1, \zeta_1']$. Obviously, for $t \in [\zeta_1', \zeta_2]$, $\|u(t)\| \leq e^{-\chi(t-\zeta_1')/4} \|u(\zeta_1')\| \leq e^{-\chi(t-\zeta_1')/4} e^{-\chi \zeta_1/8} \|u(0)\|$.

For $t = \zeta_2$, we have $\|u(\zeta_2)\| \leq e^{-\chi(\zeta_2 - \zeta_1')/4} e^{-\chi \zeta_1/8} \|u(0)\| < e^{-\chi \Delta_1/8} e^{-\chi \Delta_0/8} \|u(0)\|$. Here and below, $\Delta_k = |\zeta_{k+1} - \zeta_k|$.

Consider the interval $[\zeta_2, \zeta_3]$. From function $\|u(t)\|$, $t \in [0, \infty)$ continuity, it follows that there is an interval $[\zeta_2, \zeta_2']$ such that $|\zeta_2' - \zeta_2| < \Delta_3/10$ and $\|u(t)\| \leq e^{-\chi(\Delta_0 + \Delta_1)/8} \|u_0\|$ for $t \in [\zeta_2, \zeta_2']$. Then, if $t \in [\zeta_2', \zeta_3]$ $\|u(t)\| \leq e^{-\chi(t-\zeta_2')/4} \|u(\zeta_2')\| \leq e^{-\chi(t-\zeta_2')/4} e^{-\chi(\Delta_0 + \Delta_1)/8} \|u_0\|$, $\|u(\zeta_3)\| < e^{-\chi(\zeta_3 - \zeta_2)/8} e^{-\chi(\Delta_0 + \Delta_1)/8} \|u_0\| = e^{-\chi(\Delta_0 + \Delta_1 + \Delta_2)/8} \|u_0\|$.

Repeating the process, we have for $t \in [\zeta_k, \zeta_{k+1}]$: $\|u(\zeta_{k+1})\| < e^{-\chi(\sum_{l=0}^{k} \Delta_l)/8}$. Therefore, $t \to \infty$ $\|u(t)\| \to 0$.

Asymptotic stability is proven.

Theorem 4. *Let the following conditions be fulfilled:*
(1) the Cauchy problems (14) and (15) has a steady-state solution $x^*(t)$, $x^*(t) = (x_1^*(t), \ldots, x_n^*(t))$, $t \geq 0$;
(2) functions $a_{ij}(t, x_1, x_2, \ldots, x_n)$ are continuous with respect to variables $x_1, \ldots, x_n$ and have a set of countable discontinuities $\zeta_1, \ldots, \zeta_n, \ldots$ with respect to t. Moreover, in each finite time interval $[0, T)$, there is at most a finite number of discontinuities;
(3) at every point of continuity with respect to t, functions $a_{ij}(t, x_1, \ldots, x_n)$ have partial derivatives with respect to $x_1, \ldots, x_n$ and satisfy the Inequalities (20), (21);
(4) the conditions (22), (23) are fulfilled.

Then, a steady-state solution of the Cauchy problems (14) and (15) is asymptotically stable.

Now, we move on to the case where functions $a_i(t, u_1, \ldots, u_n)$, $i = 1, 2, \ldots, n$ have discontinuities with respect to u_i, $i = 1, 2, \ldots, n$.

For simplicity, we restrict the discussion to the case where the function $a_1(t, u_1, \ldots, u_n)$ has a discontinuity at u_1 for $u_1 = u_1^*$.

Assume that a gap occurs at time $t = \eta_1 > 0$ and $u_1(\eta_1) = u_1^*$.

Let, for $-\infty < u_1 < u_1^*$, $-\infty < u_i < \infty$, $i = 2, \ldots, n$ and for $u_1^* < u_1 < \infty$, $-\infty < u_i < \infty$, $i = 2, \ldots, n$, functions $a_i(t, u_1, \ldots, u_n)$, $i = 1, \ldots, n$ have partial derivatives that satisfy the Lipschitz condition $|D^j a_i(t, u_1, \ldots, u_n) - D^j a_i(t, v_1, \ldots, v_n)| \leq q \sum_{i=1}^{n} |u_i - v_i|$, $j = 1, 2, \ldots, n$.

Consider a time interval $[0, \eta_1)$. The conditions of Theorem 3 are verified in each $[0, b] \subset [0, \eta_1)$. Therefore, for $t \in [0, \eta_1)$, the inequality occurs $\|u(t)\| \leq e^{-\chi t/4} \delta < \delta$.

Although the function $\|u(t)\|$ is continuous for $t \in [0, \infty)$, the inequality $\|u(t)\| \leq e^{-\chi t/4} \delta$ is valid for $t \in [0, \eta_1]$.

Consider special features of the transition of the Cauchy problem solution trajectories (18) and (19) through $t = \eta_1$.

There are two possible cases:
(1) there is an interval $(\eta_1, \eta_1 + \Delta_1]$, in which $u_1(t) \neq u_1(\eta_1)$;
(2) there is a time interval $[\eta_1, \eta_1 + \Delta_2]$, in which $u_1(t) = u_1(\eta_1)$.

We will study each case separately.

First, from continuity of the function $\|u(t)\|$, it follows that there is h, $h < \eta_1/10$ so that $t \in [\eta_1, \eta_1 + h]$, $\|u(t)\| < e^{-\chi t/8} \delta$.

Therefore, for $t \in [0, \eta_1 + h]$, the inequality $\|u(t)\| \leq e^{-\chi t/8} \delta$ is valid. Clearly, $\|u(\eta_1 + h)\| \leq e^{-\chi(\eta_1 + h)/8} \delta$.

For $t \in [\eta_1 + h, \infty)$, the inequality $\|u(t)\| \leq e^{-\chi(t - \eta_1 - h)/4} \|u(\eta_1 + h)\| \leq e^{-\chi(t - \eta_1 - h)/4} e^{-\chi(\eta_1 + h)/8} \delta \leq e^{-\chi t/8} \delta$ is valid.

Therefore, $\|u(t)\| \leq e^{-\chi t/8} \delta$, for $t \in [0, \infty)$.

Thus, for the first case, the stability of the steady-state solution for the system of Equation (18) is proven.

Now, we move on to the second case. Since $u_1(t) = u_1(\eta_1)$ for $t \in [\eta_1, \eta_1 + \Delta_1]$, in this time interval instead of (18), one should observe the following system of equations

$$0 = a_1(t, u_1(\eta_1), u_2(t), \ldots, u_n(t)). \tag{25}$$

$$\frac{du_i(t)}{dt} = a_i(t, u_1(\eta_1), u_2(t), \ldots, u_n(t)), \; i = 2, \ldots, n. \tag{26}$$

The system of Equation (26) is considered under initial condition $u_i(\eta_1) = u_i$, $i = 2, 3, \ldots, n$.

We assume that functions $u_2(t), \ldots, u_n(t)$ satisfy the condition (25) for $t \in [\eta_1, \eta_1 + \Delta_1]$.

The system of Equation (26) is studied similarly to the system (18) in the space of lower dimension. Sufficient conditions of stability for the solution of the system (26) for $t \in [\eta_1, \eta_1 + \Delta_1]$ are constructed similarly to the sufficient conditions of stability for the solution of the system (18) on the time interval $t \in [0, \zeta_1]$. We omit the details. Finally, we investigate the time interval $t \in [\eta_1 + \Delta_1, \infty]$ and employ the arguments given in [48].

Now, we must consider the case of a countable set of discontinuities. It suffices to observe the case where there are discontinuities with respect to u_1 for $\bar{u}_1^i$, $i = 1, 2, \ldots$. We suggest that the discontinuities occur at the time moments t_i^*: $a_1(t_i^*, \bar{u}_1^i(t_i^*), \ldots, u_n(t_i^*))$, $i = 1, 2, \ldots$. As above, we will assume that at each finite time interval $[0, T]$, there is a finite number of discontinuities.

Here, we also must consider two cases:
(1) $u_1^i(t) \neq \bar{u}_1^i(t_i^*)$ in an interval $t \in (t_i^*, t_i^* + h_i^1)$;
(2) there is an interval $[t_i^*, t_i^* + h_i]$, where $u_1^i(t) = \bar{u}_1^i(t_i^*)$.

For convenience, we observe the first case. The second one leads to the case of a system of a lower dimension.

To each time moment t_i^*, $i = 1, 2, \ldots$ associated with a function discontinuity $a_1(t, u_1(t), \ldots, u_n(t))$ we assign a number ζ_i' so that $t_i^* < \zeta_i' < t_{i+1}^*$, $|\zeta_i' - t_i^*| \leq |t_{i+1}^* - t_i^*|/4$, $i = 1, 2, \ldots$.

Repeating the above arguments for each time interval $[0, \zeta_1']$, $[\zeta_i', \zeta_{i+1}']$, $i = 1, 2, \cdots$, we verify the validity of the following statement.

Theorem 5. *Let the following conditions be fulfilled:*
(1) the Cauchy problems (14)–(15) has a steady-state solution $x^*(t)$, $x^*(t) = (x_1^*(t), \ldots, x_n^*(t))$;
(2) functions $a_{ij}(t, x_1, \ldots, x_n)$ are continuous with respect to variables $(t, x_1, \ldots, x_n)$ everywhere except a countable set of discontinuities with respect to variables $x_1, \ldots, x_n$ that occur at time moments t_i^*, $i = 1, 2, \ldots$. Moreover, in each finite time interval, there is a finite number of discontinuities;
(3) at continuity points, functions $a_{ij}(t, x_1, \ldots, x_n)$ have partial derivatives with respect to variables $x_1, \ldots, x_n$ that satisfy the Lipschitz condition;
(4) the conditions (22), (23) are fulfilled.
Then, a steady-state solution of the Cauchy problems (14)–(15) is asymptotically stable.

4. Stability of Hopfield Neural Networks

In this section, we investigate the stability of Hopfield neural networks, which are modeled by a system of nonlinear differential equations

$$\frac{dx_i(t)}{dt} = -a_i(t)x_i(t) + \sum_{j=1}^{n} w_{i,j}(t) g_j(x_j(t)), \tag{27}$$

with discontinuous coefficients $a_i(t)$ and activation functions $g_i(x)$, $i = 1, 2, \ldots, n$.

We will perform our study of the stability of neural networks (27) in two stages. The first stage includes a case with discontinuous coefficients $a_i(t)$. The second one considers discontinuity of activation function $g_i(x)$, $i = 1, 2, \ldots, n$.

First, let functions $a_i(t)$, $i = 1, 2, \ldots, n$ have discontinuities of the first kind. It is enough to restrict ourselves to the case of one point of discontinuity. Assume that the function $a_{11}(t)$ is discontinuous at the point b_1, $0 < b_1 < \infty$. Without loss of generality, we suggest $g_j(0) = 0$, $j = 1, 2, \ldots, n$, $|g_i(x)| \leq \alpha_i |x|$, $i = 1, 2, \ldots, n$.

Now, we investigate the stability of the zero solution of the system of Equation (27). In the interval $(0, b_1]$, the norm of the solution of Equation (27) for initial value

$$x(0) = x_0, x(0) = (x_1(0), \ldots, x_n(0)), \tag{28}$$

is estimated by the inequality

$$\begin{aligned}\|x(t)\| &\leq \exp\left\{\int_0^t \Lambda(A(\tau))d\tau\right\}\|x(0)\| \\ &+ \int_0^t \exp\left\{\int_s^t \Lambda(A(\tau))d\tau\right\}\|F(t, x(s))\|ds,\end{aligned} \tag{29}$$

where $A(t) = \{a_{ij}(t)\}$, $i, j = 1, 2, \ldots, n$,

$$F(t, x(t)) = \left(\sum_{j=1}^n w_{1j}(t)g_j(x(t)), \ldots, \sum_{j=1}^n w_{nj}(t)g_j(x(t))\right)^T.$$

Proceeding with the Inequality (29), we have

$$\|x(t)\| \leq \exp\left\{\int_0^t \Lambda(A(\tau))d\tau\right\}\|x(0)\| + \gamma \int_0^t \exp\left\{\int_s^t \Lambda(A(\tau))d\tau\right\}\|x(s)\|ds, \tag{30}$$

where γ is defined from the inequality $\|F(t, x(t))\| \leq \gamma \|x(t)\|$.

From the Inequality (30), using well-known methods, we have the estimate

$$\|x(t)\| \leq \exp\left\{\int_0^t \Lambda(A(\tau))d\tau + \gamma t\right\}\|x(0)\|, t \in [0, b_1].$$

Taking $x(b_1) = (x_1(b_1), \ldots, x_n(b_1))$ as the initial value and repeating the arguments given in the proof of Theorem 1, we obtain the inequality

$$\|x(t)\| \leq \exp\left\{\int_0^t \Lambda(A(\tau))d\tau + \gamma t\right\}\|x(0)\|,$$

which is valid for $t \in [0, \infty)$.

From this inequality, it follows that when the condition

$$\left\{\int_0^t \Lambda(A(\tau))d\tau + \gamma t\right\} < 0,$$

is satisfied, the system of Equation (27) is asymptotically stable in general.

Thus, the following statement has been proven.

Theorem 6. *Let the following conditions be fulfilled:*

(1) functions $a_i, i = 1, 2, \ldots, n$ are continuous everywhere in $[0, \infty)$ except a finite number of points where they have discontinuities of the first kind;

(2) functions $g_i(t)$ are continuous;

(3) $|g_j(x(t))| \leq \alpha_j |x(t)|$;

(4) in $t \in [0, \infty)$, the following condition is satisfied

$$\int_0^t \Lambda(A(\tau))d\tau + \gamma t < 0,$$

where gamma is defined from the inequality $\|F(t, x(t))\| \leq \gamma \|x(t)\|$.

Then, the Hopfield neural network is stable in general.

Consider the case of discontinuity in synapses $w_{ij}(t), i, j = 1, 2, \ldots, n$. For convenience, we restrict ourselves to the discontinuity of the function $w_{11}(t)$ at the time moment $b_1, 0 < b_1 < \infty$.

Let us represent the system of Equation (27) as

$$\frac{dx_1(t)}{dt} = -a_1(t)x_1(t) + w_{11}(t)g_1'(0)x_1(t)$$
$$+ w_{11}(t)u_1(x_1(t)) + \sum_{j=2}^n w_{1j}(t)g_j(x_j(t)),$$

$$\frac{dx_i(t)}{dt} = -a_i(t)x_i(t) + \sum_{j=1}^n w_{ij}(t)g_j(x_j(t)), i = 2, 3, \ldots, n. \quad (31)$$

Here, $u_1(x_1(t)) = g_1(x_1(t)) - g_1'(0)x_1(t)$.

It is essential that $|u_1(x_1(t))| = o(|x_1(t)|)$, since we examine the trivial solution of the system (27). Therefore,

$$|u_1(x_1(t))| = |g(x_1(t)) - g_1(0) - g_1'(0)x_1(t)| \leq B|x_1(t)|^2,$$

where $B = \max_{0 < \theta(x_1(t)) < 1} |g''(\theta(x_1(t)))|$.

Obviously, the system of Equation (31) has a structure similar to that of the system of Equation (27). The difference is that the coefficient for $x_1(t)$ now is equal to $-a_1(t) + w_{11}(t)g_1'(0)$, and the vector function $F(x(t))$ contains $w_{11}(t)u_1(x(t))$ instead of $w_{11}(t)g_1(x(t))$.

Taking this remark into account, the assertion of Theorem 7 extends to the system (31).

Finally, we consider the case which involves discontinuous activation functions. Clearly, the system of Equation (18) is a special case of the system of Equation (18). Theorem 5's statements are readily extended to this.

5. Conclusions

In this paper, we obtain sufficient conditions of asymptotic stability for solutions of linear and nonlinear systems of ordinary differential equations with discontinuous right-hand sides. We have derived conditions for local asymptotic stability and stability in general and the obtained sufficient conditions have been used to investigate the stability of Hopfield neural networks with discontinuous synapses and activation functions. The proposed method for studying Hopfield neural networks can also be applied to other types of artificial neural networks.

The authors hope to continue their study in the following directions:

- stability of solutions of systems of differential equations with discontinuous right-hand sides and delays;
- stability of solutions of systems of parabolic equations with discontinuous right-hand sides;
- stability of solutions of systems of hyperbolic equations with discontinuous right-hand sides.

We intend to use the obtained results in the following fields:

- Ecology. There are a lot of regions with dramatic climate change. Models with discontinuities describe the dynamics of populations very well.
- Problems of automatic regulation and control.
- Mathematical models of immunology during therapy.

Author Contributions: I.B. and A.B. provided sufficient conditions for the stability of systems of differential equations with discontinuous right-hand sides. V.R. obtained stability conditions for Hopfield neural networks. A.B. reviewed the literature. All authors have read and agreed to the published version of the manuscript.

Funding: This research received no external funding.

Institutional Review Board Statement: Not applicable.

Informed Consent Statement: Not applicable.

Data Availability Statement: Not applicable.

Conflicts of Interest: The authors declare no conflict of interest

References

1. Hopfield, J.J. Neurons with graded response have collective computational properties like those of two-state neurons (associative memory/neural network/stability/action potentials). *Proc. Natl. Acad. Sci. USA* **1984**, *81*, 3088–3092. [CrossRef] [PubMed]
2. Hopfield, J.J.; David, W.T. Computing with Neural Circuits: A Model Source. *Sci. New Ser.* **1986**, *233*, 625–633.
3. Michel, A.N.; Gray, D.L. Analysis and synthesis of neural networks with lower block triangular interconnected structure. *IEEE Trans. Circuits Syst.* **1990**, *37*, 1267–1283. [CrossRef]
4. Li, J.H.; Michel, A.N.; Porod, W. Qualitative analysis and synthesis of a class of neural networks. *IEEE Trans. Circuits Syst.* **1988**, *35*, 976–985. [CrossRef]
5. Kosko, B. Bidirectional associative memories. *IEEE Trans. Syst. Man Cybern.* **1988**, *18*, 49–60. [CrossRef]
6. Chua, L.O.; Yang, L. Cellular neural networks: Theory. *IEEE Trans. Circuits Syst.* **1988**, *35*, 1257–1272. [CrossRef]
7. Varga, I.; Elek, G.; Zak, S.H. On the brain-state-in-a-convex-domain neural models. *Neural Netw.* **1996**, *9*, 1173–1184. [CrossRef]
8. Grossberg, S. Content-addresable memory storage by neural networks: A general model and global Liapunov method. In *Computational Neuroscience*; ISchwartz, E.L., Ed.; MIT Press: Cambridge, MA, USA, 1990; pp. 56–65.
9. Cohen, M.A.; Grossberg, S. Absolute stability of global pattern formation and parallel memory storage by competitive neural networks. *IEEE Trans. Syst. Man Cybern.* **1983**, *SMC-13*, 815–826. [CrossRef]
10. Hizsch, M.M. Convergent activation dynamics in continuous time networks. *Neural Netw.* **1989**, *2*, 331–349.
11. Kelly, D.G. Stability of contractive nonlinear neural networks. *IEEE Trans. Biomed. Eng.* **1990**, *3*, 231–242. [CrossRef]

12. Matsuoka, K. Stability conditions for nonlinear continuous neural networks with asymmetric connection weights. *Neural Netw.* **1992**, *5*, 495–500. [CrossRef]
13. Kaszkurewicz, E.; Bhaya, A. On a class of globally stable neural circuits. *IEEE Trans. Circuits Syst. I Fundam. Theory Appl.* **1994**, *41*, 171–174. [CrossRef]
14. Forti, M.; Manetti, S.; Marini, M. Necessary and sufficient conditions for absolute stability of neural networks. *IEEE Trans. Circuits Syst. I Fundam. Theory Appl.* **1994**, *41*, 491–494. [CrossRef]
15. Yang, H.; Dillon, T.S. Exponential stability and oscillation of Hopfield graded response neural networks. *IEEE Trans. Neural Netw.* **1994**, *5*, 719–729. [CrossRef]
16. Fang, Y.; Kincaid, T.G. Stability Analysis of Dynamical Neural Networks. *IEEE Trans. Neural Netw.* **1996**, *7*, 996–1006. [CrossRef] [PubMed]
17. Korkobi, T.; Chtourou, M.; Djemel, M. Stability Analysis of Neural Networks-Band System Identification. *Model. Simul. Eng.* **2009**, *2008*, 343940.
18. Yin, L.; Chen, Y.; Zhao, Y. Global Exponential Stability for a Class Neural Networks with Continuously Distributed Delays. *Adv. Dyn. Syst. Appl.* **2009**, *4*, 221–229.
19. Mou, S.; Gao, H.; Lam, J.; Qiang, W. A new criterion of delay-dependent asymptotic stability for hopfield neural networks with time delay. *IEEE Trans. Neural Netw.* **2008**, *19*, 532–535.
20. Sun, C.; Song, S.; Feng, C. On Global Robust Exponential Stability of Interval Neural Networks with delays. In Proceedings of the 2002 International Joint Conference on Neural Networks, Honoluu, HI, USA, 12–17 May 2002.
21. Zhao, K.; Li, Y. Robust Stability Analysis of Fuzzy Neural Network with Delays. *Math. Probl. Eng.* **2009**, *2009*, 1–13. [CrossRef]
22. Zong, G.-D.; Liu, J. New Delay-dependent Global Asymptotic Stability Condition for Hopfield Neural Networks with Time-varying Delays. *Int. J. Autom. Comput.* **2009**, *6*, 415–419. [CrossRef]
23. McCulloch, W.S.; Pitts, W. A logical calculus of the ideas immanent in nervous activity. *Bull. Math. Biophys.* **1943**, *5*, 115–133. [CrossRef]
24. Filippov, A.F. *Differential Equations with Discontinuous Right-Hand Side*; Nauka: Moscow, Russia, 1985; p. 224.
25. Boikov, I.V. *Stability of Solutions of Differential Equations*; Publishing House of Penza State University: Penza, Russia, 2008; p. 244.
26. Emel'yanov, S.V. Theory of automatic control systems with variable structure: Origin and initial stage of development. In *Nonlinar Dynamics and Control*; Emel'yanov, S.V., Korovin, S.V., Eds.; Fizmatlit: Moscow, Russia, 2004; pp. 5–16.
27. Painleve, P. *Lecons Sur le Frottement*; Hermann: Paris, France, 1895; p. 111.
28. Tan, X.; Qin, W.; Liu, X.; Yang, J.; Jiang, S. Sliding bifurcation analysis and global dynamics for a Filippov predator-prey system. *J. Nonlinear Sci. Appl.* **2016**, *9*, 3948–3961. [CrossRef]
29. Boikov, I.V. On a continuous method for solving nonlinear operator equations. *Differ. Equ.* **2012**, *48*, 1308–1314. [CrossRef]
30. Veldhuizen, V.M. On D-stability and B-stability. *Numer. Math.* **1983**, *43*, 349–357. [CrossRef]
31. Solak, M.K. A note on robust G-stability. In Proceedings of the 1990 American Control Conference, San Diego, CA, USA, 23–25 May 1990.
32. Shokri, A.; Vigo-Aguiar, J.; Mehdizadeh, K.M.; Garcia-Rubio, R. A new implicit six-step P-stable method for the numerical solution of Schrodinger equation. *Int. J. Comput. Math.* **2020**, *97*, 802–817. [CrossRef]
33. Hui, Q.; Haddad, W.M.; Bhat, S.P. Semistability, Finite-Time Stability, Differential Inclusions, and Discontinuous Dynamical Systems Having a Continuum of Equilibria. *IEEE Trans. Autom. Control* **2009**, *54*, 24–65.
34. Anosov, D.V. On stability of relay system equilibrium. *Avtomat. Telemekh.* **1959**, *20*, 135–149.
35. Losev, A.A. Stability analysis of the zero solution of a relay system of ordinary differential equations with two relays. *Differ. Equ.* **2017**, *53*, 1005–1020. [CrossRef]
36. Aleksandrov, A.Y.; Mason, O. On Diagonal Stability of Positive Systems with Switches and Delays. *Autom. Remote Control* **2018**, *79*, 2114–2127. [CrossRef]
37. Utkin, V.I.; Guldner, J.; Shi, J.X. *Sliding Mode Control in Electro-Mechanical Systems*; CRC Press: Boca Raton, FL, USA, 2009; p. 503.
38. Bainov, D.D.; Simeonov, P.S. *Systems with Impulse Effect: Stability, Theory and Applications*; Ellis Horwood Limited: Chichester, UK; John Wiley and Sons: New York, NY, USA, 1989; 255p.
39. Perestyuk, N.A.; Plotnikov, V.A.; Samoilenko, A.M.; Skripnik, N.V. *Differential Equations with Impulse Effects. Multivalued Right-Hand Sides with Discontinuities (De Gruyter Studies in Mathematics: 40)*; Walter De Gruyter GmbH Co.: Berlin, Germany; Boston, MA, USA, 2011; p. 307.
40. Anashkin, O.V.; Dovzhik, N.V.; Mit'ko, O.V. Stability of solutions of differential equations with impulse effect. *Din. Sist.* **2010**, *28*, 3–10.
41. Dudnikov, E.E.; Rybashov, M.V. Absolute Stability of a Class of Feedback Neural Networks. *Autom. Remote Control* **1999**, *12*, 33–40.
42. Borisov, J.I.; Kuz'michev, J.A.; Smolitzkii, H.P. On equilibrium states in a continuous model of neural Hopfield networks. *J. Instrum. Eng.* **1994**, *3–4*, 5–12.
43. Petryakova, E.A. Hopfield neural network with asymmetric matrix of communication coefficients between neurons. *J. Instrum. Eng.* **1994**, *37*, 24–32.
44. Gupta, M.M.; Jin, L.; Hamma, N. *Static and Dynamic Neural Networks. From Fundamentals to Advanced Theory*; Wiley Interscience: New York, NY, USA, 2005; p. 722.

45. Lukyanova, T.A. On exponential stability of Hopfield neural network on time scale. *Rep. Natl. Acad. Sci. Ukr.* **2011**, *10*, 13–17.
46. Boikov, I.V. Stability of Hopfield neural networks. *Autom. Remote Control* **2003**, *64*, 1474–1487. [CrossRef]
47. Daletskii, Y.L.; Krein, M.G. *Stability of Solutions of Differential Equations in Banach Space*; Nauka: Moscow, Russia, 1970; p. 536.
48. Boikov, I.V. Stability of Steady-State Solutions of Systems of Nonlinear Nonautonomous Delay Differential equations. *Differ. Equ.* **2018**, *54*, 1–23. [CrossRef]

MDPI
St. Alban-Anlage 66
4052 Basel
Switzerland
Tel. +41 61 683 77 34
Fax +41 61 302 89 18
www.mdpi.com

Mathematics Editorial Office
E-mail: mathematics@mdpi.com
www.mdpi.com/journal/mathematics